AF361458

Indigenous Confluences

Charlotte Cotè and Coll Thrush,
Series Editors

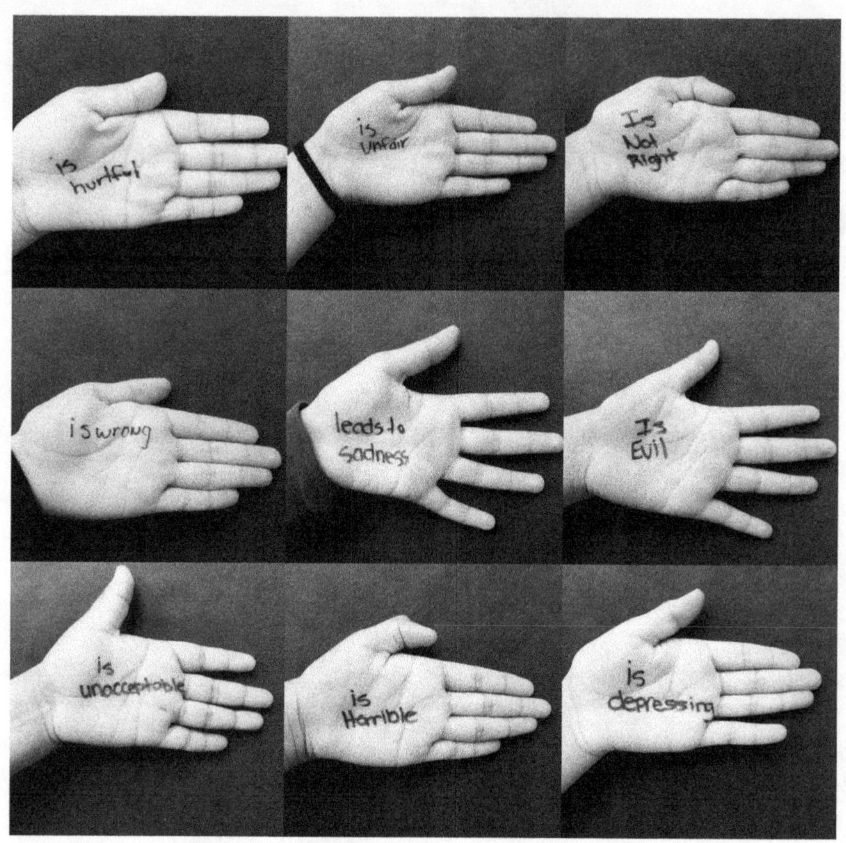

is hurtful
is unfair
Is Not Right
is wrong
leads to sadness
Is Evil
is unacceptable
is Horrible
is depressing

DISMEMBERED

*Native Disenrollment
and the Battle for
Human Rights*

DAVID E. WILKINS
and
SHELLY HULSE WILKINS

UNIVERSITY OF WASHINGTON PRESS

Seattle and London

University of Washington Press
www.washington.edu/uwpress

Library of Congress Cataloging-in-Publication Data
Names: Wilkins, David E. (David Eugene), 1954– author. |
Wilkins, Shelly Hulse, author.
Title: Dismembered : native disenrollment and the battle for
human rights / David E. Wilkins and Shelly Hulse Wilkins.
Description: Seattle : University of Washington, 2017. | Series:
Indigenous confluences | Includes bibliographical references and index.
Identifiers: LCCN 2016049328| ISBN 9780295741574 (hardcover : alk.
paper) | ISBN 9780295741581 (pbk. : alk. paper)
Subjects: LCSH: Indians of North America—Tribal citizenship. |
Human rights—United States.
Classification: LCC KIE2140 .W55 2017 | DDC 342.7308/72—dc23
LC record available at https://lccn.loc.gov/2016049328

Frontispiece: *The sixth graders from First Mesa Elementary School in Arizona express their views on disenrollment.* #stopdisenrollment
Page x photo: *Native artist, activist, and educator Louie Gong (Nooksack/Chinese/French/Scottish)*

Cover illustration: *The Dawes Roll application of Will Rogers and his family, filed on October 22, 1900.*
Source: The National Archives at Fort Worth.

CONTENTS

ACKNOWLEDGMENTS

This book was initially inspired by the banishment experience that our dear friend George Whitewolf endured twenty years ago. His traumatic but thankfully short-lived expulsion from the Monacan Nation prompted us to be more vigilant in scrutinizing membership decisions in Indian Country. As always, the scholarship and friendship of Vine Deloria Jr. compelled us to actively and honestly examine the citizenship choices that tribal leaders were making as far as their peoples were concerned.

Our greatest debt, however, is owed to the several thousand Native individuals from more than seventy Native nations who have been unceremoniously terminated, banished, or denied admission, the vast majority on the most spurious of grounds. Cathy Corey was the first disenrollee to contact us after she and her family were violently disenfranchised from the Chukchansi Nation. Her encouragement, knowledge, and abiding faith in the traditional values that her own tribal leaders no longer embodied were consistent reminders that this was a story that had to be told.

Special thanks to Carolyn Lubeneau. Carolyn wrote us after she, her family, and several others were banished from the Snoqualmie Nation for having allegedly committed treason. She immediately set out to reverse that tainted political decision and ultimately prevailed. She was eventually reinstated and then, interestingly, elected chairwoman of her nation in 2014. We also are deeply grateful to the following individuals for taking the time to talk with us during the course of our research. From Nooksack we thank Jeannie Campbell, Raeanna Rabang, Michelle Roberts, Angel Rabang, and Richard Gladstone. From the Confederated Tribes of the Grand Ronde we thank Debi Anderson, Erin Bernando, and Russell Wilkinson. From Redding Rancheria we thank Carla Foreman Maslin and Mark Maslin. From the Cahto Tribe of Laytonville Rancheria we appreciate the time and conversation with Alice Langton-Sloan and Gene William Sloan. From Lumbee we thank Reena Oxendine Locklear of the tribal enrollment office and Francine Chavis, a supreme court judge.

A hearty thanks also to Laura Wass (Mountain Maidu), who has been battling dismemberment practices for many years in California, and to the Galanda Broadman law firm of Seattle, especially Gabe Galanda, Ryan Dreveskracht, and Anthony Broadman, who have stepped up to defend the sovereignty of those facing disenrollment in several nations. Marc Benjamin, a fearless reporter for the Fresno Bee newspaper has been chronicling this debilitating subject for many years, focusing particularly on the Chukchansi of California. His outstanding reporting helped us understand the complexity and difficulty of disenrollment in that fractious nation.

And special appreciation to Julio Quan and Maralise Hood Quan, whose intelligence, warm friendship, and deep conversations helped immensely before, during, and after this book's birth.

We are also grateful for the support of our editors, Ranjit Arab and Larin McLaughlin. Their patience, advice, and belief in the undertaking were most helpful. And thanks to the two reviewers, including Tom Biolsi, who offered critically important suggestions that strengthened the final manuscript.

David Wilkins would like to thank John Coleman, dean of the College of Liberal Arts at the University of Minnesota, and the reference librarians at the University of Minnesota law school, especially Vicente Garces. Thanks also to Michelle Aguilar Wells and Yvonne Peterson who allowed me to use their offices while I was stationed at Evergreen State College in the summer and fall of 2015 where the first draft of this book was completed.

Thanks to Deron Marquez, of the San Manuel Band of Mission Indians, for his friendship and artful ideas as the manuscript developed. Katherine Spilde also provided quality commentary and scholarship that helped with key sections of the book. I appreciate the good leads that Matthew Fletcher provided early on as the research on tribal and federal court cases was gearing up. Rick Cuevas, through his website Original Pechanga, has been a stalwart defender of the rights of disenrollees for years and I extend a hearty handshake to him for his uncompromising efforts to see that justice is provided.

As always, I am grateful to my parents, Daniel and Thedis Wilkins. My mother passed away in the fall of 2015, just about the time the first draft was completed. I wish I could present her with a copy of our book now. Thanks also to my siblings, especially my brother Craig, a hard-working member of the Centers for Disease Control, and my sister Deborah, a Methodist minister. Deb's biblical knowledge about banishment and exile proved most fascinating and helped deepen and expand our understanding of these important concepts.

Finally, I am most appreciative of the love and brilliant writing of my wife, Shelly. Our collaborations and life together have helped me become a better writer and, more importantly, a better human being.

Shelly Wilkins would like to thank Senator John McCoy and Jeannie McCoy, Colleen and Frank Anderson, Amy Ruble, Sonja Silver, Jo Arlow, Sydney Forrester, Céline Planchou, Marine Le Puloch, Rachel Smith, Maureen Gallegos, Nicole Vukonich, Matt Bridges, Keith Buchholz, Gillian Maguire, Mike Delcamp, Betty Schwieterman, Chris Stancich, Richard Tierry Kirk, Kim Rehagen, Susan Vollmer and Virginia Cherry for their friendship and encouragement. Senator McCoy, along with the late Sue Crystal and her husband, Billy Frank Jr., provided critical mentorship when I began my study of tribal-state relations.

I owe much to the dedicated public servants in the Washington State Legislature, including Senators Jeannie Darneille, Bob Hasegawa, Maralyn Chase, Karen Keiser, and Sharon Nelson and Representatives Sharon Tomiko Santos, Timm Ormsby, Frank Chopp, and Joe Fitzgibbon, as well as the fine staff. The insights, institutional knowledge, and humor freely shared by Jody Olney, Majken Ryherd, Gary Wilburn, and Kevin Black have been especially appreciated.

I am also fortunate to have had mentors and friends like Nina Williams-Mbengue, Ajenai Clemmons, Rhina Villatoro, Rachel Estrella, Mary Fairchild, Mary Cate Regan, Annette Durlam, Larry Morandi, Jim Reid, and Bill Pound from my years with the National Conference of State Legislatures in Denver.

It was there that I was inspired by the foundational work of Sam Deloria and Tassie Hannah and had the chance to work with leaders from across Indian Country including Hank Adams, Fawn Sharp, W. Ron Allen, Kelly Croman-Neelands, Kate Spilde, Reggie Joule, Jack Jackson Jr., and Chris Deschene, as well as lawmakers such as Talmadge Branch (Tuscarora), Peggy Flanagan (Ojibwe), Kevin Killer (Oglala Lakota/Kiowa), Anastasia Pittman (Seminole), James Roger Madalena (Jemez Pueblo) and Carolyn Pease-Lopez (Crow).

My late parents, Alton and Peggy Sue McDonald, would have been very proud. In their stead I have had the loving support of other family members, Veda Cherneski, Ron and Naomi Shestack, Chuck and Martha Hulse, Fern and Erwin Botsch, Vernena Stowe, Rocky Jones, Lura Blankenship, Lynn Pacifico, and Duff Pacifico-Prescott. My Wilkins family fills my world with love, good humor, and banana pudding. New grandson Kai David is an unending source of happiness and hilarity.

Finally, gratitude to my husband, David, a truly fine scholar, partner, and person. There is so much joy in our lives and work together. I always look forward to our next adventure.

THE WARRIOR PROJECT
COLONIAL
DREAMS
COME
TRUE

Introduction

LIKE ALL HUMAN COMMUNITIES, NATIVE NATIONS AND THEIR GOVerning bodies are in a constant state of flux. They generate from within and absorb from without a bewildering, increasing array of issues that provide opportunities to either evolve and mature or to regress and decay. These issues include the exercise of treaty rights, the complicated dynamics of intergovernmental relations, profound environmental concerns, and the always uneven ground of land claims and sacred site battles. And these are but a few of the multitude of topics that warrant constant Native vigilance, each requiring enormous outlays of time, energy, and resources.

As critical and complicated as these topics are, they pale in comparison to what is arguably the most important question that Native nations have ever faced: what does it mean to be Tulalip, Anishinaabe, Yakama, Lumbee, Narraganset, Pechanga, or Chukchansi? What, in other words, are the defining characteristics that make an Indigenous nation just that: Indigenous and a nation? And what is required of each individual in those nations to be considered a bona fide participant, citizen, or—for lack of a better term—member of a given Native nation?

This set of intimately related questions of what it means to be an Indigenous person in a particular tribal nation has been crucial for every generation of Native nations from the moment they came into existence, as every generation has the inherent free will to self-identify as they choose. Historically, lands, languages, kinship systems, and spiritual values and traditions provided the most recognized frameworks that enabled each Native nation, and the individuals, families, and clans constituting those nations, to generally rest assured in their collective and personal identities and to not have to wonder about who they were. The bonds of organic connections were so strong and pliable, in fact, that identity crises—be they national or individual—were most likely rarely encountered within Indigenous communities.

Of course, five centuries of interactions with foreign powers have taken a mighty toll on Native peoples and their lands, cultures, and identities. During the last four and a half decades there have been increasing questions regarding how Indigenous peoples understood who they were and how they were or were no longer related to one another. Writing in 1974, Vine Deloria Jr., a leading architect of the Native sovereignty movement, succinctly noted as much when he stated: "The gut question has to do with the meaning of the tribe. Should it continue to be a quasi-political entity? [Should] it become primarily an economic structure? Or should it become, once again, a religious community? The future, perhaps the immediate future, will tell."[1]

The vital question, therefore, of who belongs to a Native nation and the grounds upon which that individual's relationship to his or her nation may be severed by the governing elites is at the heart of this book. While not as important as that most fundamental of human rights—the right to life as a free human being—the right to belong to and rest assured of one's integral place in a particular Indigenous community is critical. In an increasing number of Native nations, tribal belonging, long viewed as an absolute given by bona fide Native citizens, particularly since the early 1990s, has become more of a political privilege than a sacred and organic responsibility as defined by tribal officialdom. And since the U.S. Supreme Court's 1978 decision in *Santa Clara v. Martinez* (which affirmed a tribal nation's right to be the ultimate arbiter of its own membership requirements), an expanding list of Native peoples have disenrolled or banished an ever-growing number of otherwise legitimate Native citizens.

Such dismemberments are happening for a variety of reasons, but the two most apparent factors associated with the practice are increased gambling revenue and civil violations or criminal activity that presumably threatens community stability.[2] Interestingly, gambling revenue (or other large financial windfalls that come to some Native nations) and the way it is sometimes dispensed via per capita distribution programs, typically leads to disenrollment—that is, the legal and political termination of a tribal member's citizenship. In contrast, civil violations or criminal activity (e.g., malfeasance, drug involvement, gang activity, etc.) tends in many cases to lead to banishment—that is, physical expulsion from tribal lands and not necessarily the loss of tribal citizenship. These two concepts are often conflated, but they are in fact distinctive terms. In some contemporary tribal cases, however, they become functionally similar.

Disenrollment is a legal term of art that arose most prominently during the Indian Reorganization Act period in the 1930s. Disenrollment can broadly be divided into two categories: nonpolitically motivated disenrollments and politically motivated disenrollments. The former are arguably justifiable when due process is provided because of fraudulent enrollment, error in enrollment, dual membership, or failure to maintain contact with the home community. The latter, we argue, are never justified when driven by economic greed, political power, or personal vendettas, among other reasons. Banishment, in contrast, is an ancient concept that has been utilized by societies and states throughout the world, dating back to at least 2285 BCE.[3]

Furthermore, banishment can also be divided into two categories: nonpolitically motivated banishment for the violation of a criminal law and politically motivated banishment because of crime or purely political reasons. Historically, Indigenous nations rarely banished tribal relatives, save for the committing of grievous offenses, like premeditated murder or incest, and only then after all other attempts—ceremonies, public ridicule, restitution, shaming—had been tried to restore community harmony. When it was employed, it was used largely for rehabilitative purposes.

Native nations have always possessed the inherent authority to denationalize any tribal member. Moreover, they wield the power, unknown to any other sovereign in the United States, to formally exclude non-Natives from their territorial homelands. But this study argues that far too many tribal nations are engaging in banishment or politically or economically motivated disenrollment practices in clear violation of their own historic values and principles, which at one time utilized peacemaking, mediation, restitution, and compensation to resolve the inevitable disputes that occasionally arose within the community.

Although the 1968 Indian Civil Rights Act (ICRA) extended to all persons in Indian Country a modified version of the U.S. Bill of Rights, the only remedy spelled out in that act is the writ of habeas corpus. Habeas corpus has thus far not offered dismembered Native individuals any substantial justice. And since Native nations are also sovereign, they can and frequently do invoke the doctrine of sovereign immunity, leaving disenfranchised tribal members little legal recourse.

Dismembered Native citizens are also citizens of the states they reside in and have federal citizenship as well. Theoretically, these individuals should be the most protected class of individuals in the land, armed as they are with three distinctive layers of citizenship. Such, of course, has not proven to be the case. In regards to Native citizenship, tribal political and judicial elites can and do wield the absolute power to terminate Native citizenship—a power that not even the federal or state governments can wield over non-Native citizens. As the Supreme Court held in *Afroyim v. Rusk* (1967), citizenship is an inviolable right, and while it can be given away, it cannot be taken away. In other words, involuntary expatriation—that is, the stripping of citizenship—is not an available penalty under any state or federal statute. As the Court held, "in our country people are sovereign and the government cannot sever its relationship to the people by taking away their citizenship."

A central question this book poses and attempts to answer is the following: what does it mean that the United States, a very large, heterogeneous, secular state, has in place laws and policies that protect its citizens' rights far more comprehensively than Native nations, which are much smaller, more homogeneous, and ostensibly more kin-based polities? For if Native nations are indeed communities of kinfolk that are ancestrally, culturally, psychologically, and territorially related, then it would appear that the grounds on which to sever or terminate such a fundamentally organic set of human relationships would have to be unequivocally clear and would, in fact, rarely be carried out given the grave threat that such actions, the literal depopulation of the community's inhabitants, would pose to the continued existence of the nation. A corollary to the central question of the sanctity of U.S. citizenship in comparison to Native citizenship is the following: what does it mean that the only class of citizens in the United States who cannot avail themselves of such sacrosanct rights are Native individuals?[4]

The very concept of tribal sovereignty means that the people—the tribal community members themselves—are the sovereign, not the governing, bodies of those nations. Tribal councils and other governing institutions have merely been delegated limited authority to fulfill the needs and to protect, not destroy, the rights of the people. They do not have or should not have the power to sever their relationship to their people by taking away the most important status, the status of belonging to, of having citizenship or membership in, an Indigenous nation. Of course, for many Indigenous peoples the very notion of sovereignty is rooted in their creation accounts, suggesting that their core identity flows not from human-made constitutions, charters, or ordinances but is directly linked to their ancient origin accounts and the holy beings who initially set them upon the earth.

Why, then, is legal, political, and cultural termination of a Native nation's own kin occurring at such a heightened level now? Are the tribal government officials engaged in such harsh decisions acting in a manner that comports with the traditional notions of identity discussed earlier, or are they now acting like privileged and exclusive corporate clubs? What rights do the disenrolled or banished Native citizens have to contest this most profound of severances? Can Native nations ensure justice and individual civil rights for their citizens and still protect and exercise tribal sovereignty in membership decisions? Finally, what role, if any, should the federal government play in these contentious intratribal affairs, since those dismembered also happen to be U.S. citizens and are supposedly entitled to the same basic civil liberties as all other citizens? The United States purports to have a trust relationship with federally recognized Native nations and all of their citizens, which means that it is pledged with protecting the lands, rights, and resources of Indigenous nations by the Constitution's treaty, property, and commerce clauses; the several hundred ratified treaties forged between the federal government and Indigenous peoples; and numerous federal statutes and policy directives. When tribal governments are violating the rights of their own citizens, including their vested property interests, the federal government as the principal trust agent has a constitutional, moral, and treaty responsibility to assist those individuals suffering such violations.

GENESIS OF THIS BOOK

Two events in 1996 first brought this issue to our attention; both involved the banishment of enrolled tribal citizens. The first episode centered on the banishment of one individual, George Whitewolf, a Monacan Indian from Virginia. When new leadership was elected Whitewolf found himself on the wrong side of their political and spiritual ideology, and he was unceremoniously banished. An outcry from tribal members forced the governing body to reconsider, and within a few months his membership rights were restored. Nevertheless, that event and the pain it caused left a deep imprint.

The second episode, an important federal court ruling also involving banishment, occurred among the Seneca of New York. In this case, *Poodry v. Tonawanda Band of Seneca Indians*, a federal appellate court ruled that five Seneca citizens, who had been permanently banished by the tribal government on the grounds that they had allegedly committed treason against the Seneca nation, were entitled to a federal review of the tribe's action.[5] This was so because banishment was considered a severe enough punishment involving a sufficient restraint on their liberty and because the banished members had been evicted without a trial, prior notice, or any other form of due process. This case is discussed in greater detail in chapter 5.

As important as *Poodry* is, it has been largely ineffectual in providing those facing disenrollment or banishment any protection because in virtually all the litigation since 1996—federal, tribal, or state—courts have generally adhered to the U.S. Supreme Court's 1978 *Santa Clara* decision that Native governments are the final arbiters of membership decisions.

OVERVIEW OF THE BOOK

In this title, we will first provide a broad overview of banishment from a world historical perspective and then bring it into focus and discuss the way it was occasionally practiced among Indigenous nations. In the next chapter, we will critically examine the ascendance of the term *enrollment* as it was determined by federal judicial, congressional, and administrative officials from the mid-1800s to the early 1900s. Crime, race, and allotment factored heavily in how and why the United States intervened in tribal membership matters.

We then turn to the 1930s Indian New Deal era and the capstone 1934 Indian Reorganization Act (IRA), which formally stymied allotment and laid out a policy of tribal self-rule, including, for some nations, the formal adoption of written constitutions, bylaws, and charters of incorporation. This chapter will also critically review the language in over three hundred tribal constitutions to see precisely what they say about disenrollment, banishment, exclusion, and related terms.

In the next chapter we introduce the rise of Native nationalism and tribal sovereignty in the wake of federal policies of termination, relocation, and Public Law 280. A discussion of *Santa Clara v. Martinez* (1978) sets the stage for an examination of how tribal governments began to more forcefully assert their retained power over membership decisions. As tribal nations moved through the 1980s, Indian gambling operations began to have a major impact economically, culturally, and politically. At the same time crime became a major social problem across Indian Country. A number of Native nations began to look for ways to address membership issues unleashed by the surge of dollars, the criminal element, race, and the manner in which Native politics and culture coalesce in relation to these topics.

Next, we examine in broad fashion a number of Native nations that are disenrolling or banishing citizens. California is home to the largest concentration of Indigenous communities that are dismembering their own citizens. Tribal elites assert that they have legitimate reasons to purge membership rolls, including crimes or civil violations, treasonous activity, dual citizenship, distance from homeland, inadequate or inappropriate blood quantum, false information or documentary error, or enrollment policy changes. Disenrollees, by contrast, assert that these official rationales are masks that hide the real reasons for disenrollment: economic competition over finite resources, political power plays, personal vendettas, and racial discrimination, to name but a few. Due to the complexity of each case, we can but provide short vignettes of several nations where the process has unfolded.

In the next chapter we engage in an analysis of how both Indigenous and federal courts have addressed this vital topic. These cases reveal the difficult positions judicial bodies are placed in. On the one hand, they are the active arms of the governance structures they represent; on the other hand, they are also the one venue where those facing dismemberment feel they have the best chance at receiving a fair and impartial hearing. To further complicate matters for Native individuals facing dismemberment, not every Native nation has a court system, and of those that do tribal membership decisions are sometimes immune from challenge in those courts unless the tribal legislative body has expressly authorized such action.[6]

In the conclusion we discuss the implications of dismemberment policies and actions on Indigenous nationhood, citizenship, and the status of Native individuals in their own land and in the United States. It appears, at first glance, that a number of dismembering Native nations have embraced a corporate economic model of governance as advanced by the IRA, the Alaskan Native Claims Settlement Act (ANCSA), the Indian Gaming Regulatory Act (IGRA), and the Harvard Project on Economic Development. But this alone does not explain the rise of disenrollment or banishment as a means to deal with civil violations or criminal activity.

Finally, we assess some of the reform ideas that have been put forward by various commentators, disenrollees, and others to address dismemberment. Ideas include the formation of an intertribal human rights treaty, an intertribal appellate body, modifications to tribal constitutions or other governing documents, amendments to the ICRA (e.g., to give disenrollees an opportunity to contest their exclusion more easily in federal court), encouraging dismembered individuals to organize separately and seek acknowledgment from the federal government as separate political entities, and utilizing the United Nations Declaration on the Rights of Indigenous People and other international

Sovereigntree, the attack from within. Originally run March 4, 2016, on Indian Country Today Media Network. © 2016 Marty Two Bulls.

protocols in an effort to provide a measure of justice to dismembered individuals who have been disenfranchised.

Native governments currently engaged in or considering dismemberment actions should look deep within their own past for guidance on such important decisions. What most every nation would discover by engaging in such self-examination is that historically and until very recent times no Native leaders lightly set about to permanently banish or formally disenroll individuals or families they were organically related to. Native communities once possessed clear and well understood traditions, norms, and customs of how a civilized tribal citizen should behave in relation to his or her family, clan, community, and the larger natural order. They relied largely upon social pressures, particularly the individual's fear of embarrassing his or her relatives and clan

DISMEMBERED

members, as their primary means of determining the proper social response and penalty for violation of customary law.

The actual practice of banishment—and later disenrollment—was rarely used as it would have indicated a significant breakdown in the effectiveness of traditional dispute resolution processes. Problems were generally resolved in a peaceful, nonadversarial manner, with the emphasis being on restoring order and balance rather than mere retribution. Much less draconian sanctions existed—ostracism, ridicule, temporary removal, physical punishment—to restore balance to the community when individuals acted contrary to the laws and customs of the nation. Financial factors, DNA tests, and reliance on inadequate and often times flawed federal historical records were not used to effectively terminate the political existence of tribal citizens.

Today, in some situations, especially those centered on criminal activity, it appears that some Native nations have reluctantly determined that banishment is one social mechanism they may sometimes have to employ in order to maintain community stability; they have carefully constructed clear guidelines and procedures to carry out this difficult process. But in a majority of disenrollment cases, tribal officials exhibit no concern for human rights, tribal traditions, or due process, arbitrarily and capriciously dismembering tribal members as a means to solidify their own economic and political bases and to winnow out opposition families who disapprove of the direction the tribal leadership is headed.

If Native nations continue down the path of wholesale evictions of their own people on the most spurious of grounds, they not only may eventually provoke the federal government to step in and interfere in this most private of tribal decisions, but more importantly, they will continue to act in a manner that profoundly violates the true spirit of what it means to be an Indigenous nation: a nation in which all are related by genealogy (culturally derived, not fractions of blood), by land, by language, and by spiritual traditions and values.

Banishment

An Overview

IN JULY 2015, TWO LAKOTA NATIONS ENACTED RESOLUTIONS TO BAN-
ish all those who have been convicted of drug trafficking or related crimes.
The two nations, the Cheyenne River Sioux Tribal Council of Eagle Butte,
South Dakota, and the Standing Rock Sioux Tribe, which straddles North
and South Dakota, were reacting to a dramatic increase in the number of on-
reservation murders, suicides, assaults, and other social problems precipitated
by methamphetamine and other drugs. The Cheyenne River Tribal Council
law said that it "immediately excluded, disenrolled and/or banished for life
from the Cheyenne River Sioux Indian Reservation and all lands that the Tribe
owns" any individual over the age of eighteen who was convicted in a tribal,
state, or federal court of dealing, distributing, manufacturing, or trafficking
methamphetamine or any narcotic drug.[1] Harold C. Frazier, the chairman of
the nation, noted in signing the resolution that the intent of the law was to
send an emphatic message to any drug pusher that such behavior would no
longer be tolerated.

Four months earlier, the Saginaw Chippewa Tribe of Michigan wielded
their power to exclude as detailed in their tribal code and banish two nonmember Natives who had been accused of drug trafficking on tribal lands.
Their rationale was similar to the Cheyenne River Sioux: "Today our people
have shown that we are no longer going to tolerate people who peddle un-
healthy and life-destroying substances onto the reservation. Today we took
necessary steps to protect and uphold our members and their families against
this plague called addiction."[2]

These nations, along with several others—Grand Portage Band of Ojibwe,
Lummi, Boise Forte Band of Ojibwe, Mille Lacs Band of Ojibwe, Mashantucket
Pequot, and Lac du Flambeau, to name but a few—have decided, for a variety

of reasons, to banish, exclude, or expel enrolled tribal members, nonmember Natives, and non-Indians from tribal lands. While the reasons for these exilic actions vary, depending on the individual tribal context, the practice of banishment has been employed by ethnic groups, nations, states, and societies around the world for millennia.

BANISHMENT AND EXILE: A HISTORICAL PERSPECTIVE

Banished. Exiled. Deported. Transportation. Expelled. Outlawed. Evicted. Excluded. Each of these terms gives rise to a strong emotional and intellectual reaction, especially from those confronted by the possibility that they are to be removed. Worldwide, the political, religious, or military leadership in polities has reserved to itself or shared the power to authoritatively banish individuals, families, or even entire groups from their respective locales, typically as a punitive measure for what were considered grave offenses. As such, enforced removal from one's native land entailed a devastating loss of political, territorial, and cultural identity, since those excluded were deprived of the security and comfort of their own families, clans, and communities, as well as their religious or ethnic groups.

Banishment and *exile* are the two most commonly used terms associated with the practice of physical exclusion, which William Snider defined in its most general and benign form as "the punishment of one who has incurred the displeasure of a group to which one had previously enjoyed full membership status." Snider continues by noting that "as a means of expressing displeasure with the conduct of the banishment, the community takes the ultimate step and declares that the banished individual is no longer a part of the community."[3] The term *banished* derives from the Latin word *bannitio*, which means "exclusion by a ban or public proclamation."[4] A banished person was called a *bannitus* or "a person under a ban; an outlaw."[5]

Exile as a form of punishment was meted out by God in numerous passages in the Hebrew Bible, tracing back to God's expulsion of Adam and Eve from the Garden of Eden for their act of disobedience. Another famous biblical exile resulted from Cain's killing of his younger brother, Abel, which compelled God to banish Cain and to place a shaming mark on him.[6] Human biblical actors also engaged in exile—notably the Assyrians' expulsion of Israelites around 720 BCE and the Babylonians' exile of the leaders of the southern kingdom of Judah, including their prophet, Ezekiel, in 597 BCE.[7] In the Book of Esther, King Xerxes' advisors recommended exile for the queen.[8]

The Code of Hammurabi, a collection of legal decisions pronounced by King Hammurabi of Babylon (in the ancient state in Mesopotamia; present-day Iraq), dates back nearly 4,400 years to 2285 BCE and is the oldest codified reference to the use of banishment as a means of punishment. Number 154 of the legal code declares that "if a man has committed incest with his daughter, that man shall be banished from the city."[9]

Many other civilizations also employed exile or banishment. Ancient India prescribed exile for rapists in enacting the Laws of Manu. The Chinese exiled individuals who committed crimes specified in the Tang Code. In Europe during the Middle Ages banishment was used by the Germanic peoples, including the Danes and the Franks. In the Germanic city-state of Ulm in the latter part of the sixteenth century, expulsions accounted for nearly 40 percent of the punishments delivered to criminals. Banishment, for the city's officials, offered a "flexible tool to police the boundaries of inclusion in their community. It occupied a useful middle-ground between cruel admonitions and fines and the more severe punishments of maiming or execution."[10] Banishment was viewed as a means to reorder social and power relations by removing individuals who were viewed as undermining the community's security and prosperity.

Early Greeks and Romans used exile as a form of punishment for major crimes such as homicide, although ostracism—a variant of exile—was sometimes imposed for political reasons as well. Among Romans, prolonged, if not permanent, voluntary physical exile was one way to avoid the death penalty.[11] Voluntary expatriation, or diaspora, is, therefore, a case of immigration "where what is sought is not primarily the advantages of the place to which one goes, but essentially freedom from whatever disadvantages prevailed at home."[12] Likewise, diaspora, while it may be forced, may also be chosen. In Reimer's words, it "might involve being flung from a homeland, but might equally be a state of equilibrium and settled life. It might involve loss of identity, but it might simply imply a 'different' identity from a dominant, host culture."[13]

This voluntary or diasporic aspect of Indigenous exile will not be explored in this book, although it is certainly a subject worthy of further attention as evidenced by the bumper crop of studies that examine the continuing exodus of Natives from their reservation or trust land to metropolitan areas.[14]

The Netherlands also employed banishment with verve from the Middle Ages to the early 1800s, although the practice gradually diminished in use because of "an awareness that one did not solve the problem by just banishing someone from a small jurisdiction."[15] But during its heyday from 1650 to 1750,

97 percent of the Amsterdam court's public, noncapital cases included banishment.

As Europe emerged from the Middle Ages, banishment was used with greater frequency by officials throughout the British Empire, but especially England, which began to exile criminals to both Australia and the American colonies.[16] Banishment was initially called "abjuration," where the party accused fled to a sanctuary, confessed their crime, and took an oath to depart from the kingdom, never to return without permission. This was common practice from the thirteenth to the sixteenth centuries. Abjuration was not viewed as a punishment but as a condition of pardon.[17]

Gradually, abjuration became ineffective as a deterrent and it was replaced by the punishment of transportation. A euphemism for banishment, transportation rose dramatically in popularity in the seventeenth century. The British viewed prisons as barbarous and archaic institutions, but still needed a policy to deal with convicts and dissidents. Parliament thus enacted the Transportation Act in 1718.[18] Noncapital felons were transported—banished—for seven years. Persons convicted of capital crimes were transported for fourteen years to life. Some fifty thousand people were banished to America from the British Isles between the early 1700s and 1860s, when the practice was finally abolished in England. Banishment for political, racial, or religious purposes was, in fact, the norm rather than a penalty for criminal offenses.[19] Another 39,000 were transported to Australia, many for having belonged to radical political groups challenging British hegemony—especially in Ireland. The American colonies also made use of banishment "to rid themselves of hostile natives, rebellious settlers, religious dissidents, and fractious individuals."[20]

Colonial officials banished and transported numerous members of Native nations as slaves or as indentured servants to the West Indies or to enemy Indians, especially those engaged in wars with colonists. Conflicts such as the Virginia Indians uprising (1622), Bacon's Rebellion (1676), King Philip's War (1675–76), and the Yamasee War (1715–16) led to the expulsions of many Natives. The justification for treating Native individuals so harshly was that since they were deemed savage, colonial officials were under no obligation to abide by the rules of war or the law of nations.[21]

One case in the early 1700s involved the Nanziattico people of Virginia. When a prominent white planter, John Rowley, and his family were found murdered in Richmond County in 1704, officials captured members of Nanziattico nation, who were accused of having committed the atrocity. A trial was conducted in the local court. All the adult men were found guilty and were hung. The remaining members, over the age of twelve, were transported to England or the West Indies and sold as indentured servants for seven years. They were also banished from Virginia for life. Children under twelve were divvied up between the governor and the council members who had the right to hold them as servants until they turned twenty-four years of age.[22]

Other states also utilized this exclusionary mechanism. Ireland, Scotland, France, East Germany, Soviet Russia, Yugoslavia, and South Africa also used the practice to transport both convicts and political prisoners. France and Soviet Russia continued to exile individuals until the middle of the twentieth century.[23]

BANISHMENT IN THE UNITED STATES

Following the birth of the United States, banishment, as a form of punishment, held no appeal for the national government as a means of dealing with criminals or political dissidents.[24] This aversion to the practice as a federally administered punitive measure has never lessened. A review of U.S. Supreme Court opinions reveals that the terms *banish* or *banishment* have only been mentioned, and never fully analyzed, in six cases: *Cooper v. Telfair*,[25] *Delgadillo v. Carmichael*,[26] *Galvan v. Press*,[27] *Barber v. Gonzalez*,[28] *Trop v. Dulles*,[29] and *Costello v. Immigration and Naturalization Service*.[30] Several of these cases dealt with the deportation of aliens. Banishment differs from deportation since the latter is used to exclude aliens, not citizens, who commit crimes in the United States.[31]

The most elaborate comments about banishment are in a short paragraph in *Telfair* where Associate Justice William Cushing said, "The right to confiscate and banish, in the case of an offending citizen, must belong to every government. . . . It naturally, as well as tacitly, belongs to the legislature. However, because legislation authorizing banishment as a sentence has never been passed, an assertion of legislative authority has not actually been tested." And in *Costello* the Court merely made a comparison between banishment and deportation: "Deportation is a drastic measure and at times the equivalent of banishment or exile."

While the federal government has never utilized banishment as a sanction for citizens, since colonial times states have sometimes wielded the practice to chasten criminals by banishing, exiling, or excluding those who were viewed as having violated the rules of the community. Fifteen states currently have constitutional provisions that expressly forbid the banishment of individuals from their borders, including Alabama, Arkansas, Maryland, New

Hampshire, and Oklahoma.[32] The intent in each of these clauses is to disallow a state from exiling its own citizens beyond its borders.[33] Although some states forbid all banishment, Maryland and Tennessee only prohibit expulsion in the absence of due process. Article 24 of Maryland's constitution declares that "no man ought to be . . . exiled . . . but by the judgment of his peers, or by the Law of the land." Importantly, five states—Mississippi, Florida, Wisconsin, Oregon, and Georgia—have upheld intrastate banishment.[34] Georgia has the most active banishment record. As one example, between 1998 and 2001, Houston County banished 142 individuals for crimes ranging from drug dealing to fraud.[35]

And while no state has ever authorized banishment as a proper punishment to be carried out by judicial sentence and a majority of the state courts that have addressed the legality of banishment have held that the practice is illegal, this has not stopped judges in several states from utilizing banishment as a part of probationary sentences or as an alternative to incarceration.[36] When, in fact, banishment has been used as an executive pardon or parole, it has been upheld by the courts with the same unanimity with which sentences of banishment have been nullified.[37] As Armstrong pointed out, "trial judges and magistrates still impose banishment, often without naming it as such," and governors sometimes make banishment a condition for parole.[38]

More recently, Beckett and Herbert in their 2009 study, *Banished: The New Social Control in Urban America*, show how major cities, like Seattle, New York, Los Angeles, Portland, Las Vegas, Cincinnati, Honolulu, and others employ various strategies where "increasing swaths of urban space are delimited as zones of exclusion from which undesirables are banned."[39] These so-called banishment strategies constitute new legal tools used by city officials to deal with vagrants, criminals, and other undesirables. These exclusionary policies are rarely debated publicly in part because they "are largely deployed without much fanfare against individuals, such as the homeless."[40] Seattle, for example, adopted a parks exclusion ordinance in 1997. It authorizes police officers and park officials to "immediately remove persons for committing crimes or minor infractions of park rules and to ban them from some or all public city parks for up to one year."[41]

Banishment proponents broadly argue that the practice is justified on three grounds: rehabilitation, deterrence, and incapacitation or community protection.[42] Furthermore, prison overcrowding and the surging costs of incarceration are other arguments for the practice. But opponents of banishment muster a strong set of constitutional, policy, and moral arguments. From a constitutional perspective numerous commentators have suggested that the practice violates the First Amendment's freedom of association (to peaceably assemble); the Fifth Amendment's ban on double jeopardy and due process protections; the Seventh Amendment's cruel and unusual clause; and the Fourteenth Amendment's right to travel freely from state to state.[43]

From a policy perspective several state courts have held that in the absence of statutory authorization, banishment is not proper punishment and is impliedly prohibited by public policy as it passes off one jurisdiction's problems to another jurisdiction thus provoking retaliation.[44] Finally, opponents argue that exile is a morally bankrupt practice because it is archaic and is used more often against the poor and defenseless, is racially discriminatory, cast a "perpetual pall of criminality"[45] over the exiled, and "unconstitutionally deprives that [banished] individual of the ability to affect the political process in the geographical area in which his speech would be most relevant."[46]

Armstrong, writing in 1963, said that "banishment has retained something of the place it once shared with the thumbscrew, the rack, and other medieval refinements chiefly because of the subtle nature of its barbarism and its practical usefulness in the deflection of difficult political or social problems."[47] His view is echoed by Beckett and Herbert's 2009 study of banishment as it is being carried out in Seattle's parks and public housing complexes. They emphasize that banishment has become popular because politicians place enormous pressure on police and prosecutors to more robustly respond to the public's concerns—both real and perceived—about crime and disorder. They stress, however, that "banishment is a shortsighted and ultimately counterproductive practice. It is, to borrow a phrase from Peter Andreas, a 'politically successful policy failure.'"[48] It is viewed as successful because city officials appear tough on crime, and the short-term interest of the police, prosecuting office, and private capital all appear to benefit as well. Their research, however, shows it to be a futile and counterproductive policy failure because many targeted for banishment are ill-equipped to relocate and the practice "imperils efforts by the socially marginal to integrate with mainstream society."[49] Banishment, moreover, does nothing to address the underlying problems that create the ever-present social and economic inequality pervasive throughout society.

Banishment, in other words, is a powerful erosion of rights and does nothing to solve crime. It merely "forces the criminal element and the attendant root cause of crime upon another community."[50] As was stated in *People v. Baum* (1930), "To permit one State to dump its convicted criminals into another would entitle the State believing itself injured thereby to exercise its policies and military powers in the interest of its own peace, safety, and welfare, to repel such an invasion. It would tend to incite dissension, provoke retaliation, and disturb that fundamental equality of political rights among the several States which is the basis of the Union itself. Such a method of punishment is not authorized by statute, and is impliedly prohibited by public policy."[51]

In addition, banishment separates government from the governed. Having been denied all rights to governing mechanisms, and with no opportunity to have their dissenting voices heard, deprives the community of the banished individuals' perspective, a substantial violation of democratic principles.[52]

Chief Justice Earl Warren, in *Trop v. Dulles*, a case involving the denaturalization of a natural-born citizen, put it bluntly when describing the devastation associated with the loss of citizenship: such an individual "has lost the right to have rights" and they "may be subject to banishment, a fate universally decried by civilized peoples."[53]

BANISHMENT AND INDIGENOUS PEOPLES

As described at the beginning of this chapter, several Native nations are now actively banishing individuals—tribal citizens, nonmember Natives, and non-Indians—typically for criminal activity. Other Indigenous peoples around the world—the Maori of New Zealand and the Samoan people—have also employed banishment practices both historically and at the present time. As Lutisone Salevao noted in 2005 in discussing banishment in Samoa: "An ambitious assumption of absolute power in the village readily attracts collective censure in the form of social control mechanisms such as fines, alienation, ostracism and, in the worst-case scenario, banishment from the village."[54] Banishment's legality, even in contemporary times, has been upheld in Samoa in a series of 1990s cases, one of which declared that "it is that history and social structure [of Samoa] and those references in the Constitution which lead us now to hold that within the meaning of article 13(4), banishment from a village is, at the present time, a reasonable restriction imposed by existing law, in the interests of public order, on the exercise of the rights of freedom of movement and resident's affirmed by Article 13(1)(d)."[55]

Some First Nations in Canada (e.g., Norway House Cree Nation of Manitoba) have also in recent years adopted laws to banish Native criminals, but the Department of Indian and Northern Affairs has generally denied that they have inherent sovereign authority to enact such measures because of the Indian Act, adopted by the Canadian state in 1876, which was a powerful assimilative tool designed to subject Indigenous peoples to state law.[56] First Nations do, however, have the right to exclude non-Indians from their territorial lands.[57]

In the United States, tribal officials generally assert that they have reluctantly arrived at the decision to invoke what they claim is a historic deterrence mechanism. However, they feel compelled to do so because of the severity of the crimes, the need to protect the community, and because their criminal powers have been so constrained by federal or state laws that involuntary exile is the best option to address the problems generated by criminal deviants.

Much of the limited contemporary legal literature devoted to examining banishment in Indian Country asserts, as one commentator put it, that "banishment is an ancient punishment used by tribes to preserve order and rehabilitate tribal members." "Historically," it was noted, "tribal members who committed grievous crimes like murder would be cast out of the tribe for a period of time to reflect on their action. Such banishments helped maintain tribal cohesion, essential to cultural identity and protection."[58]

While this statement is broadly accurate, it fails to capture the complexity and rarity of the practice. In fact, Native peoples historically resorted to banishment only as a last resort or for particularly horrific acts like premeditated murder or incest with children. Institutionalized penal systems were virtually absent across Indian Country because, as the scant available documentary evidence suggests, given the familial, egalitarian, and adjudicatory nature of tribal societies—which were more focused on mediation, restitution, and compensation aimed at solving "the problem in such a manner that all could forgive and forget and continue to live within the tribal society in harmony with one another"—permanent expulsion of tribal members was rarely practiced since the clan and kinship systems were highly effective mechanisms that help regulate member conduct and any transgressions that arose.[59]

Given the kin-based nature of tribal nations and the fact that many Native societies refused to employ centralized and coercive methods of dispute resolution or formal institutions of social control, tribal citizens generally acted with great care in how they behaved toward one another. The fear of being socially ostracized or treated as an outcast was generally sufficient to maintain relatively peaceful interpersonal behavior.

However, since perfect interpersonal relationships have never existed in any human society, conflicts and disruptions sufficient to justify banishment occasionally arose in tribal communities. The Iroquois Great Law of Peace, the oldest living constitution in the world, contains several provisions addressing the subject.[60] Section 20 describes what the penalty would be if a chief of one of the Five Nations committed murder. The other chiefs, if possible, were to assemble at the place where the homicide occurred to depose the offending chief. If this could not be accomplished, the chiefs were to discuss the crime at the next council session.

The war chief was sent to remove the chief from office and to remind the deposed chief that his female relatives were also negatively affected by his actions, since his crime was a stain upon his entire family. His title of chieftain-ship was then extended to a sister family.

The war chief was also charged with making the following statement to the now despised individual:

> So you, ... did kill .... with your own hands! You
> have committed a grave crime in the eyes of the Creator. Behold the bright
> light of the Sun, and in the brightness of the sunlight, I depose you of your
> title and remove the horns, the sacred emblem of your chieftainship title. I
> remove from your brow the deer antlers which was the emblem of your posi-
> tion and token of your nobility. I now depose you and expel you and you shall
> depart at once from the territory of the League of Five Nations and never
> more return again. We, the League of Five Nations, moreover, bury your
> women relatives because the ancient chieftainship title was never intended
> to have any union with bloodshed. Henceforth, it shall not be their heritage.
> By the evil deed that you have done they have forfeited it forever.

The Great Law also contains provisions regarding voluntary emigration and the punishment that might be meted out to adopted members of the con-federacy. With regard to voluntary emigration, section 21 declares, "When a person or family belonging to the Five Nations desires to abandon their Nation and the Territory of the Five Nations, they shall inform the Chiefs of their Na-tion and the Council of the League of Five Nations shall take notice of it." In-terestingly, the chiefs reserved the right, in effect, to recall and reintegrate such individuals by sending forth a messenger bearing a belt of black shells to the émigrés. Upon hearing the messenger and seeing the belt, the émigrés understood that this was an order "for them to return to their original homes and to their Council fires."

Finally, section 75 speaks to the rights of adopted members of "alien na-tions" who, upon formal adoption, were to be extended hospitality and con-sidered "members of the Nation" and accorded "equal rights and privileges" in all ways except the right to vote in the Council of the Chiefs of the League. Adoptees were always to be on their best behavior and were not to cause "disturbance or injury." If they were found to have caused such a disturbance, their adoption, individually or collectively, could be annulled and they would be expelled by an appointed war chief who would make the following statement to the offending individual:

> You, ... (naming the nation), listen to me while I speak. I am here to inform you again of the will of the Five Nations Council. It was clearly made known to you at a former time. Now the chiefs of the Five Nations have decided to expel you and cast you out. We disown you now and annul your adoption. Therefore you must look for a path in which to go and lead away all your people. It was you, not we, who committed wrong and caused this sentence of annulment. So then go your way and depart the territory of the Five Nations and away from the League.[61]

Similarly, the Cheyenne had occasion to banish or exile the rare tribal member who murdered another Cheyenne. Again, it was a procedure seldom used, however, given the fact that, historically, murder was rarely committed in Cheyenne society. In fact, for one extended period (1835–79) there were only sixteen recorded killings. This is evidence, say Llewellyn and Hoebel "of conflict between the aggressive personal ego of the individual male and the patterns of restraint ideationally promulgated by the culture."[62]

Thus, when a killing did occur, it was a devastating cultural shock to the entire nation that affected the community spiritually. "The killing of one Cheyenne by another Cheyenne was a sin which bloodied the Sacred Arrows, endangering thereby the well-being of the people. As such it was treated as a crime against the nation."[63] Llewellyn and Hoebel graphically described the impact: "When a murder had been done, a pall fell over the Cheyenne tribe. There could be no success in war; there would be no bountifulness in available food. Game shunned the territory; it made the tribe lonesome. So pronounced Spotted Elk; so assent all Cheyennes. There is a brooding synonym for 'murder' in Cheyenne, (Cheyenne word) *putrid*. Such was the murderer's stigma."[64]

Although Llewellyn and Hoebel report that as soon as the murder had occurred, the tribal leaders would gather as a group to announce the banishment sentence, the authors admit that they were unable to learn precisely what transpired procedurally during these meetings. They pondered, for example, whether the perpetrator had an opportunity to present evidence in a trial-like setting. Although they could not find answers to these important questions since no living Cheyenne participated in an actual banishment session, they were able to learn that Cheyenne banishment was not as absolute as many had believed.

Banishment among tribal peoples has often been perceived as the equivalent of a death sentence, but, as the Cheyenne discovered, that often depended on the social and physical environment into which the offender was exiled. For instance, banished Cheyenne could sometimes be warmly received by neighboring Arapaho or Dakota so that they were not literally isolated. Nevertheless, banished Cheyenne certainly felt undeniably homesick and would seek—and were often allowed—to return to Cheyenne society if they met certain conditions. In other words, exile, even of murderers, was typically not a permanent sentence. The expulsion was usually of an indeterminate length, although it generally lasted from five to ten years, depending on three factors: (1) the absence of intent or premeditation (the death may have been accidental, or caused by drunkenness); (2) the presence of provocation (the killer had been goaded into action); and (3) the character of the murderer (a decent man who had been provoked or who had killed accidentally, or a so-called bully murderer, a man who had killed intentionally and with the degree of malice).[65] Llewellyn and Hoebel maintain that the "remission of banishment was preceded by eloquent presentation of the wretched condition of the banished man and his family, cut off as they were from association with the tribe."[66]

The chiefs retained the power to pardon exiled persons, but only after they had secured the consent of the Cheyenne military associations and the approval of representatives of the victim's family. The readmitted member could engage in many tribal functions but was permanently barred from certain activities: Renewals of the Arrows, or eating or smoking from a Cheyenne utensil, lest it pollute or stigmatize the next user.

Llewellyn and Hoebel concluded their discussion of banishment and commutation among the Cheyenne by referring to it as a "technique of multiple excellence." They noted that "by removing the murderer it lessened provocation to revenge; it disciplined the offender; allowance was made for the return of the culprit, but only when dangers of social disruption were over . . . the result was sociologically sensible, and the recorded handling of the cases compares in effective wisdom not unfavorably with that more familiar to the reader in his own society."[67]

The Cherokee nation is another tribal group that has been written about extensively. Rennard Strickland's study, *Fire and the Spirits*, details the evolution of Cherokee law from precontact to contemporary times. In detailed tables dealing with four distinctive types of deviation in Cherokee law—spirit, community, clan, and individual—Strickland identifies the legal authority that addresses the deviation, the punishment to be meted out, and the enforcement agent who carries out the prescribed punishment.[68]

Behaviors that were considered deviations included theft of sacred objects, women's taboos, assaults, hunting violations, witchcraft, arson, marriage within one's clan, sex crimes, and murder. Sanctions ranged from name-calling, public disgrace, whipping, and sickness for lesser offenses, to stoning, mutilation, and—the ultimate penalty—death for more serious offenses. Among the thirty listed offenses, "possible expulsion" was a sanction, along with whipping, insult, and outlawry,[69] for only one set of offenses: "food and field regulations, refusal to work, contribute share of working crops."[70] Interestingly, while death could be imposed for numerous deviations, including treason, arson, and witchcraft, expulsion was mentioned only once.

One final example appears in the classic novel *Waterlily* by ethnologist Ella Cara Deloria, which details life among the Dakota before white contact. Near the end of the book, the author describes a situation during the winter, when Waterlily accompanies a war party on a trek toward Blackfeet country. When a blizzard forces them to set up camp quickly, a small family group of "strange people" comes into their midst—strange because they are so isolated from their home community. The troupe consists of a mature married couple, in their fifties, their two daughters (one with child), and three small children.

They have been forced to come in because they are hungry, but it is clear after listening to the husband and observing the ill-mannered children that something is amiss in the family's circumstances. Deloria writes, "After they had gone, the warriors agreed that the man was probably a degenerate character who lived away from civilization, that is to say, the camp circle, because of some crime against society! It was impossible that his wife at her age could be mother of those small children, and since the man was the only male, the conclusion was inescapable: 'something very bad' was the way the warriors voiced their suspicion, carefully avoiding the ugly equivalent of 'incest.'"[71]

Deloria does not state whether this family, or the husband and wife, had been banished or had gone into voluntary exile. What is clear is that incest was an offense serious enough to lead to exile because it violated the kinship norms of a civilized people and that this forced or voluntary exile had terrible repercussions on the outcasts. As Waterlily muses, "Here were people unquestionably at their worst—and they did not know it! They did not know enough

to care how they must appear to the party they had evaded; they were unconscious of being judged by them. It was a tragic thing, to stay alone like this, in
a benighted state. It was better to stay with other people and try to do your
best according to the rules there."[72]

It is clear, then, that although Native nations historically had the power
to exclude, banish, or exile individuals, it was a power they rarely used, due to
the spiritually cohesive nature of tribal collectives and the assortment of in-
formal sanctions that were in place that generally worked to ensure peace and
social order in the society.

There was also an implicit understanding, as Christina Black, an Aboriginal scholar put it, that belonging was not just about belonging to a particular
group of people, but also belonging to a particular landscape—and to be banished indefinitely from one's sacred landscape had an even more debilitating
impact on the mind and spirit of the banished person, so this was something
even the offended community knew—that it ultimately did not have the spiritual authority to make a categorical decision on who "belongs to country" as
Aborigines say, because all were equally responsible in caring for one's homeland, even those who violated societal norms.[73]

Ostracism, public ridicule, or the destruction of the culprit's lodge, weapons, or other implements, was generally sufficient to resocialize the offending
individual or family and restore harmony to the community. Even when banishment was employed in Iroquois and Cheyenne societies, it could, under
certain circumstances, be of limited duration. If the offending party showed
genuine interest in rectifying the situation, he or she would be eligible for
reintegration into the community after a period of time had lapsed, certain
conditions had been met, and the injured party's family consented.

Federal Power and Citizenship in Indian Country

The Early Years

THE NATIONAL, SOVEREIGN STATUS OF NATIVE NATIONS HAS BEEN a reality since time immemorial. Indigenous sovereignty was not delegated to Native peoples by the federal government, the states, or the U.S. Supreme Court. It is an original and inherent way of being, though it has been directly impacted by thousands of federal court rulings, administrative regulations, and congressional statutes. At the same time, Native self-determination has been recognized by the United Nations, numerous European nations, and the United States via hundreds of treaties, nearly four hundred of which were ratified by the Senate and proclaimed by the president. States were forced to concede that because of the commerce clause in the U.S. Constitution and the disclaimer clauses in their own constitutions, they lack authority to politically engage Native nations, absent express federal consent.[1]

Thus, the status of individual Native citizens derives from their recognized cultural and political citizenship in a tribal nation, which is wholly unlike the status of other racial, ethnic, or religious groups in the United States. We thus begin this chapter with three premises.

First, as sovereign nations, Indigenous peoples retain as one of their core powers of self-governance the right to decide who may or may not be considered a citizen or member of their nation.

Second, many Native nations, under their powers as governments and landowners, reserved in their treaties and constitutions the right to exclude members, nonmembers, and non-Indians alike from their reserved homelands. This exclusionary power derives from two doctrines: it is a sovereign right tied to a tribal nation's ability to protect the integrity and order of its territory and the welfare of its citizens; as landowners, Native nations have the authority to decide on the conditions under which persons can be allowed to enter their lands, live there, or conduct business, so long as they do not interfere with the rights of those that are there under federal authority.

Third, the federal government, under the constitutionally problematic doctrine of congressional plenary power, has granted to itself the authority to trump the two previous premises and has on numerous occasions interfered with, blocked, or overturned Indigenous citizenship and membership decisions whenever it has suited federal purposes to do so.[2]

As citizens of distinct, autonomous, political bodies, individual tribal members had no reason to fear federal governmental intervention in the determination of a particular Native individual's legal or political status for nearly the first century of relations with the United States. The bilateral and multilateral treaty relationships that established the structure of political, legal, cultural, and territorial relations between Native nations and the federal government was void of language defining criteria for tribal membership. There were, of course, several treaties that included language about blood, especially the term *mixed blood*, but those were merely descriptions used by Native leaders and federal officials to identify a class of individuals who played important roles in treaty negotiations and were entitled to certain benefits, like land allotments and other treaty annuities.[3]

Historically, Native nations were inclusive sociocultural communities that incorporated not only mixed bloods but individuals from other Indigenous, racial, and ethnic groups. Through processes like adoption, Native peoples managed to creatively and successfully augment their numbers and thus incorporate new blood and ideas. Outsiders were frequently welcomed into tribal communities through traditional ceremonies, and later through formal tribal acts. This openness is evidence of an inherent cultural confidence and generosity that were once hallmarks of Native nations.

Thus, Native nations have always wielded the essential power to decide who belongs or no longer belongs in their communities. Nevertheless, in 1846 an important decision was handed down by the U. S. Supreme Court, *U.S. v. Rogers*, that for the first time directly addressed the issue of Native adoptions of non-Indians.[4] Here the Supreme Court was faced with the question of whether a tribally adopted white, who had been convicted of the murder of an Indian, could be excluded from the provisions of an act of Congress that exempted Indians who had committed crimes against other Indians from federal courts.

Rogers claimed that he had voluntarily moved into Cherokee territory, had subsequently been adopted by the tribe, and exercised all the rights and privileges of other Cherokee tribal citizens. Chief Justice Roger B. Taney, apparently fearing that whites might seek adoption to tribal societies just to "throw off all responsibility to the laws of the United States," disavowed Rogers's claims and asserted, "We think it very clear that a white man, who, at mature age, is adopted in an Indian tribe does not thereby become an Indian."[5] Taney acknowledged that a white "may, by such adoption, become entitled to certain privileges in the tribe, and make himself amenable to their laws and usages . . . yet he is not an Indian."[6]

Judge Taney then proceeded to construct his own definition of *tribe* and *Indian*, which contradicted his earlier acknowledgment of community recognition: Taney's more emphatic definition was based almost solely on racial criteria. The court's decision, said the chief justice, would not affect those tribal members "who by the usages and customs of the Indians are regarded as belonging to their race. It does not speak of members of the tribe, but of the race generally—of the family of Indians; and it intended to leave them both, as regarded their own tribe, and other tribes also, to be governed by Indian usages and customs."[7]

Rogers' adoption, however, was a tribal matter. Article 5 of the Cherokee Treaty of New Echota in 1835, which recognized the right of the Cherokee Nation to "make and carry into effect all such laws as they may deem necessary for the government and protection of the persons and property within their own country belonging to their people or such persons as have connected themselves with them," vested in the Cherokee people the right to determine who could be a Cherokee.[8] The Chief Justice circumvented this important aspect of self-government by relying instead on a proviso in the same article that stated that such laws "shall not be inconsistent with the Constitution of the United States and such acts of Congress as have been or may be passed regulating trade and intercourse the Indians."[9] In Taney's view, Congress's 1834 Trade and Intercourse Act, designed to regulate non-Indian involvement and activity in Indian Country, was sufficient and provided the federal government with jurisdiction over non-Indians, notwithstanding the language of article 5 of the treaty.[10] Although Taney never discussed how Cherokee tribal laws interfered with the U.S. Constitution, his opinion set the precedent on tribal adoption of non-Indians and the racial character of much federal Indian law that has often been followed in litigation since then.

As damning as *Rogers* was in denying recognition of the Cherokee Nation's adoption decision, in the late 1800s and early 1900s the U.S. Supreme Court returned to the question of tribal adoption of non-Indians and intermarried whites and handed down several rulings that actually supported tribal sovereignty over such membership decisions. In *Alberty v. U.S.*, Ed Alberty, alias Charles Burns, was an African American who had become a Cherokee citizen under the Treaty of 1866.[11] Alberty was convicted of murdering Phil Duncan, "the illegitimate child of a Choctaw Indian, by a colored woman, who was not his wife, but a slave in the Cherokee Nation."[12]

Alberty sued out a writ of error, arguing that the federal circuit court lacked jurisdiction over the case. The Supreme Court, for the purpose of jurisdiction, considered Alberty a member of the Cherokee Nation, though not an Indian. Nevertheless, although Alberty was not considered an Indian from an ethnological perspective, his political citizenship in the Cherokee Nation was sufficient to provide the Supreme Court with jurisdiction.

And in *Nofire v. U.S.*, the Supreme Court held that a white adoptee of the Cherokee Nation was indeed a Cherokee for purposes of federal jurisdiction.[13] Fred Rutherford, a white man, had been murdered by Jess and John Nofire, two "full-blooded Cherokee Indians." Under existing law, the federal courts had jurisdiction over the crime of murder, unless the murder involved "Indian parties." Justice David Brewer, writing for the court, said that Rutherford had voluntarily changed his nationality and was now recognized by the Cherokee Nation as a Cherokee. Therefore, the Cherokee courts had jurisdiction over the crime.

More explicit confirmation of Cherokee sovereignty is found in the court's statement that "since the death of Rutherford it [the Cherokee Nation] has asserted its jurisdiction over the Cherokees who did the killing—a jurisdiction which is conditioned upon the fact that the party killed was a Cherokee citizen."[14] The lower court's ruling was reversed and the case remanded. The circuit court was told to return the Nofire brothers to the appropriate Cherokee Nation authorities.

In *Roff v. Burney* the Supreme Court for the first time explicitly addressed whether or not Native nations had the power to *disenroll* non-Indians who had previously been adopted by the nation.[15] Here, A. B. Roff, a white man, had married Matilda Bourland, also white. Mrs. Bourland had been legally enfranchised by a Chickasaw Nation law in 1876. By marriage, therefore, Roff had become a Chickasaw citizen. Seven years later, in 1883, the Chickasaw Nation enacted another law that repealed and annulled the 1876 act and called for the removal of the family members as well. This, in effect, withdrew the adoptive rights the nation had extended to Roff's wife, and by extension, to Roff himself. Later, Roff brought suit against a member of the Chickasaw Nation.

The case originated in the United States Court for the Indian Territory where Roff's case was dismissed. Roff appealed to the U.S. Supreme Court. The principal question before the court was: may a white person who has lost his adoptive rights in an Indian tribe sue a member of an Indian tribe? The court unanimously answered in the affirmative. Justice Brewer, speaking for the court, first noted that although a white adopted into a tribe became a tribal citizen, this did "not necessarily cancel his citizenship" in the United States. Second, and of more importance, the court ruled that "the citizenship which the Chickasaw legislature could confer it could withdraw."[16] Moreover, said the court, "the validity of the act withdrawing citizenship from the wife of plaintiff [Roff] and the consequent withdrawal from plaintiff of all the rights and privileges of citizenship in the Chickasaw Nation have been practically determined by the authorities of that nation, and that determination is not subject to correction by any direct appeal from the judgment of Chickasaw courts."[17] Although Roff had lost his membership in the Cherokee community, having never taken an oath of allegiance to the tribe, he was still, according to the court, a U.S. citizen and entitled to seek redress in a federal court for his alleged injuries.

Reitman says that *Roff* established two basic principles that underlie all tribal citizenship cases: (1) tribes possess plenary power over citizenship, and (2) that power is ultimately subject to Congress's greater power.[18] In the Court's words, "the only restriction on the power of the Chickasaw Nation to legislate in respect to its internal affairs is that such legislation shall not conflict with the Constitution or laws of the United States, and we know of no provision of such Constitution or laws which would be set at nought by the action of a political community like this in withdrawing privilege of membership in the community once conferred."[19]

In *Glenn-Tucker v. Clayton*, the Choctaw Nation enacted a law (1882) designed to remove from Choctaw territory whites who claimed citizenship in their nation.[20] After nearly twenty years of litigation the court of appeals for the Indian Territory held for the Choctaw Nation, declaring that "the Choctaw National Council had lawfully passed judgment on the plaintiffs' [whites] citizenship, that the Department of the Interior had lawfully rejected [their appeal], and that the territorial courts of Indian Country had no jurisdiction to entertain a further action."[21]

Finally in 1906, the issue of what property rights, if any, non-Indians intermarried with Indian tribes had was brought before the U.S. Supreme Court in the *Cherokee Intermarriage Cases*.[22] The Supreme Court had dealt with the issue of tribal political citizenship for non-Indians in *Alberty* and *Nofire*, both of which involved criminal jurisdiction. This case, however, represented a situation with potentially far greater material impact on tribal nations: the disposition of tribal property to intermarried whites.

Also known as "The White Man's Case," this opinion was actually a consolidation of four cases: *Red Bird v. U.S., Cherokee Nation v. U.S., Fife v. U.S., and Persons Claiming Rights in the Cherokee Nation by Intermarriage v. U.S.*[23] It originated in the court of appeals where Cherokee Indians "by blood" filed a claim against the enrollment of 3,627 white persons who sought to participate in the distribution of the common property of the Cherokee Nation. The Cherokee's national domain then consisted of nearly 4.5 million acres of land that was about to be allotted by the federal government.

After a thorough review of the "laws and usages of the Cherokees, their earliest history, the fundamental principles of their national policy, their Constitution and statutes," the court of claims gave a three-part ruling. First, the court said that whites who acquired Cherokee citizenship by marriage before November 1, 1875, had equal per capita rights with Cherokees by blood to the Cherokee Nation's public domain lands. They were not, however, entitled to Cherokee funds.[24]

Second, whites who intermarried after November 1875 but before November 28, 1877, had no right to Cherokee property or funds unless they had paid a $500 fee to the Cherokee Nation. Finally, the claims court held that white husbands of Cherokee women who had abandoned their wives automatically forfeited all rights as Cherokee citizens, including those to property and proceeds.

This decision left many dissatisfied. Ethnic Cherokees, aggrieved intermarried whites, and the Cherokee government all soon filed appeals challenging various parts of the decision with the U.S. Supreme Court. On November 5, 1906, Chief Justice Fuller, for a unanimous court, issued his opinion affirming the court of claim's decision in all respects. The Supreme Court engaged in a meticulous review of applicable Cherokee laws and concluded that although certain whites (only 286 claimants out of 3,627 were recognized) had been recognized as Cherokees for certain purposes, "many special Cherokee laws demonstrate that the Cherokee Council did not venture to assume, nor desire to assume, the power to impart to the white adopted citizens other than civil and political rights."[25] In short, the Cherokee Nation had virtually unencumbered authority to qualify the rights of citizenship that it had bestowed.

The following day the *New York Times* ran an article with this headline: "Supreme Court Aids Indians: White Men Not Entitled to Share in Division of Lands." The frustrated white claimants turned to Congress for redress. Several bills were later introduced in both houses in the fall of 1906 with the following as their primary goals: "Providing for the enrollment of such white persons as prior to December 16, 1895, were intermarried with Cherokee, Shawnee, Delaware by blood, in accordance with the laws of the Cherokee Nation, and declaring that they should have the same status as other citizens of the tribe, but should first pay into the treasury of the United States for the benefit of the Cherokee Nation $325 each, and should avail themselves of the privilege of enrollment within six months from the approval of the act."[26]

These bills were blatant attempts to circumvent the Supreme Court's opinion and legislatively award allotments of Indian lands to whites for a minimal fee. The Commissioner of Indian Affairs, on January 4, 1907, stepped forth, largely on pragmatic grounds, in defense of the Cherokees. In reporting on one such bill, S. 6122, the commissioner "opposed the proposed legislation because it was doubtful whether there were enough Cherokee lands to give an allotment to each person entitled to enrollment exclusive of the intermarried whites."[27]

There was, however, another class of intermarried whites who stated that they believed they were entitled to citizenship because they had, in good faith, made improvements on Cherokee lands. The question was whether they should be compensated for the value of their improvements. President Theodore Roosevelt, commenting on the case in a letter to the Senate on February 11, 1907, spoke of the "urgent necessity for legislation for the relief of intermarried whites . . . adversely affected by such decisions."[28] The president had introduced a bill that was designed to allow the intermarried white citizens time to dispose of their improvements. This bill became law on March 2, 1907.[29] It gave the affected whites until May 2, 1907, to transfer their improvements to enrolled Cherokees.

The preceding cases indicate that the federal courts generally supported tribal decisions on their membership decisions (a) when they involved non-Indians, (b) if such a determination was considered especially crucial to a tribe's continued cultural existence, or (c) if such a conclusion would not infringe on Congress's assumed right to control Native property and the political relationship with Indigenous peoples. The following cases, however, are examples of judicial statements in which Congress and the Department of the Interior's power to act as the final voice in tribal membership matters was upheld.

PROPERTY AND IDENTITY

"A fundamental difference between barbarians and a civilized people is the difference between a herd and an individual. All barbarous customs tend to destroy individuality. Where everything is held in common, thrift and enterprise have no stimulus of reward and thus individual progress is rendered very improbable, if not impossible. The starting point of individualism for an Indian is the personal possession of his portion of the reservation."[30]

The operative word in the passage quoted here is *individualism*. The notion that individual ownership of a specified parcel of land was directly correlated with the civilization of tribal members probably represented the fundamental belief in the federal policymakers' paradigm from the early 1800s through the 1930s. In the formative years of the United States, individual allotments to Natives usually came as a result of specific treaty provisions or ad hoc legislation. In fact, before 1855 the federal government had, "under various treaties and laws, issued over 11,200 patents to individual Indians and 1,290 certificates of allotment."[31]

But it was in the wake of humanitarian concern for Indian reform in the post–Civil War era and the inexorable drive of Western capitalistic expansion that would catapult the idea of Indian allotment, also known as severalty, into a major federal policy directive. The national policy of allotment was pronounced in the General Allotment Act of 1887.[32] This law, hailed as "a mighty polarizing engine to break up the tribal mass," has been admirably treated by numerous scholars.[33]

Nevertheless, it is imperative that the allotment policy's fundamental components be spelled out as a prelude to discussing tribal membership rulings. Tribal membership is intimately related to allotment because although a Native nation generally has the power to determine its own citizenship, federal courts have also determined that Congress has the power "to supersede that determination when necessary for the administration of tribal property, particularly its distribution among the members of the tribe."[34]

Although various bills to allot tribal reservations had been introduced as early as the 1870s, Senator Henry L. Dawes, who became chairman of the Committee on Indian Affairs in the mid-1880s, spearheaded the final push culminating in the law's enactment on February 8, 1887. The act's major provisions were: (1) 160 acres were granted to each head of household, eighty acres to single persons eighteen years or older, and forty acres to individuals under eighteen; (2) every allottee was to receive a patent in fee to be held in trust by the United States for twenty-five years during which time the land could not be transferred or sold; (3) once a reservation had been surveyed, individuals had four years to make their selection—if they failed to act, the secretary of the interior could make the selection for them; and (4) when a person had received fee simple title to the land, they automatically became federal citizens.[35]

The Allotment Act contained several interesting provisions. First, the law was not immediately enforceable on tribal nations. The president of the United States had to first authorize a survey of a particular reservation when in his opinion the reservation seemed "advantageous for agricultural and grazing purposes." Second, the law was inapplicable to some Native nations, including the Five Civilized Tribes, the Osage, Miami, Peoria, Sac and Fox, Seneca, and Indian Territory in Nebraska that adjoined the Sioux Nation. The Five Civilized Tribes, for example, were exempt because they held fee simple title to their property, a form of title that the United States was then obligated to respect.

History shows that the General Allotment Act, as interpreted by the Supreme Court, represented, on the one hand, the foremost example of a broader federal Indian campaign— which also included Christianization, courts of Indian offenses, and Western education—designed to end tribal sovereignty by breaking up tribal lands and families and coercively assimilating Native individuals into the body politic of the United States. Before the allotment policy was terminated with enactment of the Indian Reorganization Act in 1934,[36] Native landholdings had been reduced from 138 million acres 48 million acres.[37]

Although initially exempted from the Allotment Act because of their fee simple land tenure, pressure began to mount against the Five Civilized Tribes as more non-Indians moved into Indian Territory. In 1891 President Harrison observed that "the relation of the Five Civilized Tribes now occupying the Indian Territory . . . is not, I believe, that best calculated to promote the highest advancement of these Indians." According to Harrison, the fact that there were "within our borders five independent states having no relations, except those growing out of treaties . . . was a startling anomaly."[38]

Two years later, Congress authorized the president to appoint a commission whose purpose was to convince the Five Tribes of the benefits of breaking up their communal landholdings and having them converted into individual allotments.[39] Over the next few years an unbearable amount of pressure was exerted on the Five Tribes intended to press them into entering negotiated agreements where they would cede additional chunks of tribal land in exchange for small, isolated parcels.[40] Four of the five tribes resisted, however—

the Creek, Chickasaw, Choctaw, and Cherokee. The Seminole negotiated a pre-Curtis agreement in which they consented to have their lands allotted.

While this was transpiring the Dawes Commission issued a report on May 7, 1894, which declared that the Five Civilized Tribes' separate legal and political status had to be terminated. "It is not only non-American," noted the commissioners, "but it is radically wrong, and the change is imperatively demanded in the interest of the Indian and white alike, and such change cannot be longer delayed."[41]

Congress later, by way of a provision in the Indian Appropriation Act of 1896, authorized the Dawes Commission to move directly to supplant the key right of self-government: the commission, not Native nations, was empowered to determine who could be enrolled as citizens in the Five Tribes.[42] These rolls, fraught with errors and omissions, would become determinative as to who would later be recognized as citizens of each of the Five Tribes.

A year later, on June 7, 1897, the relentless process to terminate tribal governing authority and replace it with Anglo authority was furthered with the passage of a congressional statute which gave federal courts civil and criminal jurisdiction over the Indian Territory. This transfer of jurisdiction was slated to begin January 1, 1898.[43] Congress then prepared to enact unilateral legislation to complete its dubious mission—the legal dismemberment of the Five Tribes' self-governing capabilities and the individualization of their collective lands. The tribes responded by astutely employing every political means at their disposal to head this off. For instance, the Creek and Seminole nations submitted a petition to the U.S. Senate in which they implored that body not to enact such a measure. "We desire," said the tribal politicians, "to call your attention to the fact that under the solemn treaty stipulations the right of unrestricted self-government has been guaranteed to our people."[44]

Despite these and other formidable treaty and constitutionally based arguments, Congress, on June 28, 1898, enacted the Curtis Act, which effectively gutted what remained of the Five Tribes governing powers in Indian Territory.[45] Ironically, the twenty-four-page law was entitled "An Act for the protection of the people of the Indian Territory. . ." because one of the bill's principal selling points in Congress had been that white residents in Indian Country, who outnumbered Natives 300,000 to 65,000, allegedly had to deal with tribal officials who purportedly engaged in "unlawful and fraudulent transactions."[46]

The following year the Supreme Court, in *Stephens v. Cherokee Nation*, acquiesced to the congressional trampling of tribal governing powers and upheld the federal legislation under which Congress assumed the tribal nations' power to determine membership.[47] Furthermore, the Court did not question whether the government's usurpation of tribal enrollment was proper, per se; it merely restated the falsehood of Native peoples as "wards," first articulated as an analogy by Chief Justice John Marshall in *Cherokee Nation v. Georgia* (1831) as a justification for Congress's ousting of tribal jurisdiction regarding membership.

The seven-to-two majority (Justice Edward White and Joseph McKenna dissented, but only regarding the extent of the court's jurisdiction), early in the opinion, cited Congress's "plenary power of legislation" regarding tribal citizenship.[48] This was the first federal Indian law case to employ the concept of plenary power, although congressional power was defined as exclusive and not unlimited because it remained "subject . . . to the Constitution of the United States."[49] In addition, the Court openly deferred to Congress, and quoting from *Thomas v. Gay* (1898), stated that questions such as Congress's power to enact laws that supersede treaties "are beyond the spirit of judicial cognizance, and must be met by the political department of the government."[50]

Thus this case explicitly combined plenary power, judicial deference, and the political question doctrine in a manner with devastating consequences for Native sovereignty. The Court said that "it is true that the Indian tribes were for many years allowed by the United States to make all laws and regulations [for their own people]. . . . The policy of the government, however, in dealing with the Indian nations was definitely expressed in a proviso" in 1871 that effectively stifled treaty-making between the United States and Native nations.[51]

The Court here not only legitimated Congress's questionable decision to no longer recognize tribal sovereignty via treaties, but in employing the political question doctrine, simultaneously precluded tribes from a judicial remedy. Chief Justice Melville Fuller, near the end of his opinion, concisely asserted why such immense congressional power was necessary and how it would be used: "We respect that in view of the paramount authority of Congress over the Indian tribes, and of the duties imposed on the Government by their condition of dependency, we cannot say that Congress could not empower the Dawes Commission to determine . . . who were entitled to citizenship . . . [this was] an essential preliminary to effective action and promotion of the best interests of the tribes."[52]

For the Court, the "plenary dependency" of the Native nations mandated a "plenary congressional power" to ensure their proper and steady evolution toward U.S. citizenship and assimilation. The legal fiction of wardship had been reified to such a point that even the question of tribal citizenship had to be handled by the federal government. After all, such an important determination could not be left in the hands of "incompetent wards."

While *Stephens* was the most crippling case denying tribal sovereignty insofar as allotment and membership decisions were concerned, three additional Supreme Court rulings handed down within the next two decades—*Wallace v. Adams*,[53] *U.S. ex. Rel. West v. Hitchcock*,[54] and *Sizemore v. Brady*[55]—reminded Native nations that their fundamental power to decide membership in their communities when it came to the distribution of property was subject to complete defeasance by federal authorities.

Wallace and *West*, companion cases handed down within a week of each other in 1907, elaborated on the virtually unlimited power of Congress, and the vast administrative authority of the Department of the Interior, to determine or deny tribal membership. These two cases fit well with the overall federal thrust of that year that focused on the purported plenary dependency of Native peoples and the continued assimilationist orientation of federal officials. This is evidenced by two laws enacted in March 1907. The first was a provision in the Indian Appropriation Act that authorized so-called noncompetent allotted Indians who had obtained patents to sell their tracts.[56] The second, the Lacey Act, provided for the individual allotment and distribution of Indian tribal trust funds.[57]

In *Wallace* the Court dealt with two questions: one involving procedure, one power. The procedural question focused on the defendant, Hill, who had not been made a party to the proceeding when the case arose at the trial court. They ruled, however, that this was not a problem since it was within the Supreme Court's power to "name as defendants a few individuals who are in fact the representatives of a large class having the common interest."[58]

The second and more primary question involved Congress's power: was an Indian Territory court's decree declaring the defendant, Hill, a Choctaw citizen "a finality beyond the power of Congress to in any manner disturb?"[59] Relying exclusively on the *Stephens* precedent, Associate Justice David Brewer, writing for a unanimous Court, held that: "The power of Congress over the matter of citizenship of these tribes was plenary, and it could adopt any reasonable means to ascertain who were entitled to its privileges. If the results of one measure were not satisfactory, it could try another."[60]

Less than a week after this decision, the Supreme Court dove into the parallel and equally critical issue of federal administrative power—as exemplified by the actions of the secretary of the interior over tribal lives. "The interplay," according to Cohen, "of the legislative and administrative branches of government in Indian affairs has caused the frequent application of two rules of administrative law."[61] First, so long as the adopted regulations follow statutory or treaty law they will be treated as if they are statutes and the courts will accord them proper respect. The second principle involves consistency over time. If the administrative authority has consistently acted in a certain way for an extended period, such authority will also be respected. This is especially true "if it is a rule affecting considerable property or a doubtful question."[62] Evidence of the first principle is found in the case *Wolsey v. Chapman*.[63] There, the Supreme Court posited that "the acts of the heads of departments, within the scope of their powers are in law the acts of the President."[64]

West is evidence of the second principle. In this suit, Willis C. West, a white man intermarried into the Wichita tribe of Oklahoma, had his application for an allotment rejected by the Department of the Interior, then headed by Ethan A. Hitchcock. West, according to the secretary's determination, had never been "recognized" as a tribal member. Persons considered as nonmembers, of course, were ineligible for tribal land allotments.

West lost in the lower courts and appealed to the Supreme Court. Associate Justice Oliver W. Holmes, speaking for a unified court, affirmed the appeal court's decision. The court artfully linked virtually unreviewable discretionary administrative authority—"his [Secretary's] jurisdiction did not depend upon his decision being right"—which had been delegated by the executive branch, with the similarly unreviewable and entrenched legislative authority—"the power of Congress is not doubted. The Indians have been treated as wards of the Nation."[65] "The Secretary," Holmes said, "must have authority to decide on membership in a doubtful case, and if he has it in any case he has it in all."[66] However, why must the secretary have this power? This raw assertion of administrative authority is never specifically analyzed nor made to fit within the constitutional framework. The only rationale put forth by the justices was that of "guardianship," which has no basis in the Constitution or treaty law.

Holmes did, however, paternalistically state that the secretary's power to determine tribal membership was a regulatory power "obviously made for the welfare of the rather helpless people concerned."[67] Although one scholar has narrowly construed the *West* holding regarding the secretary's immense discretionary power, in essence, the Department of the Interior may exercise the authority to disregard a tribal decision on membership so long as his action is not determined to be arbitrary.[68]

In August 1907, three months before Oklahoma became a state, members of another Native nation in Indian Territory, the Osage tribe, sent the names of 244 enrolled members[69] to the secretary of the interior insisting that they be disenrolled because they had allegedly secured enrollment fraudulently.[70] The secretary, however, after an investigation declined to disenroll those persons. McAuliff's research suggests that the individuals targeted for disenrollment were actually whites and non-Osage Indians who only claimed to be mixed-blood Osage and who happened to favor allotment.[71] Interestingly, the Osage are one of only three tribal nations that allow its members to simultaneously hold membership in another federal recognized tribe.[72]

Garfield v. Goldsby,[73] decided in 1908, is one of the few cases where the Supreme Court determined that the secretary of the interior had, indeed, acted arbitrarily in striking Goldsby and his children from the Chickasaw enrollment rolls without having first given the applicants opportunity to contest their disenrollment and having acted without congressional sanction.[74] In Associate Justice Day's words,

> In our view, this case resolves itself into a question of the power of the Secretary of the Interior in the premises, as conferred by the acts of Congress. We appreciate fully the purpose of Congress in numerous acts of legislation to confer authority upon the Secretary of the Interior to administer upon the Indian lands, and previous decisions of this court have shown its refusal to sanction a judgment interfering with the Secretary where he acts within the powers conferred by law. But, as has been affirmed by this court in former decisions, there is no place in our constitutional system for the exercise of arbitrary power, and, if the Secretary has exceeded the authority conferred upon him by law, then there is power in the courts to restore the status of the parties aggrieved by such unwarranted action.[75]

Goldsby had been enrolled in 1905 and had subsequently received a certificate of his 320-acre allotment. The court could find no language in the statute "which gave the Secretary power and authority without notice and hearing, to strike down the rights thus acquired."[76] Goldsby and his children were to be reenrolled in the Chickasaw Nation and restored to ownership of their allotment.

Six years later, in *Sizemore v. Brady*, the Supreme Court reaffirmed federal supremacy over tribal membership and elevated state power in the field as well.[77] The facts in *Sizemore* were simple enough. Ellis Grayson, a Creek Indian and an allottee, had died without a will. He was unmarried. After his death, his only surviving relatives were three first cousins, one paternal, and the other two on the maternal side. At issue, according to the court, were two questions. First, should Grayson's beneficiaries be determined by Creek tribal law or Arkansas state law? Second, did the governing law prefer either paternal or maternal relatives when "all were of the same degree?"[78] The case began in the state district court of Wagoner County, Oklahoma, where the trial court ruled for the maternal cousins. Thus, Creek law applied. The paternal cousin appealed this ruling to Oklahoma's Supreme Court which reversed the lower court's decision. The case was then appealed to the U.S. Supreme Court.

Justice Willis Van Devanter, for a unanimous court, affirmed the state Supreme Court's finding favoring state law and paternal heirship. The court first reviewed the appropriate Creek–United States agreement and other federal legislation that had terminated Creek self-government via the Curtis Act of 1898 and led to the allotment of their territory. According to Van Devanter, the act of May 27, 1902, "repealed the provision giving effect to the Creek laws of descent and distribution and substituted in their stead the laws of Arkansas."[79] Echoing prevailing congressional and popular sentiment of Native "dependency," the court held further that "like other tribal Indians, the Creeks were wards of the United States, which possessed full power, if it deemed such a course wise, to assume full control over them and their affairs, to ascertain who were members of the tribe, to distribute the lands and funds among them, and to terminate the tribal government."[80]

The Court denied that the original Creek agreement of 1901 had created vested individual property rights subject to the due process clause of the Fifth Amendment. The power of Congress, noted Van Devanter, "was not exhausted or restrained by the adoption of the original agreement, but remained the same thereafter as before, save that rights created by carrying the agreement into effect could not be divested."[81] Creek tribal law, despite explicit statutory recognition in the 1901 agreement, was submerged under both congressional authority as well as state inheritance law.

The issue of whether Indians were eligible for allotments when a mixed marriage had taken place reappeared before the Supreme Court in *Halbert v. United States* (1931).[82] In this case, a Quinault Indian woman, married to a white man, brought suit to secure an allotment for her child. Justice Willis Van Devanter said that under the usual rule, the right of individual Indians to share in tribal property depended on tribal membership and was lost when the membership ended. Under the operation of this rule, then, an Indian woman who married a non-Indian, separated from her tribe, and moved away from the reservation was deprived of her tribal membership. Van Devanter further observed that "it is the separation from the tribe rather than the marriage which puts an end to the membership." In this case, however, since the woman had remained in the tribal environment her tribal affiliation was not affected and she and her children remained legal Indians eligible for allotments.[83]

Finally, one of the more direct judicial sanctions of a congressional power that ignored the full-fledged political relationship between Native nations and the federal government was *Simmons v. Seelatsee*, a case decided by the U.S. District Court for the Eastern District of Washington.[84] The facts of this case were these: the secretary of the interior had denied the children and grandchildren of the deceased, Joseph Simmons Sr., their interest in his property on the grounds that they failed to meet the one-quarter blood tribal membership requirement imposed by Congress in a 1946 law and enforced by the secretary of the interior.[85] Simmons's children and grandchildren brought suit against the Yakima (now spelled Yakama) Nation's chief, Eagle Seelatsee, and the tribal council, challenging their denial of benefits. The United States intervened on behalf of the Yakima Nation.

Circuit Judge Walter L. Pope, not surprisingly, upheld the secretary's denial of inheritance to the Simmons offspring on the basis of Congress's self-assumed plenary power over Indian tribes. "This plenary power of Congress," said Judge Pope, "to legislate with respect to Indian rights exists regardless of whether the Indians are citizens or otherwise."[86] Included in this largely unfettered plenary power was the authority to control and decide tribal membership. "In short, Congress, or the delegated agents, had full power to define and describe those persons who should be treated and regarded as members of an Indian tribe and entitled to enrollment therein."[87]

Judge Pope continued by asserting that when Congress enacted the act of August 9, 1946, which provided that after that date only duly enrolled Yakima of one-quarter or more blood could inherit any interest in restricted or trust estates of deceased Yakima members, it clearly intended to and had to rely on blood quantum. In fact, the district court seemed enamored with blood quantum, as the following comments suggest: "It is plain that the Congress, on numerous occasions, has deemed it expedient, and within its powers to classify Indians according to their percentages of Indian blood. Indeed, if legislation is to deal with Indians at all the very reference to them implies the use of 'a criterion of race.'" "Indians," Judge Pope concluded, "can only be defined by their race."[88] The evidence addressed thus far, however, does not support Pope's conclusion. Certainly race has been an important factor, but other criteria have also been employed: community recognition, tribal self-determination, kinship relations, and so on.

The evidence just examined shows that when race, crime, or property (particularly allotments) were implicated in membership/citizenship matters, federal policymakers would generally act in a manner that reinforced federal supremacy over Native nations, especially in so far as policy was geared toward the coerced assimilation of Natives and the individualization of tribal property via the allotment process, while occasionally acting to uphold individual property rights of Natives if they had vested to the individual. A good deal of the case law just analyzed broadly supported the authority of tribal governments to determine who their members or citizens were, particularly when such questions dealt with the rights of non-Indians who had been granted tribal citizenship. But once the allotment process was fully unfurled, congressional and administrative power frequently trumped tribal power on the question of who belonged as federal officials sought to reduce the number of Natives eligible for allotments and treaty annuities.

In short, the federal court's uneven rulings on the two symbiotic issues—allotment and membership—mirrored the vacillation of federal policymakers regarding tribal sovereignty. While the courts were willing, at times, to issue occasional rulings that suggested a grudging respect for tribal self-determination on issues of membership, more often they generally acknowledged in Congress and the executive branch a significant, sometimes absolute, power over Native nations' right to decide who belonged in their communities, who were entitled to benefit from tribal resources, and who had the final say over questions of membership or citizenship.

CHAPTER 3

A New Deal for
Native Citizenship

NEARLY HALF A CENTURY OF INDIGENOUS HISTORY BOOKENDED THE General Allotment Act of 1887 and the Indian Reorganization Act of 1934. It was a cataclysmic period of social experimentation in which the federal government tried mightily—via boarding schools, the imposition of Western political and legal systems, Christian missionary activity, and especially the dramatic subdivision of Native communal property into private property increments—to "save" Natives from themselves by compelling massive changes in virtually every sphere of their lives.

As we saw in the previous chapter, private property through individual allotments became the major panacea for all the U.S.-government-created ills. The allotting of Indian Country and who was determined eligible—for one of the precious parcels or the resources appurtenant to the allotment (be it water, oil, coal, etc.) or entitled to continued trust recognition (i.e., wardship or incompetence status in the court's parlance)—became a dominant concern for federal officials and, of course, tribal nations.

During this period, if not before, we begin also to see greater evidence of factionalism or community segmentation in many Native communities. Whether driven by education (returned boarding school students versus nonformally educated students), religion (those who adopted Christianity, remained traditional, or blended the two together), geographic residence (remained on the reservation or moved away), blood quantum (full-blood, half-blood, or mixed-race), or allotment status (allotted and retained the parcel, allotted and sold or leased the parcel, or never allotted), Native communities became more divided than ever before.

It is during this era, while many Native nations struggled with allotment and the problems that policy precipitated, including for some the near destruction of their governments, that a few traditional cultural segments of tribal nations entertained the thought of voluntary exile as one way of coping with changes they no longer wanted to deal with. For example, when the U.S. Senate Select Committee on the Five Civilized Tribes visited Oklahoma in 1906, a group of Choctaw, headed by Jacob Jackson, presented the committee members with a paper requesting permission to sell their allotments and, with the funds generated by those sales, the right to emigrate to Central America. These traditional-minded Choctaw believed they had but one political right remaining and they intended to exercise it. "Surely, a race of people," they argued, "desiring to preserve the integrity of that race, who love it by reason of its traditions and their common ancestors and blood, who are proud of the fact that they belong to it may be permitted to protect themselves if in no other way by emigration. Our educated people inform us that the white man came to this country to avoid conditions which to him were not as bad as the present conditions are to us. . . . All we ask is that we may permitted to exercise the same privilege."[1] The United States, which previously had supported similar efforts by some Iroquois, Kickapoo, and Ponca, to expatriate to Canada, Mexico, and Nebraska respectively, refused to support Choctaw emigration.[2]

While Native nations experienced profound change during the years leading up to the Indian Reorganization Act (IRA), including substantive changes in their governing structures, the evidence shows that both internally and internationally, they utilized an assortment of governing approaches.[3] In other words, when John Collier proposed his New Deal for Native peoples and provided them an opportunity to exercise a measure of self-rule, the understanding of self-governance and constitutional governance were very familiar to many indigenous leaders even after having endured several decades of coercive policies aimed at the destabilization and dismantling of historic self-governing structures.

As late as the early 1930s, the incredible diversity evident in Indigenous governing structures, along with the value systems that underlay them, indicated that Native peoples were willing to embrace new legal and political mechanisms in an effort to adjust to the ever shifting landscape they lived in. Simultaneously, varying segments of many Native nations strove and had some success in maintaining precontact sociocultural norms, institutions, and traditions to distinguish themselves from other nations and several intruding political powers they had to contend with. Even in the most intensely divided nations, the vying groups sometimes still based their political, economic, and citizen decisions upon traditional beliefs, structures, and leadership styles that were deeply rooted in historic arrangements that predated the arrival of non-Indians on their lands.

Documentation of who belonged in tribal nations came from a variety of sources in the years leading up to the IRA. First, many Native peoples had signed treaties and were required to sign up to receive annuities. Second, some Native nations had formal rolls established for them, like the ones prepared by the Dawes Commission members for the Five Civilized Tribes. In other cases tribal members' names appeared on specific Indian census rolls that were gathered beginning in the 1880s by superintendents or agents. At the same time, some Native individuals' names appeared on federal census records that, beginning in the latter part of the nineteenth century, did a special enumeration of Natives on specific reservations.

Thus, by the time Franklin D. Roosevelt became president in 1933, signaling the start of the so-called Indian New Deal, there were several documentary record sets—none of which was without flaws and errors—available to both tribal and federal officials that enabled both sets of governing bodies to identify who was an enrolled Native citizen. These records provide the documentary baseline that federal policymakers and tribal leaders would come to rely on, beginning with adoption of the IRA, once it was enacted in 1934, and continuing to the present time.

NEW DEAL FOR NEW TIMES

The New Deal of Franklin D. Roosevelt brought radical changes for many Native nations. John Collier, Roosevelt's commissioner of Indian affairs, was an energetic and idealistic social scientist who understood non-Western cultures better than any of his predecessors. To assist Native nations in the stabilization and reconstitution of their political bases and to help them revitalize their cultural traditions, Collier, with the considerable help of Felix S. Cohen, introduced the IRA in 1934.[4] Although Congress amended and dramatically reduced the breadth of the bill at the insistence of various sources, including "the fears of individual Indians owning allotments, the interests of non-Indian groups leasing Indian land using Indian timber, the concerns of missionary groups operating on Indian reservations, and congressional beliefs about the appropriate relationship between Indians and the federal government," basic redefinition of critical concepts produced additional changes in indigenous status.[5]

Under the IRA, "any Indian tribe, or tribes, residing on the same reservation" had the right to organize a government and could, if they so desired, "devise a constitution and bylaws to operate under that would be recognized by the federal government."[6] In practical terms, this provision meant that tracts of land called reservations determined the status of political entities called "recognized tribes." Some tracts of land had also been set aside for individual homeless Indians. These tracts, designated as reservations, made the Indian inhabitants eligible for federal recognition. "Tribes," in some instances of less than twenty people, were thereby eligible to organize themselves under formal constitutions and bylaws. In other instances, two Indigenous nations sharing the same reservation, although with entirely different political and cultural backgrounds, including different treaties, were melded into one organic political entity under the act's provisions. Among its other provisions the IRA effectively ended allotment, restored trust protection of remaining Native lands, supported tribal political and economic organization, and, importantly, allowed tribal nations the right to choose whether they would even embrace the law's provisions.

Felix Cohen, the chief architect of the draft bill, envisioned the potential tribal constitutional governments "to be like town governments, except that they would have federal protection and their special rights."[7] After the IRA became law in the summer of 1934, 181 Native communities adopted the act, with seventy-seven choosing to reject it. Although Native peoples that adopted the measure were not required to adopt constitutions, many expressed interest in doing so, and Cohen was appointed chairman of the Tribal Organization Committee (TOC) that was in charge of helping these nations during the constitutional development process.

The process of modern tribal constitutional development has long been fraught with uncertainty and ambiguity. Many commentators have maintained that Western-style constitutions were forced on reluctant Native communities, thereby eclipsing extent traditional systems that, they argue, had survived the previous century of coercive assimilation. These authors also typically assert that the Bureau of Indian Affairs (BIA) developed a model constitution that was sent out to newly organizing tribal nations to help them structure the style and content of their organic documents, forcing a constitutional uniformity that denies the diverse nature of Native nations.

But Elmer Rusco noted in his excellent study of the IRA, *A Fateful Time,* that the allegation that a coercive and uniform model tribal constitution had been sent out was an error. While acknowledging that the idea had been considered, Rusco says that this approach was ultimately rejected by the bureau. "Perhaps," said Rusco, "the confusion arose from the fact that the Bureau did develop an outline of topics that might be included in a constitution. However, listing a membership section imposed no uniform rule for determining membership, and the same thing is true in other areas."[8]

An analysis of Cohen's private papers and a review of the little-known document he wrote on tribal constitutions, "Basic Memorandum," generally supports Rusco's interpretation of events, although there is incontrovertible evidence that some Native nations did, in fact, receive a copy of a model constitution or in some cases an outline of what a constitution might contain.[9] These instruments were meant to guide Native nations in their efforts to craft an organic document. Much more comprehensive and systematic research of all the BIA's records and the records of individual IRA Indigenous communities is required before we can definitively answer the question of precisely how many tribal peoples received the model constitution, the outline, or the model of a corporate charter. Also open to further research is the question of whether the constitutional process in Indian Country effectively displaced extent traditional systems of governance—and, indeed, which Native peoples retained traditional forms of governance by the mid-1930s.[10]

As important as the IRA was, it was actually through a series of subsequent solicitor's opinions—many written by Felix Cohen or Nathan Margold, the solicitor general—that Native nations learned what their actual political and legal powers were under federal law. Two opinions, in particular, written in the fall of 1934, established an almost contradictory set of statuses for those nations who adopted the IRA.

On October 25, 1934, an opinion by Assistant Solicitor Cohen and signed by Solicitor Margold titled "Powers of Indian Tribes" identified and elaborated on a host of inherent powers vested in Native nations under existing law—for example, the power to tax, form a government, and regulate domestic relations, among others.[11] Two additional powers are of significant import for this study. The first was outlined as such: "to define the conditions of membership within the tribe, to prescribe rules for adoption, to classify the members of the tribe and to grant or withhold the right of tribal suffrage and to make all other necessary rules and regulations governing the membership of the tribe so far as may be consistent with existing acts of Congress governing the enrollment and property rights of members." And the second: "to remove or to exclude from the limits of the reservation nonmembers of the tribe, excepting authorized Government officials and other persons now occupying reservation lands under lawful authority, and to prescribe appropriate rules and regulations governing such removal and exclusion, and governing the conditions under which nonmembers of the tribe may come upon tribal land or have dealings with tribal members, providing such acts are consistent with Federal laws governing trade with the Indian tribes."[12] These two powers provide tribal government officials with considerable authority in regards to their own citizens—though nothing expressly authorizes disenrollment, they can withhold voting privileges—and over nonmembers residents (both Natives from other tribes and non-Natives).

Cohen also declared that Native nations had historically exercised complete external and internal sovereign powers. However, two months later, on December 13, 1934, another opinion was released by Solicitor Margold that then attempted to place Native nations within the structure of federal law:

> The Indian tribes have long been recognized as vested with governmental powers, subject to limitations imposed by Federal statutes. The powers of an Indian tribe cannot be restricted or controlled by the governments of the several States. The tribe is, therefore, so far as its original absolute sovereignty has been limited, an instrumentality and agency of the Federal Government. Various statutes authorize the delegation of new powers of government to the Indian tribes. . . . The most recent of such statutes is the Wheeler-Howard Act [IRA], which sets up as one of its primary objectives, the purpose "to grant certain rights of home rule to Indians."
>
> This Act contemplates the devolution to the duly organized Indian tribes of many powers over property and personal conduct which are now exercised by officials of the Interior Department. The granting of a Federal corporate charter to an Indian tribe confirms the character of such tribe as a Federal instrumentality and agency.[13]

This conception of Native political status combined Chief Justice John Marshall's notion of domestic dependent nationhood, first articulated in *Cherokee Nation v. Georgia* (1831), with the contemporary idea of chartering federal corporations such as the Tennessee Valley Authority to produce a new entity with aspects of federalism and elements of aboriginal tribal status. In more abstract terms, Native governments were fully capable political entities except where they voluntarily surrendered aspects of self-government or where Congress had eliminated certain functions of self-government. Few people, however, understood which functions had been legally divested and which had lapsed through inattention and disuse.

Although Native governments held plenary authority over their rolls and could wield the incredible power to exclude non-citizens (with exceptions) from tribal lands, the fact that they were still subject to Congress's ultimate plenary authority and, for those who adopted the IRA and corporate charters, were viewed as "federal instrumentalities," left Native peoples in an ambiguous status politically, legally, and economically.

Despite these mixed statuses, Native nations—both IRA adoptees and non-IRA nations—set about revitalizing their communities finally armed with a stronger measure of institutional support and financial resources from their federal partners. A number of Native nations, including the Iroquois Confederacy and the Creek, Cherokee, Choctaw, and Chickasaw, had already adopted written constitutions by the mid-1850s. And by 1934, another sixty or so Native communities had crafted written constitutions or constitution-like documents before the IRA became law.

A review of more than thirty constitutions and legal codes of various tribes between 1827 and 1933 reveals that while Native communities created documents to help them cope with the tumultuous times they were in, they remained fairly cohesive, yet surprisingly inclusive communities, more intent on fortifying their numbers than in jettisoning bona fide members, though a few were keenly aware that whites sometimes needed to be removed. Take the following examples from a cross section of tribal constitutions and legal codes between 1827 and 1900:

The Cherokee Nation Constitution of 1827: And that, whenever any such citizen or citizens shall remove with their effects out of the limits of this nation, and become citizens of any other government, all their rights and privileges as citizens of this nation shall cease; provided nevertheless that the legislature shall have the power to readmit by law to all the rights of citizenship, any such person or persons, who may at any time desire to return to the nation on their memorializing the General Counsel for such readmission.

The Seneca Nation of Indians Constitution of 1848: The rights of any member of the ancient Confederacy of the Iroquois to the occupancy of our lands and other privileges shall be respected as heretofore; and the Council shall pass laws regulating the admission of any Indian of other tribes or nations to citizenship and adoption into the Seneca Nation of Indians by his or her application for his or herself or family.

Chickasaw Nation Constitution of 1856: All persons, other than Chickasaws by birth, who have been adopted as members of the Chickasaw tribe . . . shall be entitled to all the rights, privileges and immunities of this nation; provided, they are citizens of either the Choctaw or Chickasaw Nation at the time of the adoption of this Constitution. . . . The legislature shall have the power, by law, to admit, or adopt any person to citizenship in this nation, except a Negro, or descendant of a Negro: provided, however, that such an admission, or adoption, shall not give a right, further than to settle and remain in the nation, and to be subject to its laws.

Laws of the Delaware Nation of 1866: Whoever shall by violence do bodily harm to the person of another shall be arrested, and suffer such punishment as may on trial be adjudged against him and should death result from such bodily harm done to the person of another, the offender shall be arrested and suffer such punishment as may be adjudged against.

If a white man marry a member of the nation, and accumulate property by such marriage, said property shall belong to his wife and children. . . . Should such white man be expelled from the reserve, and the wife choose to follow her husband she shall forfeit all her right and interest in the reserve.

The Osage Nation Constitution of 1861: Any person or persons in the Osage Nation whether citizen or not who shall by speaking, writing, act or deed, try to subvert this Constitution and overthrow the government shall be deemed guilty of treason and on conviction suffer death as shall be prescribed by the legislative Council.

The Osage Nation Constitution of 1881: Whenever any citizen shall remove with his effects out of the limits of this Nation, and become a citizen of any other government, all his rights and privileges as a citizen of this Nation shall cease: Provided, nevertheless, that the National Council shall have power to re-admit by law, to all rights of citizenship any such persons who may at any time desire to return to the Nation, on memorializing the National Council for such readmission.

The Sisseton-Wahpeton Constitution of 1884: Any person who shall except hereinafter provided, offer to the relatives or friends of any women or girls, any money, or other valuable considerations the purpose of cohabiting with such girl or woman; and any female who shall offer herself the purpose, shall be deemed guilty of an offense against the law, and any person who shall receive or offer to receive money shall be deemed guilty of an offense against the law, and any person convicted of either of the offenses named in this section, shall pay a fine of not less than five, no more than $25, and shall be imprisoned until such fine is paid. And if any white man shall be found guilty of any of the offenses herein mentioned, he shall be immediately removed from the reservation, and not allowed to return thereto; complaint shall also be made to the civil authority.

Laws of the Pamunkey Nation in 1886/1887: Any person that becomes rude and corrupt and refuses to be submissive to the Laws of Indian Town shall be removed by the Trustees chief and councilman.

These excerpts show that Native peoples were fully capable of arriving at legal and political systems that structured governments, meted out punishment, and dealt with nonmember activity. And while Native leaders had no qualms about expelling whites, whether intermarried or not, who violated the law, with only one exception—the Pamunkey Law—did a Native nation sanction the expatriation of one of its own people.

In the decade following the IRA's passage, a substantial number of Native peoples, 161 nations in all, adopted constitutions; 131 adopted charters of incorporation.[14] The surge of constitution development unleashed after the IRA's adoption entailed the largest number of constitutions drafted in such a short span of time in world history. A number of tribal nations that opted out of the IRA or that would later establish political relations with the United States would also devise their own constitutions, some of which resembled the earlier IRA documents. Other Native nations adopted constitutions that bore little resemblance to the constitutions of the IRA.

The number of Native peoples with formal constitutions (IRA, pre-IRA, and non-IRA) has since increased to approximately 331, at least 220 that were established under the auspices of the IRA or Alaska and Oklahoma variants of the IRA established in 1936. The 236 remaining Indigenous communities (there are 567 federally-recognized Native entities as of 2016) operate with a wide assortment of governing arrangements—some are simple legal charters or town council structures, others like the Pueblos are theocracies. The sophisticated Navajo Nation has a four-volume code that details their three-branch governmental system.

CONSTITUTION AND DISMEMBERMENT LANGUAGE

Since many commentators assume that the constitutional surge that erupted in the 1930s contained the policy seeds that would ultimately culminate in the contemporary disenrollment problems of the late twentieth and early twenty-first centuries, let us examine these documents to discern what kind of disenrollment and banishment language, if any, is used by Native officials and for whom this language was intended.[15]

A comprehensive search of 330 Native nation and Alaskan Native constitutions reveals that the word *banish* or *banishment* appears in only two recent documents. The first is the modern constitution of the Pleasant Point Passamaquoddy Tribe, which in 1990 categorically declared in article 4, section 2 that "notwithstanding any provision of this Constitution, the government of the Pleasant Point Reservation shall have no power of banishment over tribal members." The second is the constitution of the Mashantucket (Western) Pequot, which states that the tribe's Elders Council, as one of its powers, may "hear and determine any matter concerning the banishment or exclusion of any person from the Mashantucket (Western) Pequot Reservation and tribal lands as necessary to preserve and protect the safety and well-being of the Tribe."

Not a single IRA constitution contains the terms *banish* or *banishment*. Until a number of tribal nations beginning in the 1990s began passing ordinances that included banishment as a form of punishment, the only prior mention by a Native nation in their legal code of what amounts to banishment—the Pamunkey used the term *removal*—is found in the Laws of the Pamunkey Tribe of Virginia, written in either 1886 or 1887, which declared that "any person that becomes rude and corrupt and refuse to be submissive to the Laws of the Indian Town shall be *removed* by the Trustees, Chief and councilmen," since they had no corporal punishment and no form of incarceration.[16] The term *exile* also does not appear in any IRA or IRA-like constitution.

Expel appears in more than eighty constitutions, with the vast majority of references having to do with laying out the grounds upon which a tribal council member or executive officer could be removed from office. For example, the constitution of the Washoe Tribe of Nevada and California states that "any councilman or other tribal officer who is proven guilty of improper conduct, or of gross neglect of duty, may be *expelled* from office by a two-thirds vote of the tribal council members."[17]

In many of the other cases, ten of which involve Alaskan Native communities, there is language like that found in the Chilkat Indian Valley Constitution

(1941), which stated that Native members after notice and an opportunity to present a defense could be "expelled by two-thirds vote of the members present for fraud or misconduct in his relations with the village or of working deliberately against the interests of the Village." Reinstatement was possible by written application with the secretary of the council and two-thirds vote of the members present.

The term *expulsion* is found in thirty-four documents, thirty of which involve how to deal with derelict legislators or executive officers. These individuals could be expulsed for neglect of duty or misconduct.

The dreaded terms *disenrolled* or *disenrollment* is found in only twelve constitutions: Grand Traverse Band, Little River Ottawa, Shoalwater, TeMoak, Pechanga (Temecula Band of Luiseno Mission Indians), Elk Valley, Graton Rancheria, Lumbee, Koyukuk, Huslia, Kaw, and Quinault. The five reasons given for disenrolling members are dual membership, failure to prove lineal descent, failure to maintain contact with the tribe, fraud, mistake, and voluntary relinquishment. These will be discussed later in the chapter.

The term *exclusion* is found in sixty-two constitutions, both IRA and non-IRA types. In thirty-two cases it refers to the power of the nation to exclude nonmembers from tribal lands when those individuals' actions or presence, in the case of the Gila River Constitution, "may be injurious to the peace, health, or welfare of the Community." In thirty cases, the tribal government reserved the power to exclude all persons who were "not legally entitled to remain thereon" (Devils Lake Sioux of North Dakota, 1946), or were not "licensed" (Calusa Indian Community, 1941), implying that non-Indians or nonmember Indians were the focus of the tribe's exclusionary power.

Further evidence that this power was aimed largely at nontribal individuals is found in the constitutions of two Washington State–based Native nations—the Shoalwater Tribe and the Skokomish people—which reference the power of the tribal leadership to not only exclude nontribal members, but also to extradite them. Shoalwater's clause reads thus: "to . . . establish procedures for the exclusion of non-tribal members from the reservation and for the extradition from areas within the jurisdiction of the Tribe of persons accused of crimes in other jurisdictions."

Numerous Native nations (e.g., Graton Rancheria, Caddo, Coquille, Grand Ronde, Ho-Chunk, Menominee, and the Duckwater Shoshone) include "voluntary relinquishment" of citizenship as one way to lose one's tribal nationality. The most emphatic language is found in the Duckwater Shoshone Constitution, first approved in 1940 and amended in 2001. Their statement declares that "the Tribal Council shall prescribe by ordinance, the rules and regulations governing loss of membership which shall be limited exclusively to voluntary relinquishment." Several tribes categorically state that if a tribal member voluntarily surrenders their citizenship they cannot at a later date regain it.

Fifteen Native communities declare that tribal members cannot be simultaneously enrolled in another Indigenous nation. Dual membership is grounds for formal disenrollment. As the Graton Rancheria put it in their revised constitution of 2015: "Any citizen who is enrolled as a member or citizen in any other federally recognized Indian tribe shall be deemed to have relinquished his or her citizenship."

The most common phrase found in Native constitutions addressing the subject is *loss of membership*. This phrase appears in 167 constitutions. In a little more than half the documents, the phrase is simply included as one of the enumerated powers of the legislative branch, typically, the tribal council. As an example, in the Absentee-Shawnee Constitution, article 3, section 5 declares that "the General Council shall have power to prescribe rules and regulations by ordinance, covering future membership including adoptions and the loss of membership."

In a number of constitutions, the secretary of the interior is acknowledged as having authority to review loss of membership ordinances. Such clauses will figure prominently in later chapters when we discuss the federal government's administrative power over this important issue.

Sixty-five Alaskan Native communities contain fairly detailed language in their organic documents on loss of membership. A fairly common refrain is that found in the Chilkat Indian Village charter which states:

> (A) Any member may give up his membership at any time upon written notice to the Secretary of the Council, in which case he shall no longer share in the activities and benefits of this Village, but he may be reinstated as a member upon written application [to] the Secretary of the Council and the majority vote of the members of the Village at any regular meeting.

> (B) Any member who, after notice and an opportunity to present his defense, is found guilty by the Village of fraud or misconduct in his relations with the Village or of working deliberately against the interests of the Village may be expelled by a two-thirds vote of the members present. . . . A person so expelled may be reinstated as a member . . . with two-thirds vote of the membership present at any regular meeting.

Other Alaskan Native villages, like Dearing, highlight the following as grounds for disenrollment: "Any member may willingly give up his membership, or his membership may be taken away for good reason by the Village, or if he moves away from the Village, intending not to return, he shall lose his membership."

Only one Native nation permits dual membership—the Native Village of Koyukuk in Alaska—but with a severe restriction: dually enrolled village residents are no longer eligible to "receive distribution of tribal assets." This financial incentive seems to be the chief justification for why many Native nations discourage multiple citizenships.

Another factor that may lead to disenrollment is failure to maintain contact with the home community. It is most widely cited in Alaskan Native villages, but several other tribal nations have similar clauses. The Bay Mills community in Michigan declares that membership can be lost "by reason of continued absence from the reservation or from Sugar Island or Drummond Island." The Chippewa Cree of Rocky Boys Reservation Constitution declares that a member can be disenrolled if they have been away for more than a decade, unless they get an extension from the tribal government. The Colville people of Washington State will disenroll those who have "abandoned tribal relations." And the Native village of Koyukuk emphasizes that its members must maintain contact "at least once every five years."

Two of the most unique grounds for disenrollment are found in the constitutions of a California nation, the Cochil Dehe Band of Wintun Indians of the Colusa Indian Community, and the Native village of Hydaburg. The Wintun state that "if a female member marries a non-Indian, she will automatically lose her membership and will be required to leave the community within ninety days after notice." This provision applied only to marriages consummated after ratification of the constitution in 1941. And the Hydaburg Cooperative Association in their 1938 charter state that a member could be disenrolled if they ceased "to engage in the fishing industry or any activity of this Association."

More than half the constitutions recognize that individuals have the right to voluntarily relinquish their citizenship and to emigrate. In some cases, tribal officials allow for readmission; in others that is not allowed. The three nations with the strongest protection of membership and citizenship rights are the Assiniboine Sioux people of Fort Peck, the Gros Ventre and Assiniboine people of Fort Belknap, and the Confederated Tribes of the Warm Springs Reservation. The Fort Belknap and Assiniboine Sioux constitutions declare that: "In no case shall a member lose his membership other than by personal request in writing to the Tribal Executive Board or establishing residence in a foreign country." And the Warm Springs document says, "in no case shall a member lose his membership other than by personal request in writing to the Tribal Council."

With regards to Fort Belknap's and Fort Peck's constitutions and their reference to "residence in a foreign country," this appears to draw from language found in federal law describing the complicated process for how U.S. citizens can lose their citizenship. While Congress has no power to expatriate without a citizen's assent, such assent can be found if an individual performs any of the following acts intending to relinquish their citizenship: (1) obtaining naturalization in a foreign state, (2) oath of allegiance to a foreign state, (3) military service in a foreign state, (4) foreign government employment—a condition of employment must be that a person acquires naturalization or swears an oath of allegiance, (5) formal renunciation of nationality (must appear in person before a U.S. consular or diplomatic officer, *in a foreign country*, normally at a U.S. embassy or consulate) and sign an oath of renunciation, and 6) acts of treason and subversion.

Even when one or more of these actions occur, the burden of proof that the acts occurred rests on the federal government. A preponderance of evidence is required and only then will there be a judicial determination that the person's act to renounce their citizenship was voluntary and intentional.

While 167 Native constitutions have language detailing the conditions under which loss of membership may occur, only one Native nation uses the term *loss of citizenship*: the Chickasaw Nation of Oklahoma. The Chickasaw, one of the Five Civilized Tribes, adopted their first constitution in 1856. In that document they refer to their people as citizens, not as members. That document lasted until 1906. The Chickasaw regained authority to adopt a new constitution in 1979. So the language in their current document works well with the history of their republic where it is stated that "the Tribal Legislature shall have the power to enact ordinances governing future citizenship, and loss of citizenship in the Chickasaw Nation."

VOLUNTARY VERSUS INVOLUNTARY DISENROLLMENT

As discussed earlier, Native nations historically were cohesive societies, organically linked by genealogy (kinship and clans), land, culture, values, and language. While they were bounded communities, they remained open and easily incorporated new individuals and groups whether through marriage, emigration, adoption, or capture. But as the political relationship with the United States intensified and became unequal, with the federal government slowly claiming the upper hand via policies of removal, reservations, allotment, and so on, and with property ever at the forefront, Native peoples' political, economic, and cultural systems had to be adjusted in ways that began to comport with those of the federal government and the larger society.

We see ample evidence of this in the constitutions' numerous references to tribal membership rather than kinship or clanship. In fact, a search of the constitutional database shows not a single reference to the word *kinship*, and only four references to *clan*, although we know that both concepts retain great cultural relevance to many Indigenous peoples. Of the four tribal constitutions that mention *clan*—Samish, Cherokee, Hopi, and Miccosukee—only the latter three indicate that clans are actively considered and remain important political, economic, and cultural institutions in those nations.

The Hopi Constitution, first adopted in 1936 and updated numerous times since, contains multiple references to clans and point to their ever prominent role in allocating farmland and regulating inheritance of property in the respective villages, and in the settlement of certain disputes, among other things. In the Miccosukee Constitution (1961), at least three clans must be represented when the tribe's general council holds their regular meetings. And the 2003 Cherokee Nation Constitution declares that tribal members have the right "to belong to a recognized clan or organization."

Today, the two most common concepts used by Native individuals to describe their connection to their own nations is as member or citizen, although tribal officialdom utilizes member and membership far more often than citizen or citizenship. A brief etymology of these two terms is revealing. *Member*, according to the *Oxford English Dictionary*, dates back to at least 1100 CE. It has been used in several senses: (1) relating to a part of a living body organism (e.g., organ of the body); (2) relating to an individual or constituent element within a social or other organizational structure (e.g., an inhabitant or native of a county or city); and (3) relating to a part of an inanimate structure or immaterial thing (e.g., a load-bearing structure).

If one understands Native peoples as genealogically or organically related communities who share a common language, values, and territory, then the term *member* is certainly apropos. After all, humans frequently use the expression "I am a family member" or "useful member of society," to distinguish themselves from others. Of course, the word *member* is also associated with social clubs (e.g., fraternities and sororities, Kiwanis, Rotary, Elk, etc.), unions, churches, and political bodies (e.g., Republican Party, member of Parliament). But given John Collier's deep understanding of the community structures, religious traditions, and value systems of Native peoples, it is doubtful that he was using the term in the latter senses.

The term *citizen* also has a long history, dating back to Aristotle and the ancient Greeks, who believed humans were political animals, and Roman law, which viewed humans as legal animals with a relationship to the state.[18] The *Oxford English Dictionary*'s earliest recorded mention of the term is in 1314. Two of its most common meanings are: (1) "an inhabitant of a city or a town, especially one possessing civic rights and privileges"; and (2) "a member of a state, an enfranchised inhabitant of the county, as opposed to an alien—in the U.S., a person, native or naturalized, who has the privilege of voting for public office, and is entitled to full protection in the exercise of private rights."

Interestingly, while blood quantum has been a feature of federal Indian policy and law since the late 1800s, dating to the 1880 federal census of "Indians not taxed" and later the Dawes Rolls and Commissioner Cato Sells' policy in 1917, and although the IRA introduced a definition of Indian to include "persons of one-half or more Indian blood," blood quantum formula were used less by Native nations in the early IRA constitutions. Kirsty Gover points out that 70 percent of Native governments presently employ blood quantum rules in their constitutions, reflecting the long-standing use of this pilloried concept by federal officials in census taking, statutes, and federal regulations.[19]

Blood rules are of two types: those measuring Indian blood (from any Indigenous people) and those measuring tribal blood (tribe specific). Only nine constitutions specifically employ the term *blood quantum*. Fractions of blood, however, are another matter. The most frequently used quantum of Native blood found in tribal constitutions is one-fourth. Seventy-four Native nations use this fraction. Only eight Native nations use one-half blood quantum: White Mountain Apache, Isleta Pueblo, Northern Cheyenne, Jamul Village, Quileute, Lac du Flambeau, Crow Creek, and the Mississippi Band of Choctaw. Fifteen constitutions employ one-eighth as the blood standard. And six documents utilize one-sixteenth as the fraction (Chemeheuvi, Chitimacha, Cowlitz, Manzanita Band of Mission Indians, Fort Independence Indian Community, and Siletz).

Blood quantum rules in Native constitutions have increased substantially since the 1930s, with nearly two-thirds of Native nations requiring some degree of blood to be recognized as a tribal member. This rise is important and blood issues form one of the more contested domains of Native identity. Gover points out that while federal lawmakers do not distinguish between "Indian blood" and "tribal blood," they still insist that Native nations be composed of Indians. "Many tribes, however, insist that applicants show genealogical ties to the community, evidenced by blood quantum rules. This difference has important normative consequences for the theories of tribalism." "It suggests," says Gover, "that tribes in the U.S. are evolving their own *sui generis* construction of membership that does not map onto the federal public law categories used to describe tribal membership in terms of race and ethnicity."[20]

The two major descent principles used are lineal descent and parental enrollment. Approximately 140 Native nations refer to the latter, with at least one parent having had to be an enrolled member at the time of the applicant's birth. Another 102 tribal nations require that applicants show lineal descent from a person on a base role. Many of the IRA-era constitutions rely on parental enrollment, whereas many written after 1960 use lineal descent.[21]

Any one of several criteria—inadequate blood quantum or blood from a different Native nation, dual membership, fraud, error, misconduct, failure to maintain contact—may be used to justify disenrollment or banishment of tribal members; nonmembers may be excluded for a variety of reasons. And when Native governments are not acting politically and provide complete due process safeguards to those being terminated, this is arguably an appropriate, if still difficult, policy choice.

But the evidence suggests that with a few exceptions, prior to the advent of the Native self-determination era in the 1970s, Native communities did not engage in disenrollment, banishment, or exclusion of bona fide members or even nonmembers very often, and when such expulsions or disenfranchisements were carried out only the rare individual was targeted, not entire families.

CHAPTER 4

Native Self-Determination

Steps Forward, Steps Backward

AS IMPORTANT AS THE INDIAN REORGANIZATION ACT (IRA) WAS FOR saving the remains of the Indigenous land estate, restoring a measure of respect for inherent Native cultural identity, and creating the political, legal, and economic infrastructure that enabled numerous tribal societies to become more stable, it also created an enormous, nearly virulent congressional backlash, with some equally impressive Native backlash, by those still intent on the further decay and ultimate absorption of Native peoples into the larger society. Within a few years, federal legislative efforts were initiated to repeal the measure. Coinciding with these developments, after multiple fits and starts Congress finally enacted the Indian Claims Commission Act (ICCA) in 1946, an important law aimed at bringing finality to Native claims for treaty violations and land undervaluations against the federal government.

Felix S. Cohen, a prominent attorney in the Department of the Interior in the 1930s and early 1940s and an architect of federal Indian law and the ICCA, said that Indian claims were "by and large, the backwash of a great national experiment in dictatorship and racial extermination."[1] As with most laws, the reasons for the ICCA's enactment in 1946 varied. The greatest impetus was the persistent effort by numerous tribal governments intent on forcing the federal government to fulfill its treaty and trust obligations. Additional support came from individuals like Cohen and John Collier, the former commissioner of Indian Affairs, who knew the importance of such a measure as a form of justice. But a number of conservative federal lawmakers also backed the act's adoption. This is attributable to the fact that many of them believed that passage of the bill would expedite the assimilation process.[2]

After the act's adoption, many Native nations filed claims under the ICCA in an effort to secure some recompense for the violations they had endured at the hands of federal officials since the assumption was that the federal government would not actually return any land to the tribes, but would only compensate those who filed successful claims.[3] Ultimately, some 170 Native communities filed 370 petitions; these were divided into more than 617 dockets during the life of the commission, which operated until 1978. The ICCA was fraught with major problems throughout its life, but eventually 274 awards were made to Native peoples who collectively received a little more than $800 million. Two hundred and four claims were dismissed. One of the problems generated by the claims process was that the monetary awards that some tribal nations secured occasionally resulted in creating or exacerbating tension between segments within those communities.

Joseph G. Jorgensen, writing about the Ute people of Colorado and Utah, described how the Confederated Utes received nearly $32 million from their first land claim in 1951. Of this amount, the Northern Ute share was $17.5 million. When the award was made "there was considerable unrest and apprehension among the Ute people."[4] Most of the Northern Ute money was used for tribal projects, but the tribe also made a $1,000 per capita distribution to eligible tribal members.[5]

Much of this intratribal tension predated the monetary award, dating back to the allotment era, irrigation projects, and tension between the so-called full-bloods and mixed-bloods of the tribe. The sudden monetary influx led to "a concomitant movement among the full bloods to expel the mixed-bloods from the tribe."[6] The mixed-blood Utes had a more individualistic orientation and wanted to have greater freedom from both tribal and federal control. The full-bloods were more oriented toward retaining their allotments under federal trust protection and in remaining in a political relationship with the federal government. With the two segments far apart, and with the federal government in 1953 having adopted the termination policy, conditions culminated on August 27, 1954, when Congress enacted Public Law 671, "An Act to Provide for the Partition and Distribution of the Assets of the Ute Indian Tribe . . . between the Mixed-Blood and Full-Blood Members Thereof; and for the Termination of Federal Supervision over the Property of the Mixed-Blood Members of Said Tribe; To Provide a Development Program for the Full-Blood Members of Said Tribe; and for Other Purposes."[7]

The Northern Ute had effectively been split into two separate communities, with the 439 mixed-bloods now being designated as the Affiliated Ute Citizens and in a terminated status with no further interest in the Ute Indian tribe of the Uintah and Ouray Reservation, which remained a federally recognized tribe now consisting entirely of full-blood Utes.

This bifurcation, at the time, seemed to suit the members of both Ute segments. The mixed-bloods and full-bloods divided the tribe's $15.8 million and 980,000 acres in proportion to their numbers.[8] The newly coined Affiliated Ute Citizens believed that "they would improve themselves socially and economically" having separated from the full-blood members. Their formal political termination occurred in 1961. The full-blood Utes (defined in the act as possessing one-half Ute blood and a total of Indian blood in excess of one-half), the remaining 1,326 members of the tribe, retained their status as members of a federally acknowledged tribal nation.

Interestingly, the mixed-blood members in section 6 had the right, but were not required, to "adopt an appropriate constitution and bylaws . . . at a special election authorized and called by the Secretary."[9] Likewise, there was ominous language for the full-blood contingent. Section 24 declared that "within three months . . . the business committee of the tribe representing the full-blood group thereof shall present to the Secretary a development program calculated to assist in making the tribe and the members thereof self-supporting, without any special Government assistance, with a view of eventually terminating all Federal supervision of the tribe and its members."[10] In keeping with the tenor of the times, the tribe, in other words, was required to draft its own termination plan.

Although the Ute had been divided, the two segments wisely agreed to jointly own and manage the remaining oil, gas, and mineral rights. In 1958 the two groups settled on and agreed to distribute the remaining tribal funds. Each mixed-blood member received $64,000; each full-blood secured $60,000.[11]

In fact, along with claims, and in addition to the termination policy of 1953, several other policies instituted in the early 1950s helped set the table for developments that would unfold in the 1960s and 1970s, developments that would create conditions that would ripen into opportunities for tribal governments to begin dismembering some of their own citizens.

Besides the Termination Resolution (HCR 108) in 1953, Congress also enacted Public Law 280, and shortly thereafter the federal government's relocation program created an exodus of native individuals from reservations to selected major metropolitan areas across the United States. These four measures—the ICCA, termination, Public Law 280, and relocation—fueled the activism that culminated in the Red Power movement that generated the contemporary Native self-determination era. It was, by most accounts, an era when Native peoples and their members won a series of important political and legal victories in their efforts to reclaim and assert inherent sovereignty. Many of these victories— which affirmed long-standing treaty rights, upheld Native claims to lands that had been illegally purchased or simply stolen, and extended federal protection of historically disregarded Native civil rights—were a result of the legal and political activism exhibited by many Native nations and committed individuals, from the occupation of Alcatraz Island (1969), the Trail of Broken Treaties (1972), and the occupation of Wounded Knee on the Pine Ridge Indian Reservation (1973) to the numerous fish-ins, marches, demonstrations, and boycotts.

At the same time, Native governments and communities participated in most of the social programs established by President Lyndon B. Johnson in the 1960s—Office of Economic Opportunity, Headstart, and Vista, among others—when his administration sought to create the Great Society. In almost every case, the eligibility sections of these congressional statutes and many of those passed in the early 1970s (e.g., the Indian Education Act of 1972, the Comprehensive Employment and Training Act of 1973, and the Indian Self-Determination and Education Assistance Act of 1975) contained a phrase placing Native peoples in a position at least comparable to states and federally charted corporations like the Tennessee Valley Authority.

Interspersed with the combination of Native activism that culminated in important political and legal victories, and the larger set of federal War on Poverty and Great Society social programs that tribal nations were eligible for because of their dire socioeconomic status, were two specific federal measures— the Indian Civil Rights Act of 1968 (ICRA)[12] and the U.S. Supreme Court's 1978 decision *Santa Clara Pueblo v. Martinez*[13]—that occupy critical positions on the spectrum of individual civil liberties and tribal sovereignty.

As part of the Fair Housing Act of 1968, Congress included the ICRA as one of the titles. The ICRA was a major law that, for the first time, imposed important segments of federal constitutional law on tribal governments, an intrusion on tribal sovereignty that many Native peoples opposed. This act dramatically changed the substance and direction of tribal courts by forcing those legal systems to enforce a modified version of the U.S. Bill of Rights protections that all reservation residents—Native and non-Native alike—were entitled to receive. Interestingly, this act, unlike many major federal laws, was sparked by complaints from some Natives who said their own tribal governments were violating their civil liberties.

Among the rights guaranteed under the ICRA are free speech and assembly, protection against unreasonable search and seizure, the right to a speedy trial, the right to hire a lawyer in a criminal case, protection against self-incrimination and cruel and unusual punishment, and the right to protection under the laws and due process. Importantly, the act excludes some constitutional provisions: for example, indictment by a grand jury, the establishment of religion clause, and the restriction against housing troops in homes. Several of the other constitutional provisions were expressly modified in the ICRA statute. The Sixth Amendment right to have an attorney for criminal prosecutions was made provisional and contingent upon the accused's ability to hire an attorney "at his own expense." Tribal nations were also not required to convene juries in civil trials or in criminal cases, or to issue grand jury indictments. Additionally, tribal governments could discriminate in voting based on race.

The act also provided only a single remedy—the writ of habeas corpus—by which litigants, whether Native or non-Native, could challenge a tribal court's decision in federal courts in certain contexts. As set forth in section 1303 it reads: "The privilege of the writ of habeas corpus shall be available to any person, in a court of the United States, to test the legality of his detention by order of an Indian tribe." A writ of habeas corpus is a court order requiring that a person being held in custody be brought before the court so that the legality of their detention may be determined. It is directed at the entity holding the accused. This process theoretically guarantees that federal courts will determine if the person being held by a tribal government is being confined in violation of the ICRA. But as we will see in the next chapter, habeas corpus has been of limited utility for the vast majority of Natives who have tried to wield it in banishment and disenrollment cases, and even when they have succeeded in invoking the clause, this has not led to reenrollment in the nation because such an act "would interfere with tribal sovereign immunity and retained tribal affairs."[14]

The ICRA is deceptive in many of its provisions, and even its description in Senate debate left a good deal to be desired as far as clarity was concerned. Senator Sam Ervin, who introduced the bill, stated that the act would "confer upon the American Indians the fundamental constitutional rights which belong by right of all Americans." But as Deloria has pointed out, "the irony of the situation is apparent. The Constitution does not apply to American Indians in their tribal relations. It does not protect Indian tribes. But, through a legislative act of Congress, some constitutional provisions were made an applicable part of the relationship between an Indian tribe and its members. As long as the situation exists, confusion and injustice will continue to be visited upon Indian tribes."[15]

For the next ten years, a number of federal court rulings were handed down that suggested that Congress, by enacting the ICRA, had waived tribal sovereign immunity regarding claimants seeking relief under the law, thus allowing individuals to file suits against tribal governments even when the claimants were not being held in custody.[16] But in *Santa Clara Pueblo v. Martinez* (1978), the Supreme Court overruled those decisions and declared that the writ of habeas corpus was the sole remedy that federal law provided under the ICRA.

In the case, the justices were asked to decide whether a federal court could determine the validity of the Santa Clara Pueblo's ordinance denying membership to the children of Julia Martinez, a recognized member of the Pueblo who had married a non-Pueblo. Her husband happened to be Navajo. The court, speaking through Associate Justice Thurgood Marshall, ruled that Martinez's sexual discrimination claim against her nation could not be brought into federal court because the provisions of the ICRA did not entail an unequivocal expression to abrogate tribal sovereign immunity by subjecting the tribal nation to civil suits in federal court.

The court, in other words, did not hold that federal courts lack jurisdiction to determine membership disputes. It simply held that the ICRA did not create a "cause of action for habeas corpus when something less than a restriction on liberty resulting from a criminal conviction is involved."[17] In short, when Congress opted to inject habeas corpus as the only remedy for ICRA violations, the court said, federal lawmakers did not waive the tribes' immunity from suit; therefore, federal courts could not hear noncustodial [not in physical custody] ICRA cases.[18]

Importantly, this decision was reached notwithstanding the extension of the equal protection guarantee to Native peoples laid out in the act, and despite a federal law extending federal courts' jurisdiction over lawsuits filed "under any act of Congress providing for the protection of civil rights." Although *Martinez* was a devastating rebuke to Ms. Martinez and her family, Native governments reveled in its affirmation of tribal sovereignty and it emboldened them to become more emphatically proactive or, in some cases, retaliatory, in their efforts to adjust their membership rolls by modifying their constitution or other organic charters' membership criteria or by enacting ordinances detailing the grounds on which members could be disenrolled or banished.

This decision and numerous other Native political and legal victories in the areas of child welfare, religious issues, hunting and fishing rights, education, and others provoked a sizable backlash among disaffected non-Indians, state governments, and annoyed federal officials. The backlash, as it unfolded, gave voice to an almost sinister mood of anger and resentment. Opponents of Native nations advocated the abrogation of Indian treaties, the abolition of the Bureau of Indian Affairs, termination of the federal trust relationship, and even the extinguishment of Indian hunting and treaty rights.

While Native leaders and their allies repelled most of these anti-Indian efforts, they could not forestall the U.S. Supreme Court from handing down a battery of decisions, also beginning in 1978, that dramatically limited tribal law enforcement powers over non-Indians (*Oliphant v. Suquamish*, 1978), weakened tribal jurisdiction over hunting and fishing by non-Indians on non-Indian land within the reservation borders (*Montana v. U.S.*, 1981), and reduced tribal water rights (*Nevada v. U.S.*, 1983).

When Ronald Reagan was sworn in as president in January 1981, his policies led to blistering and catastrophic budget cuts for the ever financially dependent Native governments. Partly to offset these financial losses, Reagan's administrative staff encouraged tribal governments to consider establishing gambling operations as one way to minimize the impact of the loss of federal dollars. Indian gambling would come to have profound economic, political, cultural, and intergovernmental consequences for the many tribal governments that ventured down that economic road.

Simultaneously, even as crime was beginning to recede in major urban areas across the United States, it was beginning to spike across Indian Country. The surge was occurring, in part, because of the jurisdictional fog that shrouds tribal lands—with the federal government, states, and Native governments each having some degree of legal authority, depending on the crime, the location, whether Public Law 280 is a factor, and the race of the parties—and with tribal governments having been largely emasculated in terms of how much punishment they could mete out. For example, under the original ICRA the harshest punishment that a tribal court could impose upon a defendant was a prison term of one year and a fine of no more than $5,000, or both.

The confluence of Indigenous nations feeling empowered by their own self-assured steps toward self-determination, combined with direct and obvious support from federal policies that supported Native autonomy, including cases like *Santa Clara*, the influx of gambling revenue, and the burst of criminal activity across Indian Country, along with other issues that varied from nation to nation, set the stage for banishment and disenrollment procedures that began during this combustible period.

The Dismembering Explodes

IN VARIOUS REGIONS OF INDIAN COUNTRY, MORE THAN SEVENTY NA-
tive governments have already acted to banish or disenroll citizens; have
provisionally acted to institute disenrollment procedures (though as of this
writing the process has not been completed); are considering whether to banish or disenroll, contingent upon not yet completed tribal enrollment audits
or other internal investigations; or have denied membership to individuals
who appear to have the bona fides necessary to be formally enrolled.

The following four tables provide a broad overview of the nations who have
or are engaging in one or more of these practices.[1] Table 5.1 is the comprehensive list of all those tribal nations we have empirical data for (though some
categories are incomplete because of lack of data) who have or are currently
involved in banishing or disenrolling citizens. It spells out the location,
whether or not the community was federally terminated, whether or not gaming is conducted, whether the tribal government provides per capita payments
to tribal members, what action is being pursued by tribal officials, and what
the official rationale(s) of the government is for engaging in the practice.

Table 5.2 shows a list of the nearly fifty communities in twenty states (excluding California) and what is transpiring in those states. The first fact that
stands out is that the number of nations that are banishing—twenty-one—is
less than the number that are disenrolling—twenty-eight. Two tribes, the
Saginaw Chippewa and the Snoqualmie, are doing both. Second, of the communities listed, thirty-four are gaming communities, or nearly 73 percent.

Official rationales provided by tribal governments to justify disenrollment
or banishment also vary. Criminal activity or civil violations are the most commonly cited reason for banishment—sixteen instances. We could find no evidence of disenrollment for such infractions. Lack of blood quantum (twelve

TABLE 5.1. Native nations that have engaged in dismemberment

Community	Location	Terminated	Gaming	Per Capita	Action	Rationale
Alabama-Quassarte Tribal Town	OK	No	No	No	Disenrollment	Insufficient blood quantum
Bear River Band of the Rohnerville Rancheria	CA	Yes	Yes	Yes	Disenrollment	—
Berry Creek Rancheria of Maidu	CA	No	Yes	Yes	Disenrollment	—
Boise Forte Band of Ojibwe	MN	No	Yes	No	Banishment	Criminal activity
Cahto Tribe of the Laytonville Rancheria	CA	No	Yes	—	Disenrollment	Dual enrollment, receipt of funds from another tribe's settlement
California Valley Miwok Tribe	CA	No	Yes	—	Disenrollment	—
Cedarville Rancheria	CA	No	No	No	Banishment	—
Cherokee Nation	OK	No	Yes	No	Disenrollment	Insufficient blood quantum
Cheyenne & Arapaho Tribes	OK	No	Yes	Yes	Banishment	Embezzlement
Cold Springs Rancheria of Mono	CA	Yes	No	No	Disenrollment	—
Comanche Nation	OK	No	Yes	Yes	Disenrollment	—
Confederated Tribes of the Colville Reservation	WA	No	Yes	No	Disenrollment	Enrollment fraud
Confederated Tribes of the Grand Ronde Community	OR	Yes	Yes	Yes	Disenrollment	Insufficient documentation
Confederated Tribes of Siletz Indians	OR	Yes	Yes	Yes	Disenrollment	Dual citizenship
Coushatta Tribe of Louisiana	LA	No	Yes	Yes	Disenrollment	Insufficient blood quantum
Coyote Valley Band of Pomo	CA	No	Yes	Yes	Disenrollment	—
Dry Creek Rancheria Band of Pomo	CA	No	Yes	Yes	Disenrollment	—
Elem Indian Colony of Pomo	CA	No	No	No	Disenrollment, Banishment	Treason, fraud, corruption, etc.
Enterprise Rancheria of Maidu	CA	No	Yes	—	Disenrollment	—

Grand Portage Band of Ojibwe	MN	No	Yes	No	Banishment	Criminal activity
Grand Traverse Band of Ottawa and Chippewa	MI	No	Yes	Yes	Disenrollment	Insufficient blood quantum
Guidiville Rancheria of Pomo	CA	Yes	Yes	No	Disenrollment	—
Ho Chunk Nation	WI	No	Yes	Yes	Disenrollment	Insufficient blood quantum
Hopland Band of Pomo	CA	Yes	Yes	Yes	Disenrollment	—
Isleta Pueblo	NM	No	Yes	No	Disenrollment	Insufficient blood quantum
Jamestown S'Klallam Tribe	WA	—	Yes	—	Disenrollment	Documentary error
Keweenaw Bay Indian Community	MI	No	Yes	—	Disenrollment	—
Klawock Cooperative Association	AK	No	Yes	No	Banishment	Criminal activity
Kootenai Tribe	ID	No	Yes	Yes	Disenrollment	—
Lac du Flambeau Band of Lake Superior Chippewa	WI	No	Yes	Yes	Banishment	Criminal activity
Las Vegas Band of Paiute	NV	No	Yes	No	Disenrollment	Insufficient blood quantum
Little River Band of Ottawa	MI	No	Yes	Yes	Disenrollment	Enrollment error, residency
Lumbee Tribe	NC	Yes	No	No	Disenrollment	Fraud, failure to maintain contact
Lummi Tribe	WA	No	Yes	No	Banishment	Criminal activity
Mashantucket Pequot	CT	No	Yes	Yes	Banishment	Criminal activity
Mattaponi Tribe	VA	No	No	No	Banishment	Criminal activity
Mille Lacs Band of Ojibwe	MN	No	Yes	Yes	Banishment	Criminal activity
Monacan Indian Nation	MD	No	No	No	Banishment	—
Mooretown Rancheria of Maidu	CA	Yes	Yes	Yes	Disenrollment	—
Narragansett Tribe	RI	No	No	No	Disenrollment	—
Native Village of Alutiig	AK	No	No	No	Banishment	Criminal activity

(continued)

TABLE 5.1. (*continued*)

Community	Location	Terminated	Gaming	Per Capita	Action	Rationale
Native Village of Tanana	AK	No	No	No	Banishment	Criminal activity
Nooksack Indian Tribe	WA	No	Yes	No	Disenrollment	Enrollment error
Oneida Nation	NY	No	Yes	No	Disenrollment	—
Osage Nation	OK	No	Yes	—	Disenrollment	Fraud
Pala Band of Luiseno Mission Indians	CA	No	Yes	Yes	Disenrollment	Insufficient blood quantum
Paskenta Band of Nomlaki Indians	CA	Yes	Yes	Yes	Disenrollment	—
Passamaquoddy Tribe	ME	No	No	No	Disenrollment	—
Pechanga Band of Luiseno Mission Indians	CA	No	Yes	Yes	Disenrollment	Failure to prove lineal descent
Picayune Rancheria of Chukchansi Indians	CA	Yes	Yes	Yes	Disenrollment, Banishment	Procedural errors, lack of documentation
Pinoleville Pomo Nation	CA	Yes	Yes	Yes	Disenrollment	—
Pitt River Tribe, Madesi Band	CA	No	Yes	—	Disenrollment	Dual enrollment
Potter Valley Rancheria of Pomo Indians	CA	Yes	—	—	Disenrollment	—
Puyallup Tribe	WA	No	Yes	Yes	Disenrollment	—
Redding Rancheria	CA	Yes	Yes	Yes	Disenrollment	—
Rincon Band of San Luiseno Indians	CA	No	Yes	Yes	Disenrollment	—
Robinson Rancheria Band of Pomo	CA	Yes	Yes	Yes	Disenrollment	—
Sac and Fox Tribal Community	OK	No	Yes	Yes	Disenrollment	Dual enrollment, insufficient blood quantum
Saginaw Chippewa	MI	No	Yes	Yes	Disenrollment, Banishment	—
San Pasqual Band of Diqueno Mission Indians	CA	No	Yes	Yes	Disenrollment	Insufficient blood quantum

Santa Rosa Indian Community of the Santa Rosa Rancheria	CA	No	No	No	Disenrollment	—
Santa Rosa Rancheria Tachi-Yokat	CA	No	Yes	Yes	Disenrollment	—
Sauk-Suiattle Indian Tribe	WA	No	Yes	Yes	Disenrollment	Insufficient blood quantum
Sault Ste. Marie Tribe of Chippewa	MI	No	Yes	No	Banishment	Criminal activity
Seminole Nation	OK	No	Yes	—	Disenrollment	Insufficient blood quantum
Shingle Springs Band of Miwok	CA	No	Yes	Yes	Disenrollment	Fraud
Shoshone-Bannock Tribe	UT	No	No	No	Banishment	Criminal activity
Snoqualmie Indian Tribe	WA	Yes	Yes	No	Disenrollment, Banishment	Insufficient blood quantum, treason
Sisseton Wahpeton Oyate	SD	No	Yes	—	Disenrollment	Dual enrollment
St. Croix Chippewa of Wisconsin	WI	No	Yes	—	Disenrollment	Fraud
Te-Moak Tribe of Western Shoshone	NV	No	Yes	No	Disenrollment	Insufficient blood quantum
Tonawanda Band of Seneca	NY	No	No	No	Banishment	Treason
Turtle Mountain Band of Chippewa	ND	No	Yes	No	Banishment	—
United Auburn Indian Community	CA	Yes	Yes	Yes	Banishment	Defamation
United Keetowah Band of Cherokee Indians	OK	No	No	No	Banishment	—
Upper Sioux Community	MN	No	Yes	Yes	Banishment	Criminal activity
Viejas Group of Capitan Grande Band of Mission Indians	CA	No	Yes	Yes	Disenrollment	—
Walker River Paiute Tribe	NV	No	No	No	Disenrollment	—
Ysleta del Sur Pueblo	TX	No	No	No	Banishment	Insufficient blood quantum, criminal activity, violation of ceremonies
Yupik Village	AK	No	No	No	Banishment	Criminal activity

TABLE 5.2. Non-California Native nations that have engaged in dismemberment

Community	Location	Terminated	Gaming	Per Capita	Action	Rationale
Alabama-Quassarte Tribal Town	OK	No	No	No	Disenrollment	Insufficient blood quantum
Boise Forte Band of Ojibwe	MN	No	Yes	No	Banishment	Criminal activity
Cherokee Nation	OK	No	Yes	No	Disenrollment	Insufficient blood quantum
Cheyenne & Arapaho Tribes	OK	No	Yes	Yes	Banishment	Embezzlement
Comanche Nation	OK	No	Yes	Yes	Disenrollment	—
Confederated Tribes of the Colville Reservation	WA	No	Yes	No	Disenrollment	Enrollment fraud
Confederated Tribes of the Grand Ronde Community	OR	Yes	Yes	Yes	Disenrollment	Insufficient documentation
Confederated Tribes of Siletz Indians	OR	No	Yes	Yes	Disenrollment	Dual citizenship
Coushatta Tribe of Louisiana	LA	No	Yes	Yes	Disenrollment	Insufficient blood quantum
Grand Portage Band of Ojibwe	MN	No	Yes	No	Banishment	Criminal activity
Grand Traverse Band of Ottawa and Chippewa	MI	No	Yes	Yes	Disenrollment	Insufficient blood quantum
Ho Chunk Nation	WI	No	Yes	Yes	Disenrollment	Insufficient blood quantum
Isleta Pueblo	NM	No	Yes	No	Disenrollment	Insufficient blood quantum
Jamestown S'Klallam Tribe	WA	—	Yes	—	Disenrollment	Documentary error
Keweenaw Bay Indian Community	MI	No	Yes	—	Disenrollment	—
Klawock Cooperative Association	AK	No	Yes	No	Banishment	Criminal activity
Kootenai Tribe	ID	No	Yes	Yes	Disenrollment	—
Lac du Flambeau Band of Lake Superior Chippewa	WI	No	Yes	Yes	Banishment	Criminal activity
Las Vegas Band of Paiute	NV	No	Yes	No	Disenrollment	Insufficient blood quantum
Little River Band of Ottawa	MI	No	Yes	Yes	Disenrollment	Enrollment error, residency
Lumbee Tribe	NC	Yes	No	No	Disenrollment	Fraud, failure to maintain contact

Lummi Tribe	WA	No	Yes	No	Banishment	Criminal activity
Mashantucket Pequot	CT	No	Yes	Yes	Banishment	Criminal activity
Mattaponi Tribe	VA	No	No	No	Banishment	Criminal activity
Mille Lacs Band of Ojibwe	MN	No	Yes	Yes	Banishment	Criminal activity
Monacan Indian Nation	MD	No	No	No	Banishment	—
Narragansett Tribe	RI	No	No	No	Disenrollment	—
Native Village of Alutiig	AK	No	No	No	Banishment	Criminal activity
Native Village of Tanana	AK	No	No	No	Banishment	Criminal activity
Nooksack Indian Tribe	WA	No	Yes	No	Disenrollment	Enrollment error
Oneida Nation	NY	No	Yes	No	Disenrollment	—
Osage Nation	OK	No	Yes		Disenrollment	Fraud
Passamaquoddy Tribe	ME	No	No	No	Disenrollment	—
Puyallup Tribe	WA	No	Yes	Yes	Disenrollment	—
Sac and Fox Tribal Community	OK	No	Yes	Yes	Disenrollment	Dual enrollment, insufficient blood quantum
Saginaw Chippewa	MI	No	Yes	Yes	Disenrollment, Banishment	—
Sauk-Suiattle Indian Tribe	WA	No	Yes	No	Disenrollment	Insufficient blood quantum
Sault Ste. Marie Tribe of Chippewa	MI	No	Yes	No	Banishment	Criminal activity
Seminole Nation	OK	No	Yes		Disenrollment	Insufficient blood quantum
Shoshone-Bannock Tribe	UT	No	No	No	Banishment	Criminal activity
Sisseton Wahpeton Oyate	SD	No	Yes		Disenrollment	Dual enrollment
Snoqualmie Indian Tribe	WA	Yes	Yes	No	Disenrollment, Banishment	Insufficient blood quantum, treason

(continued)

TABLE 5.2. (*continued*)

Community	Location	Terminated	Gaming	Per Capita	Action	Rationale
St. Croix Chippewa of Wisconsin	WI	No	Yes	—	Disenrollment	Fraud
Te-Moak Tribe of Western Shoshone	NV	No	Yes	No	Disenrollment	Insufficient blood quantum
Tonawanda Band of Seneca	NY	No	No	No	Banishment	Treason
Turtle Mountain Band of Chippewa	ND	No	Yes	No	Banishment	—
United Keetowah Band of Cherokee Indians	OK	No	No	No	Banishment	—
Upper Sioux Community	MN	No	Yes	Yes	Banishment	Criminal activity
Walker River Paiute	NV	No	No	No	Disenrollment	—
Ysleta del Sur Pueblo	TX	No	No	No	Banishment	Insufficient blood quantum, criminal activity, violation of ceremonies
Yupik Village	AK	No	No	No	Banishment	Criminal activity

TABLE 5.3. California-based Native nations that have engaged in dismemberment

Community	Terminated	Gaming	Per Capita	Action	Rationale
Bear River Band of the Rohnerville Rancheria	Yes	Yes	Yes	Disenrollment	—
Berry Creek Rancheria of Maidu	No	Yes	Yes	Disenrollment	—
Big Valley Band of Pomo	Yes	Yes	Yes	Disenrollment	—
Cahto Tribe of the Laytonville Rancheria	No	Yes	—	Disenrollment	Dual enrollment, receipt of funds from another tribe's settlement
California Valley Miwok Tribe	No	No	No	Disenrollment	—
Cedarville Rancheria	No	No	No	Banishment	—
Cold Springs Rancheria of Mono	Yes	No	No	Disenrollment	—
Coyote Valley Band of Pomo	No	Yes	Yes	Disenrollment	—
Dry Creek Rancheria Band of Pomo	No	Yes	Yes	Disenrollment	—
Elem Indian Colony of Pomo	No	No	No	Disenrollment, Banishment	Treason, fraud, corruption, etc.
Enterprise Rancheria of Maidu	No	Yes	—	Disenrollment	—
Guidiville Rancheria of Pomo	Yes	Yes	No	Disenrollment	—
Hopland Band of Pomo	Yes	Yes	Yes	Disenrollment	—
Mooretown Rancheria of Maidu	Yes	Yes	Yes	Disenrollment	—
Pala Band of Luiseno Mission Indians	No	Yes	Yes	Disenrollment	Insufficient blood quantum
Paskenta Band of Nomlaki Indians	Yes	Yes	Yes	Disenrollment	—
Pechanga Band of Luiseno Mission Indians	No	Yes	Yes	Disenrollment	Failure to prove lineal descent
Picayune Rancheria of Chukchansi Indians	Yes	Yes	Yes	Disenrollment, Banishment	Procedural errors, lack of documentation

(continued)

TABLE 5.3. (continued)

Community	Terminated	Gaming	Per Capita	Action	Rationale
Pinoleville Pomo Nation	Yes	Yes	Yes	Disenrollment	—
Pitt River Tribe, Madesi Band	No	Yes	—	Disenrollment	Dual enrollment, no lineal descent
Potter Valley Rancheria of Pomo Indians	Yes	No	No	Disenrollment	—
Redding Rancheria	Yes	Yes	Yes	Disenrollment	—
Rincon Band of San Luiseno Indians	No	Yes	Yes	Disenrollment	—
Robinson Rancheria Band of Pomo	Yes	Yes	Yes	Disenrollment	—
San Pasqual Band of Diqueno Mission Indians	No	Yes	Yes	Disenrollment	Insufficient blood quantum
Santa Rosa Indian Community of the Santa Rosa Rancheria	No	No	No	Disenrollment	—
Santa Rosa Rancheria Tachi-Yokat	No	Yes	Yes	Disenrollment	—
Shingle Springs Band of Miwok	No	Yes	Yes	Disenrollment	Fraud
United Auburn Indian Community	Yes	Yes	Yes	Banishment	Defamation
Viejas Group of Capitan Grande Band of Mission Indians	No	Yes	Yes	Disenrollment	—

TABLE 5.4. Native Nations that have engaged in denial of citizenship

Community	Location	Terminated	Gaming	Per Capita	Action	Rationale
Big Sandy Rancheria	CA	Yes	Yes	Yes	Denied Citizenship	Not recognized at restoration
Cachil DeHe Band of Wintun Indians of the Colusa	CA	No	Yes	Yes	Denied Citizenship	—
Eastern Shoshone	WY	No	Yes	No	Disenrollment, Denied Citizenship	Eligible but denied citizenship
Jackson Rancheria	CA	Yes	Yes	Yes	Denied Citizenship	Not recognized at restoration
Little Traverse Band of Odawa	MI		Yes	Yes	Denied Citizenship	Insufficient blood quantum
Mashpee Wampanoag Tribe	MA	No	No	No	Denied Citizenship	—
Mohegan Tribe	CT	No	Yes	Yes	Denied Citizenship	—
Seminole Nation	OK	No	Yes	No	Denied Citizenship	Freedman denied judgment funds, CDIB cards
Shakopee Mdewakanton Sioux Community	MN	No	Yes	Yes	Disenrollment, Denied Citizenship	Eligible but denied or postponed indefinitely.
Table Mountain Rancheria	CA	No	Yes	Yes	Denied Citizenship	Refused to process application
Yurok Tribe	CA	No	Yes	N/A	Denied Citizenship	Insufficient blood quantum

instances) is the second-most-cited rationale. Insufficient blood or the wrong type of blood from a different nation led to disenrollment, not banishment, in nine of the eleven cases. Fraud in enrollment was cited twice; both were cases of disenrollment. And there were only two cases of "error" in enrollment, which also led to disenrollment.

Table 5.3 is devoted exclusively to one state, California, which is home to the largest number of Native peoples engaging in dismemberment practices—about thirty as of July 2016. The data here are strikingly different than the data in most other states. First, the sheer number of Native communities that are dismembering is very high. The most revealing category is the action of disenrollment or banishment. Unlike the other twenty states, where the two practices are comparable, in California only two communities—Cedarville Rancheria and United Auburn—have used banishment alone. Two others are engaging in both practices—Elem Indian Colony and Picayune Rancheria. All the other communities have or are using disenrollment.

Second, all but six of the communities have gaming operations, although the Picayune Rancheria casino was shut down in October 2014 by federal decree because of a vicious intratribal conflict that has crippled the community and led to the disenrollment of more than half the community's citizenry. The casino reopened in January 2016.

Another key fact is that of the gaming tribes in California at least twenty engage in per capita distribution of at least some portion of the gambling revenue. Our data show that per capita payments, which must be established under the auspices of federal law via a Revenue Allocation Plan (RAP), play a central role in some of the tribal dismemberment battles as will be discussed later.

Table 5.4 identifies an admittedly short list of tribal governments that have not formally disenrolled or banished members, but have willfully *denied* admittance to individuals who appear to have a legitimate right to be admitted to citizenship in the nation. There may well be other nations that are denying membership, but we do not have that data.

It is impossible to definitively ascertain how many individuals—whether considered blood citizens or ethnic citizens, citizens by treaty (African American Freedmen within several of the Five Civilized Tribes), or citizens by adoption—have been dismembered in the last two decades, with figures ranging from two thousand to eight thousand. One commentator suggested that in California alone some five thousand individuals had been dismembered between 2000 and 2010.[2] We do know that the combined number of potential and actual disenrollees in two nations alone—the Cherokee Nation of Oklahoma

THE LEGACY OF DISENROLLMENT

Originally run May 31, 2013, on Indian Country Today Media Network. © 2016 Marty Two Bulls.

and its desire to disenroll some 2,800 Cherokee Freedmen (on hold for now pending a federal lawsuit), and the Chukchansi Nation of California (approximately 1,000)—suggests that the larger figure of eight thousand is likely the more accurate one.

By the late 1980s tribal governments had secured several federal legal victories, like *Santa Clara* (1978), which affirmed a tribal nation's right to deny membership, and *Chapoose v. Clark* (1985), a case involving children of Ute tribal members who fought to be enrolled, but were ousted by the assistant secretary of the interior, Ken Smith, who stated that they had insufficient blood quantum. In *Chapoose*, the district court overturned the secretary's action and said the children should be enrolled because the Northern Ute had the right to determine its own membership.

What follows are a series of short case studies that provide context for where, how, and why dismemberments are taking place throughout Indian Country. We will follow those up with an examination of some of the more important judicial cases—tribal and federal—that have been decided since the late 1980s. The case law can generally be grouped into three categories: (1) individuals looking to enroll in a particular Native nation sometimes file suit when their applications are denied; (2) in some cases, currently enrolled citizens file suits when they learn that they have been formally disenrolled; and (3) in other cases, enrolled members look to expel already enrolled members and sue when the tribal nation refuses to act upon their demands.[3]

NATIVE CASES OF BANISHMENT OR DISENROLLMENT
Case 1: Tlingit Community

In a widely publicized case in 1993, two seventeen-year-old Tlingit tribal youth who had been convicted in a state superior court in Washington for assaulting and robbing a Domino's Pizza delivery man and faced sentences of up to five-and-one-half years were instead turned over to Rudy James, a fifty-eight-year-old Klawock native, who purported to be a tribal judge of the Tlingit Nation.[4] James had convinced the state judge that if the young men were bound over to him, they would "undergo a traditional Tlingit punishment: banishment on remote, uninhabited islands, while contemplating their sins and hewing logs with which to build Whittlesey [the victim's surname] a house."[5]

Even as James convened a panel of eleven other Tlingit elders to determine the precise context for the banishment, which amounted to removal to remote islands for a period of twelve to eighteen months, "a firestorm of rumor, innuendo, and disinformation erupted, revealing rifts both within the Tlingit tribe and between the Tlingits and mainstream society that threatened the success of the experiment before it had even begun."[6] Questions arose around whether James had the authority to act on behalf of the Tlingit people, since he was not an officially recognized judge. Evidence also emerged that James and several other tribal judges had histories of bad debts and, in some cases, criminal records, and there was a question of whether banishment was even a part of Tlingit culture. Finally, Klawock's lone federally recognized Tlingit organization, the Klawock Cooperative Association, sent a letter distancing itself from the case.[7]

On May 1, 1995, the Washington Court of Appeals ruled that the two boys would still have to serve a state-sanctioned prison term once their banishment had ended.[8] However, on October 3, 1995, the trial judge who had originally referred the boys to the tribal judges ordered their banishment to cease and sentenced them to state prison. The boys were given terms of fifty-five and thirty-one months, and received credit for having served nearly two years. Finally, they were held jointly liable for $35,000 in restitution to Whittlesey.[9]

The judge preempted the banishment because he believed there were flaws in the way it was being carried out that "threatened its credibility and integrity." For example, one of the boys came to the mainland and applied for a driver's license. The judge had also been informed that the two had received visits from relatives throughout their banishment.[10]

Case 2: Tonawanda Band of Seneca Community

The Tonawanda Band of Seneca Indians, part of the Iroquois Confederacy, were parties to a federal court of appeals case in 1996, *Poodry v. Tonawanda Band of Seneca Indians*.[11] This case, in the words of Judge Cabranes, placed before the Second Circuit Court of Appeals "a question of federal Indian law not yet addressed by any federal court: whether an Indian stripped of tribal membership and 'banished' from a reservation has recourse in a federal forum to test the legality of the tribe's actions. More specifically, the issue is whether the habeas corpus provision of the Indian Civil Rights Act of 1968 . . . allows a federal court to review punitive measures imposed by a tribe upon its members, when those measures involve 'banishment' rather than imprisonment."[12]

In 1995, the district court had dismissed the applications of five Seneca citizens, Peter L. Poodry, David C. Peters, Susan LaFramboise, John A. Redeye, and Stonehouse Lone Goeman, who had been summarily convicted of treason and sentenced to permanent banishment from the reservation in 1992. The petitioners, upon their banishment, had filed applications in federal court asserting that the band's punishment order was a criminal conviction that violated their rights under the Indian Civil Rights Act. They unsuccessfully sought habeas corpus relief provided under the ICRA in the district court, which concluded that permanent banishment was not a sufficient restraint on liability to trigger the ICRA's habeas corpus protection.

The banished Seneca then appealed this ruling to the Second Circuit Court of Appeals, which vacated the district court's finding by holding that banishment was indeed a severe enough punishment involving sufficient restraint on the liberty of those banished to qualify as "detention," and thus permit federal review under the ICRA's habeas corpus rule. The case was sent back down to the district court for a resolution based on the merits. The appellate court said, in effect, that the lower court had erred in dismissing the banished individuals' petitions for writ of habeas corpus on jurisdictional grounds.[13]

First, some historical background is warranted to establish the grounds on which the individuals were banished. In the latter part of 1991, a conflict erupted on Tonawanda lands when the petitioners made accusations against members of the council of chiefs and the chairman of the council, Bernard Parker. The council is the primary legislative body of the nation. The petitioners accused the council members of "misusing tribal funds, suspending tribal elections, excluding members of the Council of Chiefs from the tribe's business affairs, and burning tribal records."[14] Allegedly, the petitioners, in consultation with other tribal members, then formed an alternative legislative body, the "Interim General Council of the Tonawanda Band."

A few weeks later, on January 24, 1992, Poodry, Peters, and LaFramboise stated that they were accosted at their homes by a group of fifteen to twenty-five Seneca who gave them notice, in writing, that they were henceforth banished from the Seneca Nation (the other two petitioners received the same notice in the mail). The language in the banishment notice is reminiscent of the language spelled out in the Great Law of Peace. The 1992 statement reads as follows:

> It is with a great deal of sorrow that we inform you that you are now banished from the territories of the Tonawanda Band of the Seneca Nation. You are to leave now and never return. According to the customs and usage of the Tonawanda Band of the Seneca Nation and the HAUDENOSAUNEE, no warnings are required before banishment for acts of murder, rape, or treason. Your actions to overthrow, or otherwise bring about the removal of, the traditional government at the Tonawanda Band of the Seneca Nation, and further by becoming a member of the Interim General Council, are considered treason. Therefore, banishment is required. According to the customs and usages of the Tonawanda Band of Seneca Nation and the HAUDENOSAUNEE, your name is removed from the tribal rolls, your Indian name is taken away, and your lands will become the responsibility of the Council of Chiefs. You are now stripped of your Indian citizenship and permanently lose any and all rights afforded our members. YOU MUST LEAVE IMMEDIATELY AND WE WILL WALK YOU TO THE OUTER BORDERS OF OUR TERRITORY.[15]

The banishment notice was signed by six of the eight council of chiefs members. The two who did not sign, Corbett Sundown and Roy Poodry, were either too sick to sign—the council's explanation for their silence—or had been excluded from the council's meeting where the banishment was set—the petitioners' explanation.

The crowds were initially unsuccessful in forcibly evicting the three petitioners. However, the petitioners asserted that they and their family members were then harassed and assaulted by the chiefs and their supporters. One of the petitioners was literally stoned, electrical services were terminated at their homes and businesses, and they were allegedly denied health services and benefits.[16] These events set the legal stage for the federal court's intervention.

The court of appeals rendered a detailed opinion that addressed the relationship between tribal sovereignty and congressional plenary power, the impact of the ICRA and the habeas corpus proviso, and the vitality of the *Santa Clara* precedent. Of importance for this study, of course, is how the court addressed the issue of treason and the meaning of banishment for tribal citizens. The chiefs said the petitioners had been convicted of treason because they had engaged in "unlawful activities," including "actions to overthrow, or otherwise bring about the removal of the traditional government" of the Tonawanda Band.[17]

In describing "permanent banishment," the court compared it with the denaturalization proceedings carried out when individuals have obtained U.S. citizenship illegally or through willful misrepresentation, or cases in which native-born American citizens must forfeit their citizenship for having committed major offenses. Both are exceedingly harsh measures reserved for the most egregious of offenses. The court described the petitioners' banishment as "the coerced and peremptory deprivation of the petitioners' membership in the tribe and their social and cultural affiliation. To determine the severity of the sanction, we need only look to the orders of banishment themselves, which suggest that banishment is imposed (without notice) only for the most severe of crimes: murder, rape, and treason."[18]

In ruling that permanent banishment as a punishment for treason amounted to a sufficient restraint on liberty to invoke federal jurisdiction in a petition for a writ of habeas corpus, the court reiterated that this was a novel question with potentially lasting significance for tribal citizens should the Supreme Court deny a writ of certiorari, which it did later that year.[19] Judge Cabranes noted that this is especially true "at a time when some Indian tribal communities have achieved unusual opportunities for wealth, thereby unavoidably creating incentives for dominant elites to 'banish' irksome dissidents for 'treason.'"[20] This is a slightly veiled reference to the gaming resources that some Native nations are amassing. Interestingly, there was no discussion in the opinion about gaming per se. Although the court concluded that the petitioners deserved the right to have the merits of their claims heard by the district court, it also held that the sovereign immunity of the Tonawanda Band must be respected and that the nation could not be sued without its express consent.

Finally, the court sent a stern warning to those tribal governments that attempt to use cultural difference to justify what the judge viewed as diminutions of the essential civil rights of individuals. In the court's words, "Here, the respondents [Council of Chiefs] adopt a stance of cultural relativism, claiming that while 'treason' may be a crime under the laws of the United States, it is a civil matter under tribal law and that while 'banishment' may be thought to be a harsh punishment under the law of the United States . . . it is necessary to and consistent with the culture and tradition of the Tonawanda Band."[21]

The court was not persuaded by these cultural arguments. While acknowledging that tribes are unique political and cultural entities, it more forcefully declared that "the respondents wish to use their connection with federal authorities as a sword, while employing notions of cultural relativism as a shield from federal court jurisdiction."[22] Judge Cabranes recognized that tribal governments have the right to govern, to establish their own criteria for citizenship, and to regulate their lands and exclude outsiders. But he also acknowledged a responsibility for those "American citizens subject to tribal authority when that authority imposes criminal sanctions in denial of rights guaranteed by the laws of the United States."[23]

Case 3: The Tigua Community of the Ysleta del Sur Pueblo

The Tigua, relative newcomers to the world of federally recognized tribes—they were formally acknowledged in 1968—inhabit territory southwest of El Paso, Texas.[24] Their banishment conflagration formally began in 1993, when the tribe's leadership failed in their efforts to negotiate a gambling compact with Texas governor Ann Richards. Despite their diplomatic failure, the tribe proceeded to build a bingo hall and later expanded the operation to include pull-tab gaming, blackjack, and other games.[25] Within a short period of time, the Tigua's gaming operation was bringing in an estimated sixty million dollars annually. It remained successful until it was shut down by federal officials in 2002 for failure to comply with the Indian Gaming Regulatory Act because of the tribe's inability to forge a gaming compact with the state.[26]

The Tigua dismemberment saga entails a combination of gaming revenue, sacred objects, and sibling camaraderie that would ensnare this small nation in a bitter banishment struggle. In 1990, a twenty-seven-year-old Tigua member, Marty Silvas, was named a war captain and was given the responsibility to be caretaker of one of the tribe's most sacred objects, a drum. Three years later, his brother, Manny Silvas, who was the tribe's lieutenant governor, was suspected by the tribal council of having misappropriated $70,000 of the tribe's money. The council and the tribal chief, Enrique Paiz, were split on whether the accusations were true, but the council eventually voted, over Paiz's vigorous objections, to deny Silvas the opportunity to run for reelection.

Because Paiz had supported his embattled lieutenant governor, the council then took the unprecedented step of removing him from office as well. As result of these actions, Marty Silvas then called for the entire council to step down, hiding the sacred drum he had been entrusted with as war captain. He also refused to join in a tribal ceremony. While the tribe was exploring legal means to recover the sacred item, it wiped Marty Silvas's name from the tribe's rolls and sent tribal police to remove him from tribal lands in May 1996.[27] Silvas was ordered at gunpoint to reveal where he had hidden the drum. When he refused, "he was driven by car to the edge of the reservation and told that he was no longer a part of these people . . . [and that he] did not belong here anymore."[28]

The banishment conflict expanded dramatically in 1996 as the tribe's wealth increased and as the new Tigua governor, Vince Munoz, consolidated his power. The banishment zeal soon included many additional families, and pitted two factions against one another: those who supported the Silvas brothers and Chief Paiz, and those who supported the council and Governor Munoz. As Everett Saucedo reports, "the tribal leaders confirmed the families' fears when they announced they would re-examine the tribal rolls in order to correct alleged disparities created by the inclusion, in tribal membership, of those who did not meet bloodline requirements. Those who lacked the minimum blood requirements were to be removed from the tribe's rolls."[29]

As the conflict continued to expand in 1998, several of Marty Silvas's supporters were first fired from their government jobs and then, four days later, officially banished for allegedly lacking the necessary requirement of Tigua blood. Some of those banished were given small financial settlements, and they departed voluntarily. But several other families fought the banishment proceedings in state district court. Their suit, however, was dismissed.

Armed with this judicial ruling, the tribe more aggressively sought to banish certain families and individuals that were still on tribal lands until all had been forcibly evicted. One of the last to be expelled was Grace Vela who, by

January 1999, faced nearly unrelenting pressure from tribal police officers to leave. Finally, on February 18, police officers knocked down Vela's front door, placed her in handcuffs, and removed her from tribal lands.[30]

When Governor Munoz was asked whether his government's decision to banish those members had anything to do with consolidating his power base or the tribe's fiscal affairs, he insisted that he was acting under "pressure from the Bureau of Indian Affairs [BIA]," which, he alleged, "had threatened to reduce the tribe's federal funding unless the membership rolls were reexamined."[31] But according to Saucedo, who wrote a lengthy article on this case, neither the BIA nor the tribe would comment on the issue, declaring that it was an "internal tribal matter."[32]

Case 4: Nooksack

The Nooksack Tribe, located within Washington State, has undertaken to disenroll 306 of its two thousand citizens, in a case popularly referred to as "the Nooksack 306." A majority of the tribal council, along with the chairman of the tribe, Bob Kelly, who was adopted into the community as a child, has led the effort to disenroll the 306 individuals. As of this writing, June 2016, the 306 are still provisionally enrolled, although they have been denied the benefits and services other members are entitled to. Pending BIA and federal court action will ultimately determine their political fate.

A federally terminated tribe, the Nooksack people worked hard to become reinstated by providing historical evidence of their continued existence. They also sought out those directly descended from known ancestors who had left their traditional home places in order to bolster their numbers and thus their case for rerecognition. Three families, tracing their lines through Annie George, were actively recruited by the tribe's leadership to move back to their territory. These are the citizens whose legitimacy is now called into question.

Anthropologists and legal counsel provided ample evidence of Annie George's Nooksack heritage in 2013 before then tribal court chief judge, Raquel Montoya-Lewis, herself a disenrollee from the Isleta Pueblo in New Mexico.[33] Judge Montoya-Lewis ruled against the Nooksack 306, reasoning that the proof of lineage was irrelevant given that the tribal chair and council possessed the sovereign power to set membership rules as they saw fit.

In December 2014, Judge Montoya-Lewis was tapped by Washington State governor Jay Inslee to serve on the Whatcom County Superior Court. She is the first Native judge to be appointed for a superior court judgeship in Washington.

She was replaced by Susan Alexander, a non-Indian, who assumed her post in June 2015. Alexander arrived with a wealth of judicial experience, having served as a tribal judge for several Native courts over a twenty-year career. Alexander was immediately ensnared by the disenrollment fracas. Without going into a detailed analysis of all the intricacies of this nation's enrollment saga, a few choice bullet points will highlight how bizarre and deeply frustrating the situation has become for those facing dismemberment.

January 2016:	Judge Alexander rules that the Nooksack Tribal Council (NTC) could not prevent any qualified Nooksack 306 member from voting in the impending tribal elections slated for March 2016.
February 2016:	The NTC suspends benefits for elder citizens who have been targeted for disenrollment.
February 2016:	The NTC enacts a resolution barring (or disbarring) the Galanda Broadman law firm representing the Nooksack 306 from practicing in the tribal court or engaging in any other business activity.
March 2016:	Judge Alexander in a bold ruling in *Belmont v. Kelly*, having ordered the NTC to show what due process it had provided to the Galanda Broadman law firm, found that no due process had been provided to the attorneys. Her opinion states emphatically that "it appeared to the Court that Galanda Broadman had not received notice and an opportunity to be heard." Alexander went on to note that "the tactics employed by Defendants [Chairman Kelly and several of the tribal council members] are surely confounding" and she chided them for sending the Nooksack 306 attorneys "in a wild goose chase" as they sought to meet the council's convoluted and ever-changing rules.
March 2016:	The Nooksack Tribal Court of Appeals also rules against the NTC legislative actions against the Galanda Broadman law firm.
March 2016:	The NTC cancels the scheduled tribal elections mandated by the tribe's constitution and the Tribal Election Ordinance.

March 2016:   The Nooksack Tribal Enrollment Director sends notices
                     to some forty members (not members of the 306 group)
                     informing them that they face disenrollment for having
                     dual membership in Nooksack and the Tlingit and Haida
                     Tribes of Alaska. They are given thirty days to relinquish
                     membership in the Alaska Native groups or face expulsion
                     from Nooksack.

March 2016:   Judge Alexander is informed she must take a "random"
                     drug test, although she is later told by tribe's general
                     manager that her March 21st *Belmont* decision "under-
                     mines the authority of the general manager." On March
                     28th she is told that she passed the drug test, but within
                     an hour she is informed that she has been terminated
                     "without cause."

April 2016:   NTC member Carmen S. Tageant, who voted against the
                     disbarment of Galanda Broadman and supported the
                     Nooksack 306, is subject to a recall election on April 22.
                     In a complaint filed by Tageant on April 25, she asserts
                     that "the entire recall petition was instituted by Defen-
                     dants [Kelly and other council members] to target Plain-
                     tiff [Tageant] for her views, which disagreed with those
                     of the defendants."

April 2016:   The Nooksack Tribal Court of Appeals quashes an appeal
                     by the tribe's leadership, and insists the council must
                     share resolutions it had passed in February that blocked
                     the Galanda Broadman firm from representing the Nook-
                     sack 306.

April 2016:   The forty individuals targeted for disenrollment in March
                     for alleged dual membership in an Alaskan Native tribe
                     file a lawsuit, *Gladstone v. Kelly,* in which they assert that
                     they have been slated for disenrollment by Chairman
                     Kelly and the council as retaliation "for supporting the
                     Plaintiffs who are subject to disenrollment and commonly
                     known as 'the Nooksack 306.'"

June 2016:   Nooksack Tribal Court of Appeals orders the Nooksack
                     Tribal Council to appoint a judge to either hear the chal-

	lenge of Michelle Roberts, a member of the Nooksack 306, or "to refrain from taking any further action to disenroll her."
June 2016:	Raymond G. Dodge Jr., formerly a lawyer for the Nooksack tribe, is appointed chief judge of the Nooksack Tribal Court.
July 2016:	A special election, convened as the Nooksack General Council, is held to select four interim tribal council members to fill four vacant seats. This special process is necessary as the council had failed to hold a constitutionally required election in March 2016. Chairman Kelly, unhappy with the makeup of the new council, claims the results are invalid.
August 2016:	The Nooksack Court of Appeals denies the motion by Michelle Roberts to expand the court's jurisdiction to include all 272 plaintiffs/potential disenrollees.
September 2016:	Gabriel Galanda files a petition before the Nooksack Tribal Court seeking an order that his disbarment was "illegal and invalid."

Thus, while Nooksack's leadership has not yet succeeded in dismembering nearly 350 of its members, they have taken substantive steps to curtail property rights, denied due process to lawyers and sitting tribal judges and legislators, and barred otherwise bona fide citizens from participation in tribal meetings and gatherings.

When interviewed, several pending disenrollees said they believed personal vendettas were the root cause of the disenrollment effort. While not critical of traditional adoption, they spoke of the irony of an adoptee—the tribal chairman—questioning the legitimacy of family members who had been sought after and accepted as blood relatives more than thirty years earlier. Interestingly, in 2014 the council voted to suspend all tribal adoptions.

In December of 2015 the tribe's first major economic initiative, the River Casino, closed its doors. The closure occurred in part because of financial problems and competition from other casinos in the area, but also, according to Michelle Roberts, a former human resources manager for the casino and one of the targeted Nooksack 306, because of the disenrollment squabbles in the community. She noted that "if they [tribal officials] weren't so focused on putting all their energy into disenrollment, they could have put more energy into the business."[34]

And the actions of Chairman Kelly and council members in March of 2016 to seek to disenroll another forty tribal members for allegedly having dual membership in an Alaskan tribal nation is a clear example of political retaliation for those members' staunch support of the Nooksack 306.

Case 5: Confederated Tribes of the Grand Ronde (CTGR)

The CTGR in Oregon was officially terminated by federal decree in 1954. They were restored to recognized status in 1983. In 2015, the CTGR stripped citizenship from eighty-six members, seventy-nine living and seven deceased, including the descendants of their well-known chief, Tumulth, an original signatory of the 1855 Kalapuya Treaty. (Tribal court cases involving the CTGR will be discussed in the ensuing chapter.)

The disenrollment process was triggered by a controversial audit of the CTGR membership rolls. Critics claimed the audit violated then tribal law because enrollment records and personal information left the reservation and were viewed by nontribal citizens. The New Mexico consulting firm hired to review the records found what it deemed to be inconsistencies and errors in numerous member records. These alleged inaccuracies formed the basis for subsequent disenrollment proceedings.

James Shaw, a Portland-based nontribal attorney appointed by tribal leadership as their tribal judge, ruled against the disenrollees in several cases that will later be analyzed. He based his decisions, in part, on Chief Tumulth's "lack of relocation to the CTGR area" after settlement commenced in 1855 and establishment was formalized in 1857. Judge Shaw did not consider that the chief was unable to relocate from his family home to the newly established reservation as he was executed by the U.S. Army in 1856. Citing spelling inconsistencies, the judge also dismissed the evidence of the disenrollees' matrilineal descent from Chief Tumulth's wife, Susan Tomolcha, who was listed on the 1872 Tribal Census roll.

Among the nearly ninety dismembered citizens were native language speakers and elders, many of whom had been enlisted by the Grand Ronde government to showcase the nation's strong cultural ties to the area when they sought to block neighboring tribes' efforts to engage in traditional practices and economic development. The CTGR continues to claim Chief Tumulth's territory as part of their ceded lands even though they have now stripped his very descendants of their citizenship.

Case 6: Picayune Rancheria of Chukchansi Indians

Due to the complexity of this nation's dismemberment situation, we begin with a historical timeline to provide some necessary context.

Timeline

12,000 BCE	Chukchansi people settle in the San Joaquin Valley.
1848	Discovery of gold in California leads to profound trauma and demographic collapse for the Chukchansi and other Native nations in the region.
1912	U.S. President Taft issues an executive order establishing the eighty-acre Picayune Rancheria for the homeless Chukchansi people.
1958	Chukchansi is one of forty-one tribal nations targeted for termination by the California Rancheria Act.
1963	Chukchansi Nation is officially terminated by federal statute. The rancheria lands are distributed to two individuals: Maryan Ramirez and her brother, Gordon Wyatt.
1983	Chukchansi is officially rerecognized by the federal government via the *Tillie Hardwick v. U.S.* court decision. There are twenty-three members in the nation at the time.
1986	The first tribal council is seated.
	Tribal dispute erupts over a proposal to establish a bingo hall.
	The tribe has three significant groups that are often at odds: (1) Distributees: These are members who are descendants of the Rancheria's founders and who sold the Rancheria during the termination era, but then formed the nucleus after the 1983 *Tillie Hardwick* case. (2) Allottees: These are individuals or their direct lineal descendants who received land allotments under the 1887 General Allotment Act. (3) Petitioners: These are landless individuals who did not live on the rancheria when it was officially terminated in 1963. They may become members if they have Chukchansi blood and they applied for membership by October 1989.
1988	Chukchansi community adopts its first constitution.

1989	Chukchansi prepares its first official tribal roll.
1990	Tribal roll is adopted by tribal resolution and sent to the BIA for approval. The tribal council approves six hundred new applications for membership. Another seven hundred individuals are approved shortly thereafter.
1992	Intratribal conflict mounts, and a recall effort is begun by one faction to remove Jane Wyatt Lawhon as chairwoman. Lawhon files three appeals with the BIA; all are denied. During this tumultuous period much of the tribe's office equipment, vehicles, and nearly all the enrollment files and applications are removed. The tribal council disenrolls the Ramirez descendants.
1995	The former chairwoman, Wyatt-Lawhon, and nearly a dozen family members are disenrolled for theft, embezzlement, and the taking of enrollment records. The tribal council reenrolls most of these individuals in the tribe in 2001 without the knowledge or consent of the general council.
1998	Chukchansi tribal leaders clear twenty-seven acres of land in Madera County in the hope that they will eventually receive federal authorization to build a casino. The process, however, angers a rival group of Chukchansi, descendants of the rancheria's founders, who complain that the land preparation has destroyed their homeland, including several burial sites. Chukchansi membership is now at over 1,500.
1999	Chairwoman Daisy Liedkie in June is forced out of office. Two months later she and two hundred other members are formally disenrolled. They are given no explanation for their termination.
2003	Chukchansi Gold Resort and Casino, a 300,000 square-foot operation, opens in June at a cost of nearly 200 million. Tribal membership is listed at over 1,800 by Chairman Dixie Jackson.

2005	The Chukchansi conducts an enrollment audit pursuant to a resolution, ostensibly to determine whether those enrolled in the tribe meet the constitutional criteria for membership. Disenrollment could occur for dual enrollment, enrollment through error, or for "fraudulent documentation or misrepresentation." The tribe's official correspondence in February admits that "adding to the problems we face . . . is the fact that many of the enrollment records have been lost, stolen, or destroyed. This may make it impossible to determine which petitioners were accepted within one year specified in the Constitution."
	Tribal membership votes to stop disenrollments. The tribal council declares the vote invalid because some members who voted face pending disenrollment hearings.
2006	Disenrollment hearings begin in September and last until early 2007. Some six hundred members are disenrolled.
2007	Tribal membership is now at approximately nine hundred.
2007–8	Chairman Dustin Graham sees that nearly one hundred family members and others are enrolled just prior to being voted out of office.
2008	Harold Hammond, a tribal council member, declares, "We didn't disenroll anybody. We just corrected our paperwork."
2011	Fifty-seven members from one family are disenrolled, including a former tribal chairman, Gilbert Cordero. Another two hundred members are slated for disenrollment.
2012	A near riot erupts when a faction of fifty, led by Morris Reid, who had sought to be sworn in as a tribal council member in December 2011 but was denied, breaks into the tribe's office to claim their positions. Another faction led by Reggie Lewis, reporting to be the tribal council, is stationed at the tribe's Economic Development Administration building. A third faction, led by Nancy Ayala, operates out of a small building near the tribe's casino.
	A group of Chukchansi distributees, the Ayala and Ramirez family members, file a federal lawsuit in San Jose. They

claim the Chukchansi should only be comprised of forty-six members from their two families. A federal judge dismisses the case.

Approximately one hundred members are set to be disenrolled.

Chukchansi membership is now at approximately 691.

A 250-million-dollar agreement is reached when the tribe's Economic Development Authority restructures its financing after the tribe struggles to pay its debt to Wells Fargo, which holds the note for casino investors.

2013   Fresno State University hosts a public panel discussion titled "The Chukchansi's Legitimacy Crisis: One Year Later" to discuss developments in the community.

2014   BIA issues a ruling reappointing the 2010 tribal council in an attempt to quell the bitter factionalism wracking the tribe. Amy Dutschke, the regional director for the BIA, chooses that date because that was allegedly the last year there was a relatively uncontested election. In reality, virtually all elections since 2006 have been hotly contested. The 2010 council membership apparently favors factions led by Morris Reid and Reggie Lewis.

A federal administrative law judge overturns the BIA's decision to return control of the tribe to the council elected in 2010.

The ongoing intratribal conflict leads the National Indian Gaming Commission and the California State Attorney General to close the tribe's casino and hotel in late October largely because "imminent jeopardy exists because of the real and immediate threat to human health and well-being, which if uncorrected, could result in serious harm or death." The casino complex and the tribe's Economic Development Authority has a "fund deficit of $49.6 million in 2013."

2015   To further complicate internal affairs, a fourth faction arises within the tribe—this one is composed of the descendants of the tribe's original forty-three voting members who were recognized when the Chukchansi were restored to federal status in 1983. The other factions are the Tex MacDonald group, the Lewis/Ayala group, and the Reid group.

The BIA's Interior Board of Indian Appeals rules that the tribe should be governed by the group that had been elected in 2010—as in 2014 allegedly because that was the last election without real dispute. That council included Reggie Lewis, Nancy Ayala, Morris Reid, and several others.

The tribal council in a highly contentious four-to-three vote opts to reenroll all those who had been disenrolled since 2010. This decision, which as of this writing had not been fully carried out, ignores the nearly eight hundred former members who had been disenrolled from the early 1990s to 2010.

The tribal council hires Phil Hogen, former head of the National Indian Gaming Commission, to advise them on gaming regulatory issues in the hopes that this will expedite the tribe's attempt to reopen their casino.

2016   The tribal casino, Chukshansi Gold, reopens in January.

The tribal council adopts a resolution in May that determines the membership of the tribe to be all those officially listed on the tribal rolls as of December 2008. This action, if carried out, would reenroll those disenrolled in 2010 and 2012 but would exclude at least eight hundred people who were disenrolled in 2000, 2006, and 2007.

Forty-six members, many of them involved with other political factions within the tribe, are served with letters for disenrollment for allegedly having been "dually enrolled in another tribe." Hearings are held in August and September but no final decisions have been made public as of this writing.

Of the many tribal nations engaging in dismemberment practices, the people of the Picayune Rancheria of Chukchansi offer arguably the most complicated and combustible instance as the timeline attests. In sheer numbers alone, with the single exception of the Cherokee Nation of Oklahoma which is seeking to dismember nearly 2,800 African American freedmen, the Chukchansi has terminated more of its citizens than any other Indigenous people. As of 2016, the tribal government—as fractured as it is—has formally terminated well over one half of its population over the past two dozen years. At one time the population was as high as 1,800; it has now been reduced to between six hundred and eight hundred people. The story of this small nation's dismemberment activity warrants a full-length book, given its complicated twists and turns. This short case study can but skim the surface. Readers are encouraged to peruse the excellent work of Marc Benjamin and Chris Collins, journalists for the *Fresno Bee*, who have covered the Chukchansi's saga for several years. In addition, Kevin Fagan of the *San Francisco Chronicle* wrote a major story about Chukchansi that was facilitated by the American Indian Movement's Laura Wass.

Like most Native nations in what is now California, the arc of the Chukchansi's historical struggles since their arrival several millennia ago ranged across the harsh Spanish colonial period, marked by missions, slavery, and disease, through the brief Mexican occupation period (1821–48), and on to the arrival of U.S. jurisdiction in the late 1840s. In 1848 white settlers discovered gold in the Sierra Mountains and the resulting influx of fortune hunters led to genocidal activities and policies blatantly designed to eradicate the Indigenous population in the region in order to make room for these new settlers. These actions precipitated massive social, demographic, cultural, and territorial changes in the lives of the Chukchansi people.[35]

At nearly every turn the Chukchansi, like other Native nations, were attacked and undermined. First came state policies that officially sanctioned their extermination in 1851. The following year federal policies were introduced, which initially produced eighteen treaties between the United States and scores of tribal nations. However, immediately after the treaties were signed by the California Nations, the documents were secretly tabled and never ratified by the U.S. Senate because of strong state and federal opposition.

For a century, the tribes struggled to survive without treaty protections while the California juggernaut put increasing pressure on their territories and resources. As the U.S. entered into the postwar termination era, conditions worsened for the region's beleaguered Indian peoples. In 1953, Public Law 280 granted the state of California criminal jurisdiction over Indian Country within its boundaries. The transfer of authority culminated in the federal termination of the legal and political status of the Chukchansi and thirty-seven other Native nations under the Rancheria Act (72 Stat. 619) introduced in 1958.[36] When the Chukchansi's individual termination measure was finally prepared in 1963, the community's former lands were distributed to two individuals, Maryan Ramirez and her brother, Gordon Wyatt.

The trauma associated with such destructive state and federal policies generated and exacerbated profound socioeconomic problems in the Chukchansi community: inflated alcoholism rates, acute poverty, high dropout rates, and the like. But when the Chukchansi (along with sixteen other rancherias) were restored to federal status by the court ruling *Tillie Hardwick v. U.S.* (1983), hope mounted that the community was moving in a better direction. Tribal membership at the time stood at a mere twenty-three individuals.[37]

In 1986 a tribal council was formed and tensions escalated as talk of building a bingo hall began. In 1988 the tribe adopted its first constitution and then set about developing a tribal roll that the BIA then approved. In 1990 the tribe's two major families, the Ramirezes and the Wyatts, oversaw a significant tribal enrollment and expansion of nearly 1,300 new citizens in an effort to strengthen the tribe and secure a greater amount of federal funds. As the tribal council admitted in 2005, "the greater our membership numbers, the more dollars we received from the BIA."[38] But intratribal conflict continued to fester and in 1992 the first of several major disenrollments occurred, with the Ramirez descendants and several others being terminated by tribal decree.

In 1998, tribal leaders, led by Chairman Gilbert Cordero, ratcheted up their plans for a casino and cleared twenty-eight acres of land in Madera County. Some of the cleared land belonged to another segment of the tribe who complained that the land being developed had disturbed several of their ancestors' burial sites.[39] By the end of 1998, Cordero had been ousted as chairman and Daisy Liedkie, an elder, was chosen as chairwoman. Liedkie's tenure was short-lived, however, and by the fall of 1999 she and nearly two hundred other citizens had been disenrolled. These disenrollees received no explanation as to why they had been dismembered, although Liedkie said she believed she had been exiled because she pushed the Cascade Entertainment Group, in charge of helping the tribe establish the casino, "too hard for contractual concessions that would benefit the tribe at the expense of the management company."[40]

Liedkie valiantly challenged her dismemberment and the BIA agreed that she and her followers had been disenrolled without due process. The bureau sent a letter threatening to "suspend federal recognition if it [the tribe] didn't eliminate the influence of political factions."[41] Liedkie and other disenrollees also hired attorneys and had DNA tests completed to verify their heritage. Their disenrollments were not overturned and the BIA meted out no sanctions against the tribal government.

In 2003 the tribe opened the Chukchansi Gold Resort and Casino at a cost of nearly $200 million. This major development set the stage for several more rounds of disenrollments, some of which dated to an internal enrollment audit that was initiated in 2003, pursuant to a tribal resolution. The tribe's estimated population in 2003 was around 1,800.

Those facing disenrollment were confronted by a damning and insoluble problem: most of the tribe's enrollment records had been lost, stolen, or destroyed in the early 1990s, making it virtually impossible for most to meet the documentary threshold required retain membership—proof of Chukchansi blood, listing in a federal document that presaged their Congressional termination in 1963, or proof of descendancy from someone who had received an allotment under the 1887 General Allotment Act.

Although the tribe's membership voted in 2005 to stop disenrollments, the tribal council declared the vote invalid "because some members who voted had pending disenrollment hearings." Beginning in 2006 and continuing into 2007, the tribal council disenrolled another six hundred citizens. Initially, each disenrollee was given a hearing of at least forty-five minutes to contest the tribe's action. But because of the sheer numbers involved, the council soon reduced the length of each hearing to only twenty minutes. Laura Wass (Mountain Maidu), the Central California Director of the American Indian Movement and a longtime advocate for those who have been disenrolled, noted that pending disenrollees often brought more than ample documentation, despite the problem of lost or pilfered enrollment records, but even that did not protect them from dismemberment. The council usually did not deny that these were persons of Chukchansi descent. "Instead, they insisted the members had failed to meet other criteria, like applying for membership before an April 1990 cutoff date."[42]

Laura Wass and Cathy Corey, one of the six hundred disenrolled, both emphasize that money was a central factor in this particular tribal purge. Corey pointed out that at the July 2006 meeting of the tribal council, tribal leaders voted to "give themselves $250 each for every disenrollment hearing." In fact, not only were council members paid for each hearing they attended, but so were the enrollment committee members, the enrollment specialist, and the tribe's attorneys. The amount each received—ranging from $200 to $350—depended on the individual's position in the tribe.

And Wass has noted that while the tribe's official line is that it is correcting its membership rolls by following blood criteria spelled out in the constitution, "the real motive is money." "There was," she said, "no such thing as disenrollment before casinos."[43] By 2007 Chukchansi's membership had been reduced to approximately nine hundred citizens.

The tribe's inner turmoil continued, culminating in another wave of disenrollments in 2011, when another fifty-seven citizens were disenrolled in October, including the former chairman of the tribe, Gilbert Cordero. A month later, two hundred other members were notified that they, too, faced political liquidation. The tribe's attorney, Rob Rosette, insisted that the decision to disenroll so many was not so that remaining members might gain additional money. The tribe, he said, "was following their written laws to a T. It's not arbitrary. It's objective, and it's well-founded in the law."[44] But opponents mustered substantial arguments that indicated that politics, arbitrariness, and money were, in fact, the three major dynamics pushing the citizenship purges.

In late December 2011 and early 2012, conditions deteriorated even further when tribal elections were held and the results were intensely contested. A near riot erupted in February 2012 that left three people injured between the three competing factions.[45] In August, another one hundred members were slated for termination.

The intense and deep factionalism continued to increase, culminating in February 2014 in a ruling by Amy Dutschke, the regional director of the BIA, that effectively reappointed the council that had been elected in 2010 as that was deemed the most recent election that was relatively uncontested.[46] That decision, however, was short-lived because a federal administrative judge in April overturned Dutschke's ruling. Judge Steven Linscheid declared that the regional director's decision had not "articulated the . . . reasoning for why she believes making the decision effective immediately would preserve the public health and safety."[47]

In October 2014, the tribe's problems compelled a joint decision by the National Indian Gaming Commission and the California State Attorney General to shutter the tribe's casino and resort complex, largely because of concerns about the health, safety, and well-being of those frequenting the casino operations, after members of one of the tribe's factions had entered the casino bearing weapons. The tribe's own Economic Development Authority showed a fund deficit of nearly $50 million in 2013.[48] The casino was finally reopened in January 2016.

In a potentially positive move, the tribal council in June 2015, in a tightly contested vote, opted to reenroll those Chukchansi who had been disenrolled—but only the ones terminated since 2010—leaving over eight hundred other former citizens nationless. Despite this vote, as of September 2016 those slated for reenrollment had not received formal notification of their readmitted status, leaving many to question whether or not they have been reenrolled.

Finally, in July 2016 another forty-six tribal members, many involved with other political factions of the tribe, received formal letters from the Chukchansi tribal government informing them they faced disenrollment because of alleged dual enrollment in another tribe. Hearings were held in August and September, but no decisions had been publicly disseminated as of late September.

These case studies confirm how complicated and diverse dismemberments are across Indian Country. Time factors, confidentiality concerns, and insufficient and reliable data make it extremely difficult to arrive at anything more than a sketchy overview of these several tribal situations. That said, certain recurrent themes became evident in the course of examining these and other nations: (1) there were few checks and balances in place in many Native governments that might have forestalled some of problems disenrollees face; (2) nepotism—a practice in which officeholders award positions, favor, and power to family members—is a gnawing issue that has caused substantial problems in numerous cases; (3) without any support, Native political elites in numerous cases created in their organic documents (be it a constitution or other document) a multitude of new doctrines, rules, regulations that are ever changing, thus depriving or dramatically minimizing those facing dismemberment of due process and a fair opportunity to challenge the charges that have been made against them; (4) as one Grand Ronde elder put it, "it's all about the money," and this theme resonates in numerous, though not all, cases; (5) tribal officials frequently use exaggerated and fabricated appeals to necessity, emergency, fear, and prejudice to justify the denial of fundamental human rights and constitutional/traditional safeguards to those facing dismemberment; (6) race and geography matter—in some cases having the "wrong" ethnic ancestry (whether it be Filipino ancestry in Nooksack, Spanish or African American ancestry in the case of some California Native nations, or African American ancestry in Cherokee country) or living "outside" what are considered the core or central homelands is sufficient grounds to deny or terminate tribal citizenship; (7) interfamily conflicts, sometimes dating back several generations, appear to be a leading factor in numerous cases; and (8) the powerful role played by lawyers who work for tribal governments, and particular organizations like the California Indian Legal Services entity, which was cited numerous times by several disenrollees from California-based nations. Lawyers were cited several times as being the culprits in crafting disenrollment policies, revising enrollment procedures to make it easier to disenroll, and in pursuing lawsuits that enrich law firm coffers while financially crippling those facing disenrollment.

Much more detailed research is required of each and every community that has or is currently engaged in dismembering otherwise bona fide members. But without complete and unfiltered access to all the required historical, genealogical, cultural, legal, and other data necessary to understand how and why these tribal nations opted to banish or disenroll citizens, we are denied the opportunity to fully comprehend the full scope of these particular intra-tribal citizenship scenarios.

CHAPTER 6

Judicial Interpretations
of Dismemberment

Indigenous and Federal

THIS CHAPTER ANALYZES SOME OF THE JUDICIAL LITERATURE NATIVE
and federal courts generated in their efforts to cope with tribal dismemberment policies.[1] While most commentators focus on the U.S. Supreme Court's
Santa Clara Pueblo v. Martinez decision in 1978, we examine a sample of cases
handed down by Native trial and appellate courts, which are typically the first
ones to hear these matters. Important caveat: while the federal and individual
state constitutions outline the structure and power of the multitiered court
system found in those polities—trial, appellate, and supreme—and authorize
the development of specialized courts like the U.S. Court of Military Appeals
and the U.S. Court of Claims, approximately 350 of the 567 federally recognized Native nations have functioning judicial systems.[2]

As described earlier, Native peoples historically had a variety of methods
to resolve the inevitable disputes that occasionally arose prior to the impositions made by the federal government. The first federally imposed courts were
the so-called Courts of Indian Offenses, introduced by the Department of the
Interior in 1883. These were staffed by judges the local Bureau of Indian Affairs
(BIA) agent or superintendent handpicked. Their broad function was to suppress Indigenous values and practices that were considered detrimental to the
assimilation process.

It was not until the 1934 Indian Reorganization Act that Native communities received support to establish their own judicial systems as part of their
general political revitalization. While a number of nations opted for constitutions and corporate charters, fewer established independent court systems.

Of those that chose to create courts, many were established under the authority granted them by the tribe's legislative body. Hence, the doctrine of separation of powers, a hallmark of the federal and state systems, was not as fully implemented in Indian Country. This continues to be a complicated, sometimes debilitating, dynamic in many tribal nations today.

Across Indian Country, there are several distinctive justice systems currently in place, including modern tribal courts; a remaining handful of Courts of Indian Offenses, often referred to as CFR courts because they operate under title 25 of the Code of Federal Regulations; and a number of peacemaking courts that draw upon traditional nonadversarial means for handling disputes.

Finally, in some states Native nations do not operate any court system at all or have systems in place that hear only a limited number of cases (i.e., hunting and fishing violations or child welfare issues). The reason for this is Congress's 1953 law, Public Law 280, that assigned several states—Minnesota (except Red Lake), Wisconsin (except Menominee), California, Nebraska, and Oregon (except Warm Springs), and later Alaska—mandatory criminal jurisdiction over Indian Country and allowed other states the option to assume this vast power if they determined it was in their best interest to do so. In Public Law 280, state courts prosecute all persons who commit crimes on tribal land and also hear private disputes such as divorce, personal injury cases, and contract disputes.[3]

Thus, the judicial process in Indian Country is fraught with more complexity than in any other jurisdiction. The reasons for this are many. First, many Native communities lack functioning tribal court systems. Second, assuming a tribal court is available, securing judicial review is not always attainable, as tribal legislatures may invoke the doctrine of sovereign immunity from suit, thus limiting their exposure to lawsuits. Third, challenges to tribal enrollment decisions often cannot even be heard in tribal courts unless the tribe's legislative branch has expressly authorized the court to hear such cases. And since disenrollment actions are frequently born in the legislative chamber of a nation, those bodies only sometimes allow suits to be taken to the tribal court for fear of being overturned. Fourth, Congress, in the modern era, has not authorized federal courts to become involved in tribal membership disputes. The only exception is banishment, but even that is a limited federal intervention. Finally, the BIA is extremely reluctant to step in when disenrollment problems flare up and will do so only if the tribe's constitution mandates such review, or if Congress insists on it.

Notwithstanding all these constraints, a detailed analysis of a range of tribal and federal court opinions reveals the complexity and frustration of this incendiary topic and provides insights on the problems that arise from inadequate checks and balances, but also as to what might be done to rectify some of the more egregious human and civil rights violations confronting those being dismembered.

NATIVE JUDICIAL PROCEEDINGS DEALING WITH ENROLLMENT AND DISENROLLMENT

As previously discussed, one of the central powers of Native governments is the right to decide who is or is not eligible for membership or citizenship in their nations. Some of these member-related cases would have first been litigated in a tribal court proceeding.

As of 2016, approximately 350 of the 567 federally recognized tribal nations operated tribal courts.[4] It would take a massive tome and free-flowing information from tribal governments and the BIA to determine how many of these courts had been authorized to hear enrollment/disenrollment cases, a project far beyond our scope. But we have gathered and will now discuss two categories of tribal opinions that have addressed membership issues: cases where the tribal courts side with the plenary power of the nation's political and administrative branches of government to either deny applications for membership or sanction a tribe's power to disenroll bona fide citizens, whether alive or deceased; and cases where those courts deny tribal officials the power to terminate a tribal member's citizenship status.

These decisions are critically important because Native nations have plenary authority to determine membership for tribal purposes. The BIA, Congress, and the federal courts will intervene in tribal enrollment determinations in only a limited manner (habeas corpus) or for broader reasons such as federal distribution of tribal land (e.g., allotments) or money or regarding the creation of programs specifically for Indians. In these cases the federal government "determines who is eligible, and it may ignore a tribe's membership list and adopt a different standard."[5]

TRIBAL CASES DENYING AND TERMINATING TRIBAL CITIZENSHIP

Bailey v. Grand Traverse of Ottawa and Chippewa Indians (1999)

Ronald Bailey's application for membership into the tribe had been denied.[6] Judge Michael Petoskey, himself a tribal member, saw no evidence that tribal administration officials acted arbitrarily, capriciously, or outside the scope of their duties in denying plaintiff's membership application. Apparently, Bailey

The trouble with sovereignty. Originally run May 13, 2015, on Indian Country Today Media Network. © 2016 Marty Two Bulls.

failed to meet the legal requirements for membership as set forth in the tribe's constitution. Petoskey did say, however, that "the plaintiff still has the opportunity to apply for adoption into the band, in accordance with article 2 of the constitution."

Ross v. Little River Band of Ottawa Indians (2004)

Dorian Ross and several others filed suit claiming that they met the requirements of the tribe's enrollment ordinance and a judgment distribution plan called the 80/20 plan connected to the Michigan Indian Land Claims Settlement Act of 1997.[7] The plaintiffs asserted that they were currently members of the Little River Band of Ottawa Indians and as such were entitled to a share of the per capita distribution as established by the Judgment Fund plan. The tribe claimed it was immune from suit for damages and that the "plaintiffs did not meet the definition of 'qualified tribal member'" for a one-time per capita payment under the settlement act.

Ross and most of the other plaintiffs had applied for enrollment in 1997 and 1998. One of the plaintiffs, Delia Ross, was enrolled; the rest received letters of denial. The plaintiffs again tendered applications in March and April of 2001 and they were enrolled as members of the band. Subsequently, they formally initiated their request for eligibility for the aforementioned per capita distribution plan. The tribal council determined that they did not meet the criteria established under the Judgment Fund and refused to grant a per capita distribution to them as to do so would have been an action outside the scope of the payment plan.

The tribal court said that "it is undisputed that the plaintiffs are not on the rolls established pursuant to the 80/20 plan. Most likely, the reason the plaintiffs' names did not appear on the rolls was due to their failure to appeal their denial in the manner required." In summary, the court dismissed the case, relying upon the tribe's sovereign immunity stance.

Cooke v. Yurok Tribe (2005)

Bernard Cooke applied for membership in the Yurok tribe in early 2004.[8] Cooke was the biological child of Joseph Cooke, deceased and a non-Indian, and Ivora Nelson Cooke, deceased and an enrolled member of the Hoopa Valley tribe at the time of her death in 1990. In June of 2004, the tribe's enrollment committee determined that Bernard was not eligible. But following a notice of intent to appeal from Cooke and an evidentiary hearing on August 26, 2004, the enrollment committee reversed itself and voted to recommend that the Yurok Tribal Council approve his application for enrollment. On September 9, contrary to the recommendation of the enrollment committee, the tribal council denied Cooke's application. He then appealed the decision to the Yurok Tribal Court. On January 31, 2005, holding that the Yurok Tribal Council properly interpreted the relevant provisions of the Yurok Constitution, the tribal court granted the tribe's motion for summary judgment. Cooke appealed the decision to the tribe's court of appeals.

"This case," said the three-judge panel, "requires interpretation of the Yurok Tribal Constitution. Because he meets the blood quantum requirement (one-eighth Yurok) and because his grandfather was a Yurok allottee, Cooke appears to qualify for enrollment under the 'Extraordinary Circumstances' provision of the Yurok Constitution. The tribe argued that because Cooke's mother was a Hoopa tribal member and neither of his parents were Yurok, he had been properly denied membership. The judges noted in citing the U.S. Supreme Court's *Santa Clara* decision, "as the tribe argues, it is well settled that one of the most fundamental rights of a sovereign nation is the right to determine qualifications for the enrollment of its members." And, "regardless of whatever sympathies the members of this court may have for Mr. Cooke or any other person who meets the blood quantum requirement for membership in the Yurok tribe but is deemed ineligible for membership because of the combined actions of their parents and the drafters of the Yurok Constitution, it is simply not within the power of this court to rewrite or ignore that Constitution." Thus, Cooke was denied membership.

Hopkins v. Little Traverse Bay Bands of Odawa Indians (2006)

Brian Hopkins sought a review of the tribal council's decision to deny his application for tribal membership.[9] He had applied to become a member in November 2004. His application was denied on April 3, 2005, "for the reason that the applicant was deemed to have less than one-quarter or more Indian blood quantum as required by tribal law to become an enrolled member of the tribe." He argued that he should be accepted as several of his extended family members were enrolled as a result of the tribe "grandfathering" enrollment of individuals, an action that was later determined to have been done in error. "When the tribe corrected its mistake, it recognized the unfairness of disenrollment of those who had gained membership because of the mistake the tribe had made. Thus, those members were allowed to remain enrolled." Hopkins expressed the belief that the court had the authority to overturn the tribe's enrollment decision.

But Judge Michael Petoskey said that "plaintiff has not demonstrated clear error in the declination of his membership application. His application for tribal membership was received after the window of full-blood presumption was closed. It is unfortunate that the mistake made by the Tribal Council has these unintended consequences, but this court has no authority absent a finding of clear error, to overturn the enrollment decision."

In re the Membership Revocation of Julie Bill Meza et al. v. Sauk-Suiattle Indian Tribal Council and Enrollment Committee Members (2006)

In this case, seven members of the Sauk-Suiattle challenged their disenrollment.[10] The trial court had affirmed the council's decision to revoke the individuals' membership. They had been enrolled via tribal resolutions, but those resolutions were later overridden on the grounds that those individuals were not direct descendants from a proper person, Emily (Joe) Bill, listed on the Skagit-Suiattle (public domain) census roll of January 1, 1942. Bill had been listed as a tribal member, but her inclusion was proven to be an error. The council then revoked the appellants' membership, concluding that they did not meet the qualifications for enrollment in the tribe because they had no direct descendancy from anyone listed on the 1942 census.

Moreover, the three appellate judges held that the seven individuals did not qualify under the tribe's constitution and that the council had not corrected its membership roll to add any of the individuals. The court did say it was "sympathetic to the appellants because the evidence relied on by the Tribal Council in enacting [the termination resolution of 2005] was lost or missing." But this was not enough to overcome the fatal fact that their ancestor, Emily Joe Bill, should have been listed on the 1942 census. The court of appeals finally held that the appellants had (1) failed to establish that the council's action was clearly unsupported by the record, (2) failed to establish a denial of due process, and (3) failed to establish a basis for equitable estoppel.[11]

Lomeli v. Kelly (May 20, 2013), *Roberts v. Kelly* (October 17, 2013), and *Roberts v. Kelly* (March 18, 2014)

In three cases involving the Nooksack people of Washington State, the Nooksack trial court and the tribe's court of appeals handed down rulings that dealt crippling, though not fatal as of this writing, blows to the citizenship status of 306 tribal members. The plaintiffs, represented by Gabriel Galanda of the Indian-owned law firm Galanda Broadman, entered the process with a clear understanding that their legal battles would be fraught with difficulty because the tribal courts are creatures of the Nooksack tribal council and thus there is no formal separation of powers between the legislative and judicial branches of the Nooksack government.

Still, the chief judge, Raquel Montoya-Lewis, had established a solid judicial reputation. There was also reason to believe she would have a unique insight into the plaintiffs' situation as she, herself, had experienced disenrollment. Of Laguna and Isleta ancestry, she unsuccessfully sued Isleta officials and the Department of the Interior after being disenrolled from Isleta in the early 2000s.

In the first case, *Lomeli*, the issue before the court, according to Chief Judge Raquel Montoya-Lewis, centered on a "fairly narrow question: should the tribal court issue a preliminary injunction prohibiting the Tribal Council from moving forward with disenroll in the Plaintiffs under Resolution 13-02?"[12] The judge determined that it was necessary to examine the plaintiff's contention that the Nooksack government violated the Nooksack Tribal Constitution and the Enrollment Ordinance of the Nooksack Tribal Code. Specifically that the actions the council and Chairman Robert Kelly had taken were outside the scope of their authority and that the doctrine of sovereign immunity did not protect them from legal actions in this instance.

"The facts," said the judge, were not in "substantial dispute." In December 2012, plaintiff Terry St. Germain submitted paperwork for his children's enrollment. On December 19, 2012, at a special meeting called by Chairman Kelly, the tribal council addressed the question of the children's eligibility for Nooksack citizenship. Enrollment officer Roy Bailey, according to Judge Montoya-Lewis, indicated that he had no information at that time that would have proven the children were indeed qualified for enrollment. Secretary Rudy St. Germain, who was not a plaintiff to this proceeding, questioned why his relatives were not presented for enrollment. Mr. Bailey replied that the applicants did not appear to meet the requirements at this time and Secretary St. Germain objected, stating that if those applicants were ineligible, so was he. Chairman Kelly said he would research the issue.

Three weeks later, at the January 8, 2013, tribal council meeting, Roy Bailey reported that not only had he and Chairman Kelly failed to find supporting documentation for the St. Germain children in the Bureau of Indian Affairs records, they also discovered that three hundred other enrolled Nooksack citizens were "missing" these critical documents, including Nooksack Tribal Council members Secretary Rudy St. Germain and Michelle Roberts.

Chairman Kelly then called an executive session of the tribal council on February 11, 2013, to be held the next day. At that session, four resolutions were passed. Prior to the consideration of those resolutions, Secretary St. Germain and Council Member Roberts were instructed that they "could not participate in the discussion or vote on those resolutions because they were included in the approximately 300 individuals who would be subject to disenrollment by Resolution 13-02 and their participation in these discussions would be a conflict of interest." Each of the resolutions were discussed and enacted by a unanimous vote of five to zero. Following a February 12 meeting, approximately three hundred Notices of Intent to Disenroll were mailed to each of the tribal members identified as having been enrolled "erroneously." These notices informed the recipients that they were subject to disenrollment and instructed them that they could request a meeting with the tribal council to challenge their pending disenrollment.

The plaintiffs argued that Chairman Kelly, the other members of the tribal council who voted in favor of the resolutions, enrollment officer Roy Bailey, and then enrollment officer Jewell Jefferson all acted outside the scope of their authority during process. The trial judge, after reviewing all the evidence, said that "first, the court finds that the Nooksack Tribal Council intends to assert its sovereign immunity to the fullest extent possible in the tribal code." She went on to note that "under Title 63, the Tribe must prove that those who face loss of membership have been enrolled either from 'fraudulent submissions, mistakes in blood degree computations, or inadequate research. . . . It is the Tribe's burden to prove a member has been enrolled erroneously, not a tribal member's. The Tribal Council must become involved in disenrollment proceedings because it is its responsibility to prove the reason for the loss of membership."

Judge Montoya-Lewis found that the tribal council had authority under title 63 of the constitution to determine both enrollment and disenrollment issues and that it had not acted outside the procedures established in the title. She denied the plaintiffs' motion for a preliminary injunction.

Five months later, in October, Judge Montoya-Lewis followed up her earlier ruling by again affirming the tribal council's action. Here she supported the Nooksack tribe's request to dismiss the lawsuit on the grounds that the tribe had provided sufficient to process safeguards and that "the cloak of sovereign immunity protects the Defendants." The judge artfully noted in her conclusion that the case presented "difficult and complex issues" for the Nooksack community and that there was "no 'obvious' answer, despite the entreaties of both sides that the answers to these issues are settled and obvious. They are neither."

Even as she affirmed the power of Nooksack, a sovereign nation, to set its own membership criteria, the judge managed to devalue the very essence of Native nationhood by negatively comparing Native loss of citizenship to that of non-Native loss of U.S. citizenship. To her credit, it appeared that the judge was attempting to console the disenrollees and explain a decision that gravely disappointed them. Unfortunately, she also utilized words that profoundly diminished Indigenous sovereignty:

> While the Court recognizes the important entitlements at stake for the proposed disenrollees, this is a fundamentally different proceeding than a loss of United States citizenship. . . . In the case of tribal disenrollees, the disen-

rollee loses critical and important rights, but they are not equal to the loss
of U.S. citizenship. A person who is disenrolled from her tribe loses access
to the privileges of tribal membership, but she is not stateless. Though she
loses the right, for example, to apply for and obtain tribal housing through
the Tribe, her ability to obtain housing in general is unaffected; though she
loses the right to vote in tribal elections, she does not lose the right to vote in
federal, state, and local elections. While the impact on the disenrollee is serious and detrimental, it is not akin to becoming stateless.

Whatever one's views on the way each Native nation chooses to exercise
their sovereignty with regard to defining membership, the chief judge's view
of Native nationhood is chilling. By ruling that the termination of a Native
person's citizenship "is not equal to the loss of U.S. citizenship" and the loss of
tribal membership is "not akin to becoming stateless," she placed Native citizenship in a position clearly inferior to U.S. citizenship. The implications are profound. It is not realistic to expect to maintain true government-to-government
relations with states and the federal government if Native judges begin by di-
minishing their own tribal citizens' status as citizens of sovereign nations.

That a Native judge would consider tribal nationhood and citizenship in-
ferior to U.S. statehood and citizenship is an unnerving perception to fathom.
It is difficult to believe she intended to weaken the idea of sovereignty even as
her ruling assuredly reaffirmed it. It is this unconscious paradigm shift within
Indigenous communities that may potentially do the most profound harm to
Native peoples.

In contrast, the value of tribal citizenship was well expressed by a judge
who sat on the federal court of appeals for the second circuit. In the important
case *Poodry v. Tonawanda Band of Seneca Indians* (1996), discussed in the previous chapter, Judge Jose A. Cabranes provided a profound defense of Indigenous citizenship, which equated the deprivation of a Native's citizenship to
that of a U.S. citizen's denaturalization.

In discussing both, Judge Cabranes, relying on prior Supreme Court
precedent, reminded readers that "a deprivation of citizenship is an extraordinarily severe penalty with consequences that may be more grave than
consequences that flow from conviction for crimes." He also said that the loss
of citizenship—be it indigenous or federal—entailed the "total destruction of
the individual's status and organized society. . . . It is a form of punishment
more primitive than torture, for it destroys for the individual the political
existence that was centuries in the development."

Finally, Cabranes directly addressed how damaging tribal loss of Native citizenship was.

> [Such a deprivation] does more than merely restrict one's freedom to go or to remain where others have the right to be: it often works a destruction of one's social, cultural, and political existence. To measure whether summary banishment from a tribe constitutes a severe deprivation solely by reference to the liberties of other Americans is tantamount to suggesting that the petitioners [the five banished Senecas] cannot live among members of their nation simply because other Americans cannot do so; and that the coerced loss of an individual's social, cultural, and political affiliations is unimportant because other Americans do not share them. Such an approach renders the concept of liberty hollow indeed.

Judge Cabranes's analysis of the deep and lasting deprivation banished Native individuals experience is arguably even more fitting for Natives facing legal disenrollment. And nowhere in his account did he suggest that the loss of Native citizenship was somehow less onerous than the loss of U.S. citizenship.

Judge Montoya-Lewis's ruling was appealed to the three-member Nooksack Court of Appeals, which, in March 2014, handed down *Roberts v. Kelly*.[13] While acknowledging that tribal membership was a constitutionally protected property right that brings with it "not only certain benefits, but a cultural, familial and spiritual identity," the appellate judges adopted the tribal court judge's assertion that being deprived of tribal membership was "not analogous to [losing] U.S. citizenship," since tribal disenrollees were "not rendered stateless by the loss of tribal membership." The court emphasized that the tribal interest was equally as strong as that of the appellants, and approvingly cited *Santa Clara*'s declaration that the tribe's right to define its own membership was "central to its existence" and because of that "membership determinations are committed to the sole discretion of a tribe."

The judges went on to note that the burden to prove a member did not meet the tribe's membership criteria rested on the tribal government, not the member. And this burden was to be met by "providing documentation supporting disenrollment to the disenrollee establishing why he or she does not meet the Nooksack constitutional requirements under which they were originally enrolled."

The 306 Nooksack facing disenrollment were to be given written notice twenty-one days in advance of their hearing, provided an opportunity to contest their disenrollment in writing—a two-page limit—and were to have a hearing of no more than ten minutes. Their attorneys argued that the spatial and temporal limitations were onerous and did not provide adequate due process to those facing political and legal termination. The appellate judges disagreed and stated that the requirements were "rationally related to the Council's need to organize the materials and evidence, and to ensure the decision-makers are easily able to read and decipher the materials with minimal effort."

The two victories for the appellants, those facing disenrollment, were that the court agreed with the trial court that the potential disenrollees were entitled to legal representation and that the council did not have authority to arbitrarily shorten the twenty-one-day notice if a person was served notice and then was provided a chance to have a telephone hearing. Despite those small wins, the court found, in conclusion, that the tribe's disenrollment resolution had not violated the due process rights of the 306 under the Nooksack Constitution. More importantly, the court declared that those changes and all procedural rules governing disenrollment proceedings had to be adopted via an ordinance "and the ordinance [had to be] approved by the Secretary of the Interior as provided for in the Nooksack Constitution." The case was then sent back to the trial court and the judge was ordered to address the deficiencies raised by the appeal court.

Two weeks later, the trial court responded to the appellate court's mandate and issued a permanent injunction against Chairman Robert Kelly and the tribal government, enjoining them from undertaking the disenrollments as prescribed under Resolution 13-111 because the proposed measure had not been constitutionally adopted by law and had not been approved by the secretary of the interior. The Kelly-led government responded by modifying the tribe's disenrollment ordinance and then forwarded it to the secretary of the interior for validation. In January 2015, the secretary approved the revised ordinance. Despite that, the Nooksack 306 were not formally dismembered. As noted in chapter 5, the litigation and tribal dysfunction continues, with no signs of clear resolution as of September 2016. For example, the official terms of four council members of the Kelly-led government expired on March 24, 2016, but elections were delayed for several months. Decisions, including those related to the 306, continued to be made by the council even though they lacked a quorum and official authority under the Nooksack constitution.

One of those decisions was to ban plaintiffs' counsel from the Galanda Broadman law firm from practicing law in Nooksack court. Based on this action, the Tribe's court clerk, Betty Leathers, refused to accept filings or other documents submitted by the disbarred attorneys. The Tribe's appellate court found her in contempt for her actions and ordered her arrest, but the Tribe's police chief refused to make the arrest and he, too, was held in contempt. As of September 2016, while the refusals of filings continue, the appellate court-ordered sanctions have not been enforced.

These latest episodes convinced Nooksack elder and the Tribe's election superintendent, George Adams, to get involved. He called for a General Council election that was held on July 14, a gathering of all eligible adults, to elect four interim council members. With that election, a majority of the council is now opposed to disenrollment. But Chairman Kelly and his supporters immediately challenged the validity of the election and circulated a petition to disenroll the 306.

The Nooksack 306 still exist in a nebulous status—not having been formally disenrolled; yet being denied benefits as tribal citizens.

Crocker v. Tribal Council of the Confederated Tribes of the Grand Ronde Community of Oregon, Williams v. The Confederated Tribes of the Grand Ronde Community, and Alexander, Val et al. v. The Confederated Tribes of the Grand Ronde Community

Finally, we turn to the Confederated Tribes of the Grand Ronde community of Oregon, which has been involved in a hellish disenrollment struggle for several years.[14] In this trifecta of cases—all handed down in late August and early September 2015—the tribe's chief judge, David D. Shaw (a non-Indian), issued a damning set of rulings that terminated the political and legal membership of over eighty living Grand Ronde citizens and, more disturbingly, several deceased individuals.

Two months before the decisions, on July 2, the tribal council held a special meeting to allow citizens an opportunity to testify for or against a proposed emergency enrollment ordinance, whereby the council sought to delegate its constitutional authority to involuntarily dismember citizens. At issue was whether or not the council should give the enrollment committee the power to make the final decision. The committee, made up of tribal members the council had selected, had already studied the situation and recommended the dismemberment of the more than eighty tribal members.

At the conclusion of a nearly three-hour discussion, the council narrowly adopted the ordinance and set into motion an expedited disenrollment process. Exactly three weeks later, on July 24, the enrollment committee would follow up on its early recommendations and vote to formally dismember eighty-six tribal citizens, both living and deceased.

This public meeting revealed several interesting dynamics. First, the testimony of the family members facing dismemberment and that of their allies was riveting and intellectually compelling as they described their clear genealogical connection to Chief Tumulth, a signer of the 1855 treaty. Second, these individuals were profoundly dismayed at the council's last-minute attempt to abdicate its express constitutional responsibility to an inferior administrative unit, the tribe's enrollment committee. Third, they were concerned about the loss of checks and balances reflected by the council's proposed action. And they astutely suggested that the so-called emergency action was a mere smokescreen designed to protect the chances of several council members facing reelection.

In contrast, those in favor of the ordinance argued with equal fervor that the decision to introduce the measure was indeed an emergency because the disenrollment issue had become so contentious and divisive that it was eclipsing other tribal business. They also maintained that it was well within their power to delegate this authority because the enrollment committee's members were professional and had acquired expert knowledge of each disenrollee's case. They further emphasized that checks and balances remained in place because disenrollees could appeal their loss of citizenship to the tribal court where they would have a chance to contest the committee's decision.

Reflecting on this further, it was plain that all those involved—those about to be cast out and those preparing to do the deed—sincerely believed their position was sound and the right path for their nation. Traditional Native nations, while never utopias, all operated with institutions and values that generally enabled them to weather serious internal disputes without deliberately endangering the lives or livelihoods of their members. Since each and every tribal soul had a fundamental right to exist, the entire community shared a fundamental responsibility to see that every member—no matter their racial admixture, bloodlines, gender, age, abilities, adoptive status, distinctive life, and personality—should be respected and supported. The success of the whole depended on an intense recognition of the personal autonomy of each individual member.

Furthermore, it is clear that Native communities have become more diversified over time. All nations were severely impacted by the might and seductive qualities of external forces such as the Western educational system, capitalism's raw benefits, the installment of foreign political and legal institutions, and Judeo-Christian religious traditions. The changes wrought are reflected in the emergence of tribal perspectives that fundamentally diverge from older ways, not so much because of racial, ethnic, or biological changes, but because of what Vine Deloria Jr. referred to as "differences of metaphysical viewpoint, of ways of looking at, understanding and interpreting the events and experiences of the world."[15]

This certainly seemed to be a factor with the Grand Ronde people. Whatever their personal motivations, the council members who supported dismemberment fervently believed that their newly prescribed administrative process for deciding membership was a real improvement over the status quo and thus this action was in the best interests of the entire community. Council members do the off-reservation work, interact with local, state, and federal governments to protect their nation's sovereignty, and make sure that treaty rights and the trust relationship are honored by the federal government. Like all elected officials, they walk a fine line between enacting the will of their people and making sure the rules for engagement with other governments are met. Of necessity, these individuals must take many of their cues from the federal government. They have convinced themselves that only by adhering to the rules, procedures, and protocols agreed upon during the Native self-determination era will ensure that their tribe continues to receive the benefits and privileges they feel they are entitled to by the federal government.

Those with the difficult task of working to represent their nations from without and within work constantly to maintain this difficult balance. However, once this group accepts federal measurements of time, success, history, and identity—whether opportunistically or with the sincere belief that this is the path for continued survival—their metaphysical viewpoint begins to diverge from those, like the disenrollees, who adhere to more traditional ways of perceiving the world and its relationships.

By contrast, those facing dismemberment generally are more representative of traditional perceptions. When the Grand Ronde members facing disenrollment stated emphatically that a new, expedited administrative process should never be used to decide something as important and as substantive as who belongs to their nation, they were harkening back to older ways of walking through the world. Frequently, they cited the value of history, the sacredness of treaties (not just the utility), the power and bond generated by shared experiences, and moral character. All these things are profound and necessary for survival. These people, too, knew, without a doubt, that their position to remain Grand Ronde was in the best interests of the entire community.

Those facing expulsion and their supporters expressed deep appreciation of the idea of peoplehood that Vine Deloria Jr. said "transcends temporary political organizations and speaks to generations of people, people past and people yet to come."[16] They were calling out for recognition of a connection that is being destroyed from the inside out.

It could very well be argued that this worldview is not sustainable given the outside pressures for change. In modern times, survival is treated more as an individual endeavor, synonymous with the acquisition of money. In contrast, that Indigenous peoples have survived is a tribute to interdependence. Native peoples historically worked with the earth, other creatures, the spirits, and with all other tribal members in order to acquire food, shelter, and, ultimately, to gain understanding and meaning. Today, Native peoples now work not with what they can see, feel or eat, but with grants from the federal government, studies by for-profit and philanthropic organizations, and university economic development projects. All are entities that require Native nations to measure success based on the generation of capital and the construction of political and legal systems that more often resemble non-Native bodies.

The soon-to-be-dismembered Grand Ronde citizens were concerned with the substance of Native life and what they were about to lose from the inside. The enrollment committee and those on the council that supported dismemberment appeared more focused on minimizing what could be taken away by outsiders. In the minds of some of those on the council, the more professional and efficient the processes that they relied upon were, the more credible the nation would appear to other governments and powerful outside entities and the more they, too, would benefit personally.

The tragedy is that both these groups are made up of tribal members who want the best for their nation. The leaders recognize and respond to external threats; the members recognize and respond to internal threats.

Tribal nations will have to challenge unreasonable and unsustainable demands of the larger political and economic regimes that surround them and decide how they will define themselves in order to continue to remain true to their histories, their lands, and their ancestors. If success is to be based largely on measures like accumulation of capital or outside assessments of membership, then Native peoples are engaging in what we call suicidal sovereignty; they will also hollow themselves out from the inside until being Native is nothing more than an archaic and impractical ideal.

By the end of August 2015, Judge Shaw had arrived at his findings. In the first case, Rebecca Janice Crocker appealed the tribal council's 2013 decision to have her disenrolled from the tribe. Shaw denied her petition but said in his introduction "that prior to engaging in the analysis, the court is compelled to comment that this judicial opinion speaks only to a legal proceeding and does not intend to unnecessarily comment on the personal issue of the petitioner's sense of self and personal identity."

Crocker had been a member of the Grand Ronde community for nearly twenty-seven years. Her history, however, "included a period of slightly over three months when she was dually enrolled with the Confederated Tribes of the Grand Ronde (CTGR) and the Confederated Tribes of the Siletz Indians of Oregon (Siletz)."[17] Importantly, that extremely brief overlap of membership was thirty years ago. The CTGR Constitution, like many Native nations' constitutions, prohibits an individual from qualifying for membership in the tribe if the person is also a member of another tribe.

In April 2013, Crocker was notified by letter that a recent enrollment audit had indicated she had been enrolled with Siletz at the time she was enrolled in the CTGR in 1986. The enrollment audit was conducted by a third party hired by the tribe to act as its authorized agent. Despite that extremely short overlap of dual membership from some thirty years ago, the tribe's Enrollment Department recommended that Crocker be removed from tribal membership. Crocker argued that the tribe's disenrollment action was unconstitutional and she asserted that the tribal constitution provided only limited grounds for disenrollment. Moreover, she emphasized that her sole membership in the CTGR for the past thirty years mattered more than the brief overlap of her citizenship in Siletz.

The tribe responded that the constitution provided authority for correction of a member enrolled by error and that a person could not achieve a vested enrollment status if their enrollment was based on an error. The tribe further argued that it had the sovereign authority to "make a policy choice to forego providing conditional steps to allow correction or repair of a prior enrollment error."

Judge Shaw then made an interesting statement indicating that his views were clearly in line with those of the tribal council.

> As a general matter, linguistic tension between 'an action to correct a prior enrollment error' and 'a disenrollment action' theoretically exists. And there may in time be a case before this Court where the facts stretch the linguistic tether of a claimed action to correct the prior enrollment error so far as to snap it from its Constitutional moorings. However, despite the passage of approximately twenty-seven years, the facts of this case did not represent such a situation. The actions below are reasonably viewed as correcting an error of the Petitioner being dual enrolled at the time of enrollment at CTGR,

and as such the actions of the relevant Tribal parties are authorized by the Constitution and Tribal ordinance.

Less than a month later, on August 31, Shaw rendered six rulings all dealing with the disturbing practice of disenrollment of deceased tribal members—termed *posthumous enrollments* by the court—who were related by family and lineal descent to living members who were also facing disenrollment. In one of the cases, *Williams v. The Confederated Tribes of the Grand Ronde Community*, those representing the deceased member, one Arthur Williams, claimed the right to receive formal notice and the other administrative procedures and substantive rights authorized under the tribe's enrollment ordinance when subject to a "posthumous disenrollment action that follows a disenrollment action for a living relative with the same allegation of membership ineligibility."[18]

Despite the fact that the tribe's constitution made no reference to posthumous membership matters, and that the tribe's actions, as the petitioner argued, profoundly violated cultural norms in Indian Country regarding respect to those who have passed on, Shaw dismissed this and the other cases by declaring that such dismemberments did not violate the constitution, the enrollment ordinance, or even Indigenous cultural norms. Shaw admitted that the ordinance was "far from a picture of clarity" on how a deceased tribal member should be treated when that individual was related to a living member who was subject to disenrollment. And while acknowledging the cultural queasiness linked to such a practice, the judge went so far as to say:

> These cultural norms do not dictate that the Tribe has exceeded its constitutional authority to administer the Tribal membership rolls and enact a Tribal Enrollment Ordinance that fails to provide a process for how deceased members are removed from the membership roll when related to an unsuccessful appeal of a similarly situated living relative. Instead, they perhaps merely reference policy choices that the membership and the Tribal electorate can address in a different forum than this court of law. Here, the Enrollment Ordinance is interpreted as legally sufficient to provide a process to only living members to appeal their own proposed disenrollment. The Tribe is also interpreted to hold the Constitutional authority to remove deceased members after an administrative process is complete on a similarly situated living relative, and without a related obligation to provide independent notice and an independent administrative appeal.

But Shaw's words and the tribal council's "policy choice" to purge their tribal rolls, not just of their living relatives, but even of their dead, easily allows current tribal officials to then wield the legal authority to disenroll descendants who are currently enrolled tribal citizens.

The actions are inhumane and, unfortunately, they are not limited to the Grand Ronde people. The Shakopee Mdewakanton Sioux of Minnesota adopted an ordinance, 6-13-75, in 1975, concerning loss of membership. It provided for the "removal of deceased members from the membership roll, voluntary relinquishment, and disenrollment of dead members."[19] The Saginaw Chippewa of Michigan also have laws allowing the practice.

In one California case, elected leaders of the Redding Rancheria required the exhumations and DNA testing of the bodies of revered elders, the grandmother, and great-grandmother of a citizen fighting her disenrollment, Carla Foreman Maslin. Maslin is the daughter of the late Bob Foreman, the Redding Rancheria tribe's first modern chairman and a leader in health policy for all of Northern California's Native peoples. In spite of his recognized leadership and contributions to the revitalization of the tribe, Foreman and his entire family were disenrolled in 2004.

When the family expressed shock at the idea of disturbing the remains of their revered loved ones in order to add further proof to their already well-documented history, the tribal chair supporting their ouster responded that since the grandmothers were now "nothing more than a bag of bones," it shouldn't be of concern.

Carla Maslin made the agonizing decision to disinter her grandmothers in order to finally put an end to her family's ordeal and restore honor to her father. Astonishingly, even though the DNA tests clearly confirmed Maslin's ancestors as genetically bona fide members of the Redding Rancheria, thus scientifically legitimizing the citizenship of her and her family members, the names of the long deceased women and seventy-six of their descendants were unceremoniously erased from the tribe's rolls.

Exhumation and DNA testing are actions that Native nations often fight against when outsiders want to invade the gravesites of their ancestors. Recall the incredibly spirited effort put forth to defend the dignity and humanity of Techaminsh Oytpamanatityt, the Ancient One, also known as Kennewick Man in Washington State.

Some tribal officials, in their zeal to purge their rolls of political enemies or otherwise inconvenient tribal citizens, have now stooped to a level of institutional behavior unparalleled in the narrative of Indigenous history—a narrative that considered the ashes of the dead as sacred ingredients for the ongoing life of their nations. In *God Is Red*, Vine Deloria Jr. said that Indigenous peoples historically understood that death in a very real sense fulfilled their destiny—for as their bodies became dust they once again contributed to the ongoing life cycle of creation.

It is difficult to fathom why any Indigenous people would want to take up the federal government's work of casting out living tribal members in either this world or the next. But tribal officials who violate the sacred dead so that they can more easily destroy the political and legal rights of living tribal citizens have undertaken a repulsive, spiritually perverted practice that has outraged many inside and outside Indian Country. Such actions are irrevocably damaging their nations' foundational sovereignty by disrespecting, violating, and denying their ancestors' sacred identities. As with any structure, a foundation must be tended. If allowed to weaken, the overall structure starts to shift and sag. If pieces are removed, the entire living unit collapses. Native ancestors were the foundational blocks of their communities and when even one of them is disrespected through exhumation or disenrollment, the people-based and historically grounded sovereignty of Native peoples is forever damaged.

Chief Seattle, in famously attributed remarks spoken in 1854 before early white settlers, observed: "Your dead cease to love you and the land of their nativity as soon as they pass and wander away beyond the stars. They are soon forgotten and never return." He went on to explain how for Native peoples the dead are not "powerless," for while their bodies blend with the earth, spirits of the deceased travel on because "there is no death, only a change of worlds."

Chief Seattle was not saying that the settlers failed to mourn or respect their dead—although they most certainly did so in a fashion much different from Native peoples—but rather that their dead no longer played a dynamic role in the day-to-day existence of the living. He was trying to explain an interconnectedness that was incomprehensible to the colonizing culture. For Native peoples then, as now, those on the other side continue as vital members of Native societies. Centered between human beings and the Great Mysterious, they are able to bridge the worlds. They are conduits, providing critical guidance necessary for the continuance of Indigenous peoples. Unless tribal governments end postmortem disenrollments, as Seattle noted, Native dead will cease to love those of the living and there will be nothing here in this realm that will keep them from wandering away beyond the stars, never to return.

In the third case, *Alexander, Val, et al. v. The Confederated Tribes of the Grand*

Ronde Community, rendered September 1, 2015, a number of individuals facing disenrollment, represented by Gabriel Galanda, Joe Sexton, Amber Penn-Roco, and Anthony Broadman of the Indian-owned law firm Galanda Broadman, challenged the enrollment committee's July 22, 2014, final decision to have them removed from the tribe. Judge Shaw, as he had in the previous cases, denied their petition on the same grounds he used earlier. After restating the history of the tribe from their well-known chief, Tumulth, who signed the Willamette Valley Treaty in 1855, to the tribe's subsequent termination by Congress in 1959 and congressional restoration of recognition in 1983, Shaw noted that the first members of Chief Tumulth's family to become members of the tribe achieved the status in 1986, after restoration of the tribe's federal relationship and the adoption and approval of the tribe's constitution in 1984. The enrollment staff and committee at that time found that none of these ancestral applicants related to the current petitioners were ever previously enrolled at Grand Ronde, but the committee determined that "these relevant applicants *would have been eligible* for enrollment before termination because they descended from a treaty signer and membership was provided on this basis" (emphasis in the original).[20]

Shaw then admitted that the tribal government had frequently exploited Chief Tumulth's legacy "to advance its interests." Nevertheless, in 2013 an enrollment audit determined that members claiming descent from Chief Tumulth lacked the relevant constitutional membership requirement of descent from a lineal ancestor listed on any roll or record of Grand Ronde membership. Shaw supported the enrollment committee's determination that "the Willamette Valley Treaty, signed by Chief Tumulth, did not constitute a valid roll of Grand Ronde members." He also asserted that since Tumulth had never lived on the yet to be determined reservation he merely had "eligibility for CTGRC membership that was [never] effectuated."

Shaw then brushed aside the other arguments made by Tumulth's descendants. He acknowledged that "it is uncontroverted that the process used below fell short of a full judicial hearing, perceived imperfections occurred, and Petitioners' counsel had to overcome some obstacles to making its presentation." But these laws did not amount to a failure of due process, in Shaw's opinion.

The petitioners also argued that the tribe's actions violated their related property (membership benefits such as housing, healthcare, etc.) and liberty interests (the identity and name as a tribal member) in tribal membership. But for Shaw such claims "must allege (and then prove) governmental actions that

Back to the future. Originally run November 10, 2006, on Indian Country Today Media Network. © 2016 Marty Two Bulls.

'shock the conscience.' Stated otherwise, Petitioners must show that the Tribal action at issue was 'clearly arbitrary and unreasonable having no substantial relation to the public health, safety, morals, or general welfare.'"

Shaw concluded his opinion by stating that "an allegation that Tribal governmental actors proposed Petitioners for disenrollment due to an audit that alleged that Petitioners did not have proper lineal descent, and then conducted administrative hearings as referenced herein, may arguably appear negligent or even strongly disagreeable to Petitioners but based on the current record does not rise to the level of an intentional or recklessly indifferent act intended to harm the Petitioners with no sufficient relation to the public health, safety, morals, or general welfare. Under the totality of these facts and context, procedural and substantive due process has been met."

A day after Shaw's final decision, the petitions, opinions, and legal briefs of the tribe's attorneys and the disenrollees were posted on the Turtle Talk website, maintained by Michigan State University's Indian Law program.[21] Simultaneously, Gabriel Galanda posted the Turtle Talk link on his Facebook page. The tribe's attorneys filed a motion with the tribal court requesting that Galanda "cease and desist" in publicizing the briefs and related materials because of privacy concerns about enrollment data being viewed by the public. Kimberly S. D'Aguila and Deneen A. Keller, the tribe's attorneys, argued that such a posting violated an agreed-upon September 18 order that "no briefs . . . shall be available to the general public until after the parties have submitted arguments on this topic."[22]

In effect, the tribal government was demanding that the "entire record" in this matter remain sealed from public scrutiny. Interestingly, one of the arguments used by the tribe's attorneys was that this was purely an intratribal matter and since tribes deal with enrollment conflicts "in accordance with their respective customs, traditions, and laws and those resolutions have no precedential value beyond the individual tribe," the publication of the material only satisfies the public's curiosity and is an attempt to "improperly influence proceedings through the use of the media."[23]

But tribal judges, just like state, federal, and even international jurists frequently rely on opinions from other jurisdictions and use them as precedential authority or at least as data that can help illuminate their own particular case. This is a fundamental tenet of common law and the concept of judicial comity—respect shown by a court of one state to a court of another state—has long been practiced throughout the United States.

On October 26, 2015, Judge Shaw issued a final ruling in accordance with the tribe's enrollment ordinance ordering "that the Confederated Tribes of Grand Ronde Enrollment Staff remove the Appellants' [Alexander, Val, and more than eighty other members] names from the Tribal Roll."[24] Those formally disenrolled filed an appeal to the tribe's appellate court, which according to the tribe's own official document repository had only published two opinions involving disenrollment since 2003.

On June 13, 2016, the CTGR defended posthumous disenrollment before the tribal appellate court and judges Douglas Nash, Robert Miller, and Patricia Paul by arguing that as Chief Tumulth had signed a treaty that neither designated a reservation location nor named the Confederated Tribes of the Grand Ronde—neither of which would be defined until after the chief's execution by the U.S. government—he was not a CTGR member and thus should never have been considered a tribal citizen. They also contended that the dead had no right to citizenship by virtue of being deceased and that no one living, even direct descendants whose citizenship depended on lineage, had legal standing to defend their status.

The following day, the living disenrollees appealed their disenrollments. The arguments used by the tribal attorneys speaking on behalf of the CTGR were similar to those employed in other judicial proceedings. Of note was a response to appellate court judge Robert Miller, who asked about sovereign rights of tribal citizens. The CTGR attorney astonishingly contended that individuals hold no sovereign power and that sovereignty is only possessed and wielded by tribal governments. She went on to echo the views of former Nooksack judge Montoya-Lewis that the disenrollees were not stateless, as they would maintain their U.S. citizenship. Judge Miller observed that the tribe's line of reasoning meant that any tribal member, living or dead, from any nation, could be stripped of their citizenship at any time and for any reason that a sitting tribal council chose to employ.

On August 5, 2016, the appellate court reversed the lower court's ruling and found in favor of the disenrollees. The judges reasoned that as the targeted citizens had been enrolled in good faith for more than twenty-seven years, current tribal leaders could not reopen the issue of their enrollment status. A similar rationale was used by the tribal court to force reinstatement of five members disenrolled by the St. Croix Chippewa: "Tribal governments and their administrative bodies must be bound to bring their causes of action in a timely manner; because an orderly and efficient operation of the tribal government requires it. To do otherwise will cause chaos, mistrust, rivalry and political in-fighting."

While the living disenrollees were reinstated, the dead were not so fortunate. The court found that the living had no standing to intervene on behalf of their ancestors, therefore, Grand Ronde treaty-signer Chief Tumulth was posthumously disenrolled. As of this writing, tribal leadership has chosen to end its effort to remove Chief Tumulth's living descendants from their rolls.

CASES AFFIRMING TRIBAL MEMBERSHIP AND /OR CITIZENSHIP

DeVerney v. Grand Traverse Band of Ottawa and Chippewa (2000)

In this appellate case, Angus DeVerney and his children brought suit challenging their automatic termination of membership status.[25] DeVerney and his offspring had been enrolled with the Sault Ste. Marie Band of Chippewa in 1976 and did not rescind that membership before enrolling in the Grand Traverse Band. The family later rescinded their membership in the other tribe and was fully accepted as members of the Grand Traverse Band.

The tribe's trial court ruled in favor of the father and his children; the tribal government appealed. Unlike the Grand Ronde tribal court, which had held that a tribal member's three-month dual membership in another tribe twenty-seven years earlier was grounds for disenrollment, the Grand Traverse Band's appellate court said just the opposite. While affirming that the tribal council's political authority on membership decisions was due deference, Judge Ronald G. Douglas said that "once membership is granted, the court must give due process except where the Tribal Constitution expressly removes that court's discretion or jurisdiction."

And since membership is a property right and the family had been consistently enrolled since they rescinded their membership in the other tribe, they retained their membership rights in Grand Traverse and were to be reenrolled. Said membership also made the DeVerney's eligible for some per capita and docket fund (from a court of claims award) monies, despite the tribal council's attempt to invoke sovereign immunity as a defense against the distribution of the funds. In the court's words, the funds were "a membership benefit" and "a property right spelled out in tribal law and already intended for distribution."

Maltos v. Sauk-Suiattle (2003)

In this case, Nino Maltos brought suit against the tribe and the tribal council for having disenrolled him.[26] He claimed personal injury and that the tribe's action violated its own code and federal statutes. The tribe asserted sovereign immunity. Chief Judge Martin Bohl of the Sauk-Suiattle Tribal Court issued an order granting the tribe's motion to dismiss on sovereign immunity grounds, but directed notice of a rehearing for Maltos because he had been denied due process. Maltos then appealed.

The tribe's appellate court agreed that the trial court had jurisdiction to order a rehearing, but also held that sovereign immunity did not apply in this case. "The rehearing," said Justice Richard Woodrow, "is an administrative remedy and as such does not constitute a suit against the tribe." In their two-to-one decision for Maltos, the justices stated that "the enrollment ordinance is ambiguous. It is unclear if a member may appeal a disenrollment or a relinquishment of membership in the tribe. This court holds that a member may appeal a loss of membership in which privileges of membership are revoked by the Tribal Council or the enrollment committee."

More importantly, the court determined that there was no discernible distinction between "loss of membership" and a "denial of membership." This conclusion was based on the following facts:

> (1) the membership is a valuable property right and all members must be afforded due process when that right is taken by the tribe; (2) tribal members should have the same appeal rights as other Indians seeking to become tribal members; (3) the Enrollment Ordinance is ambiguous regarding appeals rights and this ambiguity should be resolved in favor of the tribal members; (4) there does not appear to be any appeal process or right to reapply for membership if a member is disenrolled or relinquishes membership brought by the motion of the Tribal Council or the Enrollment Committee. There should always be a remedy for mistake.

The justices, in a footnote, identified a fundamental flaw and bizarre irony in the tribe's enrollment policy, noting the different treatments of nonmember Indians compared to member Indians: "nonmember Indians are given a right to appeal their rejection, are given a right to present evidence, a right to counsel, a right to file again for membership, and a right to appeal to Tribal Court. Member Indians that are disenrolled have no such rights."

In conclusion, the justices, having already rejected the tribe's sovereign immunity stance, then said more emphatically that "tribal sovereignty was never at issue in this case." What mattered to the court was the fact that Maltos had been denied due process—not being informed of his right to appeal his disenrollment—a clear violation of his sovereign rights as a citizen of the Sauk-Suiattle Nation.

The Saginaw Chippewa of Michigan have been at the forefront of the disenrollment and banishment issue for least two decades and they are one of only a few tribes that have acted to dismember deceased members. As recently as August 2015, the tribe's appeal court determined that more than two hundred living and dead tribal members could be disenrolled.[27]

Ten years earlier, however, the same court, composed of three different justices—Carey N. Vicenti (a Jicarilla Apache and the chief justice), Michael Petoskey (a Grand Traverse Band citizen), and Frank Pommersheim (a non-Indian professor of law at the University of South Dakota and an author of several books on federal Indian law) issued a dramatically different ruling,

Snowden & Hinmon v. Saginaw Chippewa Indian Tribe of Michigan, when confronted with the question of whether the tribe had authority to disenroll two deceased tribal members, Malinda Hinmon and Mary Lee (Tipkey) Snowden.[28]

The court, in an opinion by Pommersheim, issued what is arguably the most eloquent opinion affirming the civil rights of those facing dismemberment. This case involved Hinmon and Snowden, and, by extension, their descendants, which included two members of a previous tribal council and a former tribal court chief judge. The two deceased members had been disenrolled in 2001. When a new council was elected in 2003, their descendants filed a motion to have the decision to disenroll reversed. They also requested a new hearing before the newly created Office of Administrative Hearing, which was a body set up to hear disenrollment cases.

But the two parties—the tribe and the descendants—also requested that the tribal court first address the underlying question of "the Tribal Council's authority to initiate disenrollment proceedings within the limits of the Tribal Constitution." The case, in other words, was not a specific review of the tribe's determination to disenroll those two individuals but was rather "an appeal requesting that this court determine the *tribal* constitutional standard as to the *implied substantive* grounds, if any, for possible disenrollment" (emphasis in original).

The single issue before the court was "whether the Tribal Council's power to disenroll currently enrolled members is limited to the narrow grounds expressly identified in the Tribal Constitution and if not, what are the Tribal constitutional boundaries in establishing (substantive) grounds for disenrollment." Displaying a solid understanding of federal Indian policy, Pommersheim then provided a brief overview of the tribe's constitutional history, dating back to the Indian Reorganization Act and how the tribe "became enmeshed in the coils of an unknowing and meddlesome BIA and Federal Government."

The commissioner of Indian Affairs from 1935 through 1937, William Zimmerman, directly interfered as the tribe worked to adopt a constitution, forcing them to adopt a narrower more geographically rigid definition of which communities and which individuals could belong. Zimmerman also unilaterally altered language in the constitution's preamble and modified representation on the tribal council by insisting that all council members be elected from within the reservation and all tribal members reside on reservation lands. The constitution was adopted by tribal vote in 1937. The process of its formation and its adoption, according to the court, "sowed the seeds of membership confusion and discontent that yielded the bitter harvest at the core of this most challenging, even heart wrenching, litigation about the cultural and legal aspects of tribal belonging."

The court discussed the structural arrangement and type of constitution then in operation on Saginaw Chippewa land. The 1986 constitution, which modified the original document, like that of the United States, is one that limits the powers of governing officials by clearly enumerating those powers that the governing branches may wield, with all nonenumerated powers residing in "the people."

After perusing the constitution's language on membership, the court "found that" the only *express* constitutional authority to disenroll is limited to certain situations involving "adopted" tribal members and tribal members who "abandon" Saginaw Chippewa Tribal membership by enrolling in another federal recognized tribe" (emphasis in original).

The court then examined the constitution to see if there was any language that could be interpreted as authorizing an implied power to disenroll. After reviewing the relevant constitutional data for the Saginaw Chippewa and then conducting a survey of other tribal constitutions, the justices found that "no tribal constitution cited by the parties or otherwise known by the Court contains any express provision to disenroll on such basic grounds like 'fraud and mistake.'"

A study of 330 tribal constitutions confirmed that no tribal constitution mentions fraud or mistake as grounds for formal disenrollment.[29] Two Alaskan Native communities, the village of Chilkat and the Sitka community state that individuals can be expelled for fraud or misconduct, but this is not a permanent status for the expellee and those vanquished can be reinstated, in the case of Chilkat, upon the vote of two-thirds of the village members.

Pommersheim then noted that this did not mean that the power to disenroll was nonexistent, but rather that "it is so basic and ingrained in the understanding of what is necessary to become a (legitimate) tribal member that there is a very, very limited *implied* power to disenroll on grounds of fraud and mistake that inheres in the right to enroll itself." In other words, tribal governments needed to retain an implied power to terminate a citizen or else they would be left without a remedy to address the rare occasion when the case of fraud or error did occur during the enrollment process.

The court then emphatically declared its finding: "No, the Tribe may not disenroll people for whatever 'good' reasons it might identify. No, the Constitution does not (and cannot) condone any constitutional failure of justice that would potentially endorse (constitutional) fraud and mistake in obtaining membership. Beyond such quite limited constitutional authority to disenroll on grounds of fraud or mistake, there are *no* other *implied* grounds for disenrollment" (emphasis in original).

Tribal membership, said Pommersheim, was not just a constitutional status, but was "the ultimate indication of cultural belonging," and "for it to be stripped from a citizen required a detailed ordinance that laid out the precise grounds for dismemberment and that also provided procedural to process safeguards for those facing such action."

LaHaye v. Enrollment Commission (2006)

In *LaHaye*, the Little River Band of Ottawa Indians Tribal Court overruled the Enrollment Commission's July 14, 2005, decision to disenroll a descendant of Ephraim LaHaye, having decided that he was not Native and could not be a member of the tribe.[30] It also addressed whether or not another forty-six individuals who traced their ancestry to persons listed on the Durant Roll 1908 were entitled to membership.

The primary issue raised in this appeal was whether the Enrollment Commission exceeded its authority by failing to follow the directive of the tribe's enrollment ordinance section 4.04, which stated that if the Durant Roll is the only source of information regarding a person's blood quantum, that person is presumed to be a full-blooded member of the tribe.

The trial court invalidated the commission's decision to disenroll and to make the other membership and blood quantum changes it sought because it had erroneously relied on documentary sources beyond those it was constitutionally allowed to use—the Durant Roll and the 1870 Annuity Roll.

Lucy Allen v. Cherokee Nation Tribal Council (2006)

The next case garnered a great deal of national media attention when some 2,800 tribal citizens were disenrolled by the Cherokee Nation of Oklahoma.[31] The so-called Cherokee Freedmen are descendants of African Americans who prior to the U.S. Civil War had been enslaved by some Cherokees, but were subsequently freed and incorporated as citizens under a provision of the 1866 treaty between the Cherokee Nation and the United States.[32]

The Cherokee were the first Native nation to formally adopt a secular national constitution in 1827 that effectively supplanted the traditional political system based on clan structures, decentralized towns, and oral traditions. In key respects it was mostly modeled after the U.S. and state constitutions in its stipulation of three branches of government, bicameralism, denial of voting privileges to African Americans and Cherokee women, and free exercise of religion. Yet it also contained specific provisions (e.g., communal land ownership) that sustained a measure of traditional Cherokee values and property notions.[33]

By the 1890s the Cherokee, along with the other so-called Five Civilized Tribes, faced unrelenting pressure to cede land to the ever-encroaching white population. The Dawes Commission was convened in 1893 to compel the Five Tribes to negotiate agreements with the federal government calling for the allotment of their fee-simple owned territories. Five years later, Congress enacted the Curtis Act which unilaterally and in direct violation of treaty and statutory laws terminated the legal existence of the Five Tribes. These and other developments transformed these peoples from an independent and wealthy status to one of stark poverty that would take decades to rise above. So dominant was federal power over the Cherokee that from 1906 to 1970 the U.S. president actually appointed the Cherokee nation's chief executive.

As part of their resurgence during the self-determination era that robustly began in the 1970s, the Cherokee adopted a new constitution in 1975. In that document, Cherokee citizenship was broadly defined to include not only those who were ethnologically Cherokee, but also included African American, Shawnee, and Delaware individuals who had long been politically incorporated into the Cherokee Nation. But in 2002 the tribal council adopted much more stringent and racially based language, declaring "tribal membership is derived only through proof of Cherokee blood based on the Final Rolls."

This action effectively deprived the nearly 2,800 Freedmen descendants of their citizenship in the Cherokee Nation. In 2004 Lucy Allen, a descendant of individuals listed on the Dawes Commission Rolls as "Cherokee Freedmen," filed a lawsuit against the tribal council asking the nation's court to declare chapter 11 CNCA section 12 unconstitutional because it was more restrictive than the membership criteria set forth in article 3 of the 1975 constitution.

The Cherokee Nation Judicial Appeals Tribunal rendered its two-to-one decision in the spring of 2006, holding that the Freedmen were entitled to citizenship under the tribe's constitution and that the council's more restrictive membership criteria were improper and invalid. As Stacey Leeds wrote for the court: "When they [the Cherokee people] adopted the 1975 Constitution, they did not limit membership to people who possess Cherokee blood. Instead, they extended membership to all the people who were 'citizens' of the Cherokee Nation as listed on the Dawes Commission Rolls."

Continuing, Leeds noted that while providing proof of Cherokee blood was one way to be a member, it was not the only way. In fact, she said "Article 3 expressly mentions Shawnee and Delaware, who possess some Indian blood, but not Cherokee blood. The Shawnee and Delaware are not citizens 'by blood' of the Cherokee Nation. Article 3 expressly includes all people who can prove that they were 'citizens' on the Dawes Commission rolls with no mention (one way or the other) about Cherokee or Indian blood quantum. The Cherokee Freedmen, the Shawnee and Delaware were all citizens at the time the Dawes rolls were finalized and they all continue as citizens to this day."

Leeds did, however, lay out a constitutional prescription for how the Cherokee people could change their organic law since they were the "ultimate authority" on citizenship. The constitution could be amended to require that all tribal members possess Cherokee blood. But if they chose this option it would have to be done in a transparent fashion.

The Cherokee Nation's leadership, led by Principal Chief Chad Smith, moved quickly to implement the blood-based requirement the court had said would have to be sanctioned by the people. The council approved and then circulated a nationwide petition calling for a referendum vote on an amendment to the 1975 constitution that would create a blood requirement for Cherokee citizenship. In October 2006, the Cherokee Supreme Court ruled that supporters had gathered enough signatures and that a special election was set for March 3, 2007. The proposed amendment was adopted by a large margin: 77 percent (6,693 votes) for the amendment, and 23 percent (2,040 votes) against it. With this action, the Cherokee terminated the Freedmen's Cherokee citizenship.[34]

In 2011, the disenrolled Cherokee Freedmen filed a class-action lawsuit in the district court of the Cherokee Nation challenging the tribal referendum that had culminated in the constitutional amendment that led to their dismemberment. In *Nash v. Cherokee Nation*, the district court reminded the Cherokee national government and the Cherokee people of the moral and legal import of the treaties their nation's ancestors had signed with the United States.[35] The 1866 treaty, said the judge, "was an agreement which, to this date, has not been modified or abrogated by any action heretofore taken either through Constitutional change or Amendment thereto and the Nation is still bound by such provisions. The Cherokee Constitutional Amendment of March 3, 2007, by virtue of the provisions of the Treaty of 1866 and subsequent actions taken in furtherance thereof, are hereby determined to be void as a matter of law."

The Freedmen were restored to their status as it was before the 2007 amendment had been enacted. Less than a year later, however, the Cherokee Nation Supreme Court reversed the district court's decision and declared that the Cherokee people had the right to change the definition of Cherokee Nation citizenship and had properly done so by a national referendum in 2007 and the ensuing constitutional amendment.

The Cherokee Freedmen, as of September 2016, are still members of the Cherokee Nation and receive benefits as such. A moratorium, however, has been placed on those Freedmen seeking new membership. A federal district court judge, Thomas Hogan, is set to issue a decision in late 2016 that may finally clarify the rights of these 2,800 Cherokee citizens. Whatever Hogan decides will likely be appealed.

Samuelson v. Little River Band of Ottawa Indians

The Little River Band of Ottawa Indians' appellate court, speaking through Ryan L. Champagne, faced two issues: "whether the Enrollment Commission had the authority to examine and use extrinsic evidence outside of the Durant Roll of 1910 and the Annuity payrolls of 1870 and whether the tribal court had the authority to order the individual's membership status and the fixing of an individual's specific blood quantum for the purposes of determining eligibility for enrollment with the Little River Band of Ottawa Indians."[36]

This case affirmed the trial court's *LaHaye* decision of 2006, that the tribal court did, indeed, have authority to render decisions on member-related matters and that the Enrollment Commission did not have authority to rely upon data outside the two constitutionally recognized sources: the Durant Roll and the Annuity Rolls.

More important, for our purposes, was the language the appellate judges used to describe what belonging to a Native nation meant. "Tribal membership," said Justice Champagne, for Native people "is more than mere citizenship in an Indian tribe. It is the essence of one's identity, belonging to community, connection to one's heritage and an affirmation of their human being place in this life and world. In short, it is not an overstatement to say that it is everything. In fact, it would be an understatement to say anything less. Tribal membership completes the circle for the member's physical, mental, emotional, and spiritual aspects of human life. Thus, to strip all of this away is indeed a very serious matter and therefore ought to stand the highest levels of scrutiny."

Graveratte et al. v. The Saginaw Chippewa Tribe

In 2010, the Saginaw Chippewa Tribal Court of Appeals heard a set of consolidated cases that once again involved a review of the interpretation of the tribe's enrollment ordinance by the Office of Administrative Hearing and the Tribal Certifier.[37] Those two bodies had interpreted the ordinance as limiting the evidence that an applicant for membership could present in trying to establish Saginaw Chippewa blood. The tribe's community court had upheld the denial of enrollment of Skylar Graveratte and others, but they appealed and the three justices, one of whom was Kevin K. Washburn, who would later serve as the assistant secretary of Indian Affairs, ruled in favor of the plaintiffs by declaring that the applicants were entitled to present whatever evidence they could muster in support of their application.

Reiterating the importance of the procedural rights of the applicants, the justices noted that "membership in the Tribe involves important features of personal identity for the applicant which reaches beyond liberty or property interests into whether the applicant possesses hereditary birthright to participation in the Tribal community. It is, therefore, incumbent upon this Court to ensure that the laws of the Tribe are interpreted in a manner which fully comports with the promise of Article 3, Section 1b that an applicant born to a member of the Tribe who possesses one-quarter Indian blood shall be eligible for enrollment in the Tribe."

In another 2010 decision involving a Midwestern Native people, the Ho-Chunk, the tribal court heard the case of Jenna Littlegeorge, who had been targeted for disenrollment, notwithstanding a vote by the general council in 2009, which had rejected the motion to have her disenrolled.[38] The enrollment committee then ordered Littlegeorge and her relatives to submit to a DNA test in 2010 in an attempt to verify her Ho-Chunk lineage.

Littlegeorge argued that the general council was the final arbiter of membership questions and that the constitution did not expressly afford the committee any right of appellate review of the general council action, granting this right instead only to the affected member. The general council, in fact, had sole authority to decide membership and the tribal government had to respect the peoples' decision.

Russell Chivis et al. v. Nottawaseppi Huron Band
of the Potawatomi Tribal Council

In this case, eight enrolled tribal members filed a petition with the court seeking a writ of mandamus against the tribal council, urging the council to act upon the request to have a number of tribal members disenrolled because of their concern that they had been erroneously enrolled.[39] The court, however, held that while the appellants had a right to be concerned about the community's membership criteria, the council was under no legal obligation to take the actions requested of them by those filing the suit.

Phebus v. Las Vegas Tribe of Paiute Indians (2013)

Chief Judge William A. Thorne Jr. and two others addressed the situation of whether the tribal government could criminally prosecute a disenrolled tribal member, Christopher Phebus.[40] Phebus, along with others, had been disenrolled in 1999. According to the court, he was "outraged" by his disenrollment and his conduct since that time had "crossed the line of acceptable behavior." Most recently, in November 2012, he was convicted of improper influence in official matters and sentenced to six months of incarceration.

On May 6, 2013, Chief Judge Thorne issued an immediate stay of that sentence and ordered that Phebus be released. The tribe appealed this release as it wanted to punish Phebus for having violated tribal law. Yet as the court noted, the council had "specifically deprived [the] Appellant of his enrolled status, and continued to do so even in the face of a 2005 court decision to the contrary. In so doing they left [the] Appellant with the status of Indian *only* in terms of certain services definitions, e.g., Indian Health Service. So that if respondent had criminal conduct jurisdiction over the Appellant it must flow from that status and/or unless as the Chief Judge noted the basis for that assertion somehow resulted from his status as a 'generic Indian'" (emphasis in original).

But the court declared that "generic Indian" status "is not, nor has it ever been, successfully claimed as a basis for tribal court criminal jurisdiction. Criminal jurisdiction on Indian reservations has many limitations. The most important limitation for the purpose of this discussion is the need for the defendant to be an Indian. Indian in this situation is very specifically defined as ENROLLED Tribal member, which was initially taken to mean enrolled tribal member of the Tribe seeking to prosecute."[41] Judge Thorne could find no constitutional or statutory language extending the tribe's criminal jurisdiction to nonenrolled tribal members. Since that was the case the tribe had no jurisdiction over Phebus and could not legally prosecute him.

"The act of disenrollment," said the court, "so long as it stands, precludes criminal prosecution by Respondent [Tribe]. Basic concepts of estoppel and fairness prevent the tribe from depriving appellant [Phebus] of tribal member-

ship and then prosecuting him criminally as they would have been entitled to
do had he not been disenrolled." The appellate judges cautioned Phebus, however, that criminal prosecution by the state was not precluded, emphasizing
that their decision was not a "free passage to engage in criminal behavior."

The court went so far as to implore the tribal government to take political
action to reverse Phebus's disenrollment. They expressed concern that further
criminal actions would result in harsh consequences and not lead to resolution
of this "essentially political question." In conclusion, the court said that "based
on the above it is our decision that the underlying criminal conviction and
sentence be vacated and Appellant suffer no further legal consequences from
said conviction."

The tribe appealed this decision to the U.S. District Court for the District
of Nevada, which agreed with the tribe that it could exercise criminal jurisdiction over "any person qualifying as an Indian under the Indian Civil Rights
Act," but insisted that the tribe had to "prove Indian status beyond a reasonable
doubt," and that the accused was entitled to a jury trial if faced with imprisonment. Finally, the district court said that if the tribe wanted to prosecute a
member it had disenrolled, "the Indian status analysis in such a prosecution
may not rely upon political affiliation with the Tribe, but only upon actual or
de facto membership in another tribe."[42]

FEDERAL JUDICIAL PROCEEDINGS
DEALING WITH DISMEMBERMENT

In previous chapters we discussed a number of federal, not state, rulings that
have examined the issue of Native citizenship and membership.[43] And more
recently published legal literature provides detailed analysis of numerous federal cases that we need not repeat.[44] Prior to the Native self-determination era,
federal courts were not averse to intervening in such matters, whether involving purely internal tribal matters or external, federally derived sources.

Since the *Santa Clara* decision in 1978, and notwithstanding the Indian
Civil Rights Act of 1968, federal courts have been much more reluctant to get
directly involved in membership battles unless there is specific language in a
tribe's constitution or other organic document requiring such involvement.
Thus, at the present time, dismembered individuals have extremely limited
rights to challenge their termination under existing federal tribal law, despite
the promise of the *Poodry* ruling in 1996.

A review of much of the federal case law since *Poodry*[45] reveals that in virtually all of the litigation, federal courts have generally adhered to the *Santa Clara* precedent that tribal governments are the final arbiters of membership decisions and that their sovereign immunity broadly shields them from lawsuits filed by tribal members.[46] As the court said in *Payer,* "the decision of the United States Supreme Court in *Santa Clara Pueblo v. Martinez* reduces the degree of federal interference in tribal government and requires that enforcement of the Indian Civil Rights Act rest primarily in the Tribal Courts."[47]

The Ninth Circuit Court of Appeals in *Lewis v. Norton* (2005) was even more blunt in reminding disenrollees of their limited rights: "Although their claim to membership appears to be a strong one, as their father is a recognized member of the tribe, their claim cannot survive the double jurisdictional whammy of sovereign immunity and lack of federal court jurisdiction to intervene in tribal membership disputes."[48]

There is, however, one crucial area where the federal courts have in a few cases—*Sweet v. Hinzman* (2008) and *Sweet v. Hinzman* (2009)—provided a semblance of support for those facing dismemberment, and that is when banishment is involved rather than disenrollment.[49] Recall that in *Poodry* (1996), the U.S. Court of Appeals for the Second Circuit held that the permanent banishment of five Seneca citizens was a severe enough restraint on liberty to warrant habeas jurisdiction under the 1968 Indian Civil Rights Act. Two years later, the same circuit court was called upon to hear the complaints of several members of the Oneida Indian Nation of New York, the prominent Shenandoah family, then led by a clan mother, Maisie Shenandoah, who had been disenrolled for challenging the tribal government's authority.[50]

The Shenandoahs had lost in the district court and appealed. They claimed that their disenrollment entailed loss of employment, termination of healthcare benefits, destruction of property, being banned from certain businesses (including the tribal casino), loss of membership, and so on. The disenrolled members said that these punishments constituted severe restraints on their individual liberty interests and that they were therefore entitled to habeas corpus relief under the Indian Civil Rights Act (ICRA). The Oneida Nation, led by Ray Halbritter, invoked sovereign immunity and said that the plaintiffs had not exhausted administrative remedies.

The second circuit held that even if all the plaintiffs' allegations of misconduct were true, while these would be serious offenses, they were still insufficient to bring them within the habeas provision. "Habeas relief," said the court, "does address more than actual physical custody, and includes parole, probation, and release on one's own recognizance pending sentencing or trial, and permanent banishment."[51] In other words, the judges stressed that the banished Seneca faced considerably more serious punishment than the Oneida plaintiffs because they had been convicted of treason, faced permanent banishment, and had been stripped of their citizenship and removed from the tribe's rolls. The Oneidas, by contrast, had not been banished, deprived of tribal membership, convicted of any crime, or faced expulsion demands, and therefore had not actually experienced a "severe actual or potential restraint on [their] liberty" sufficient to justify habeas corpus relief.

The second circuit, in effect, had modified its stance on dismemberment by holding that habeas jurisdiction could be invoked for *banishment*, but not for *disenrollment*. That disturbing judicial logic has generally governed the federal courts' decisions on such matters since *Shenandoah*. We say disturbing because formal disenrollment is far more detrimental than banishment alone, because disenfranchisement is an absolute denial of the legal, political, and cultural rights of a citizen; whereas banishment alone—unless it is joined with disenrollment—is a physical expulsion from the community but does not necessarily entail a loss of citizenship. As the Supreme Court held in *Klapprott v. U.S.*[52], "a deprivation of citizenship is an extraordinarily severe penalty with consequences that may be more grave than consequences that flow from conviction for crimes."[53]

While most of the judicial precedent continues to vigorously enforce the *Santa Clara* holding, a few judges have more recently begun to contend that banished individuals and disenrollees should have more rights under the law to dispute their expulsion or termination of citizenship. In a case involving several Snoqualmie tribal members who had been banished in 2008, *Sweet v. Hinzman*, a federal district court ruled that the five banished members' due process rights had, indeed, been violated under the ICRA because they had not been given adequate notice of a tribal meeting where their permanent banishment was determined. Equally important, the court held that the doctrine of tribal sovereign immunity did not shield tribal officials "in their official capacity for alleged unlawful acts" associated with the banishment proceedings.

And in *Jeffredo v. Macarro*, a case involving the Pechanga Band of Luiseno Mission Indians, Judge Claudia Wilken gave a stirring dissent after noting that the tribe's membership criteria had not been established until 1979; that the procedures used to disenroll were not put into place until 1988; and that the "Tribal Council did not begin [to] disenroll . . . large numbers of members until recently, when the Tribe's casino profits became a major source of revenue."[54]

She said: "Although with disenrollment Appellants retain their United States citizenship and will not be physically stateless, they have been stripped of their lifelong citizenship and identity as Pechangans. This is more than just a loss of a label; it is a loss of a political, ethnic, racial, and social association. Such a loss constitutes a restraint on liberty that, combined with the actual and potential restraints described above, satisfies the detention requirement under Sec. 1303, in my opinion."[55]

Finally, in two cases involving membership issues within the Santa Rosa Rancheria Tachi Indian Tribe—*Quair v. Sisco (Quair I)*[56] and *Quair v. Sisco (Quair II)*[57]—two tribal members, Rosalind Quair and Charlotte Berna, were disenrolled and banished in 2000 for having allegedly misused tribal funds, privacy violations, defamation, and "undermining the government" for having hired an attorney to pursue legal action against the tribe. They challenged the tribe's decision and petitioned for a writ of habeas corpus, claiming that their procedural and substantive rights had been violated under the Indian Civil Rights Act.

In *Quair I* the federal district court of the eastern district of California handed down an important victory for those facing dismemberment. It agreed, in part, that Quair and Berna's petitions met the requirements for seeking habeas review. More importantly, it established a categorical rule that "disenrollment from tribal membership and subsequent banishment from the reservation constitute detention in the sense of a severe restriction on petitioners' liberty not shared by other members of the Tribe."[58]

The court also held that the plaintiffs had the right to sue the tribal council, notwithstanding the doctrine of sovereign immunity. More broadly, the court made two other statements that indicated some pushback against both the broad concept of carte blanche tribal sovereignty and the meaning of *Santa Clara*: "While Congress has deferred with regularity to tribal membership determinations . . . there is little question that the power to define membership is subject to limitations by Congress. Whether section 1302 of the ICRA does in fact impose any limits on tribal authority to determine questions of membership in the tribe is a question on the merits, and not one resolved in *Santa Clara Pueblo*."[59] And equally important, the judges said that "although we did not reach the question here, we note that Title I of the ICRA may well be a federal statute that imposes limitations on a tribe's power to summarily banish its members."

Following this ruling, the general council called a new hearing and made sure in advance to provide written notice to Quair and Berna and to let them know they were entitled to be represented and to call witnesses. The two women refused to participate, insisting that the process was biased. In October 2004 the council met and voted on two separate resolutions to disenroll and then banish the two women.[60]

Quair and Berna once again challenged these actions in federal court, arguing that their due process rights had been violated under the ICRA. The court determined that habeas jurisdiction was proper for both disenrollment and banishment actions, so long as they inhibit the petitioner's freedom of movement. But having said that, the judges relied on a so-called geographic movement assessment and found that the petitioner's disenrollments did not limit their physical mobility but only affected their interests in "tangible tribal benefits," like gaming revenue, health insurance, housing allotments, and others. The court also dismissed the petitioners' complaint on the grounds that they had failed to prove that their individual interests in procedural safeguards "surpass any countervailing tribal interests."

According to Patrice Kunesh, *Quair II* announced several important stipulations and provides greater clarity as to when disaffected tribal members can invoke habeas corpus under the Indian Civil Rights Act:

First, tribal banishment decisions are criminal proceedings for purposes of federal habeas corpus under the ICRA. Second, a federal court will consider tribal disenrollment and banishment decisions as separate and distinct sanctions when the tribe has independently deliberated each matter. Third, each tribal decision will be subject to the *Poodry* test, as expanded in *Quair I* (criminal proceeding, detention, and exhaustion of tribal remedies). Fourth, although cautiously prescribed, a tribal disenrollment decision will warrant habeas corpus review if it meets all three prongs of the *Quair I* test and the tribal member has proven that the disenrollment decision affects the member's physical freedom to a degree tantamount to detention. Finally, the court will apply the Randall balancing test when the tribe follows a model of adjudication substantially different from the Anglo-American judicial system, meaning that whenever a tribe makes a decision based on tribal customary or traditional law, its interest in maintaining its cultural identity and the traditional values of the tribal community will likely be weighed against the individual tribal member's interest in certain—but not yet fully defined—procedural, and perhaps substantive, protections in the tribe's decision-making process.[61]

A number of fundamental issues remain unresolved. For instance, what type of hearing is required for banishment proceeding—criminal trial or a civil hearing? What is the full panoply of due process due to individuals facing banishment or disenrollment? Finally, what kinds of remedies can a federal court order in such cases?[62]

More importantly, even the few federal cases that can be considered legal victories for those who have been dismembered—*Poodry*, *Sweet*, and *Quair I*—are limited rulings because they point to the real impotence of habeas corpus review as the lone remedy. This was stated most unequivocally in *Quair I* where although the court found that it had jurisdiction over petitioners' claims for a writ of habeas corpus, the proposed remedy left to those facing dismemberment was insubstantial. In the court's words: "If the court concludes that petitioners were denied their rights to procedural due process in connection with the decisions to disenroll them and banish them from the reservation, the remedy is not reinstatement, which would interfere with tribal sovereign immunity and internal tribal affairs but, rather, a direction to provide appropriate due process, essentially a re-hearing."[63]

Conclusion

HISTORICALLY, NATIVE NATIONS WERE BOUNDED BUT INCLUSIVE SOCIO-cultural communities that prided themselves on maintaining distinctive religious-cultural identities while also incorporating—whether through force, invitation, or acceptance—individuals from other Indigenous, racial, and ethnic groups. Native peoples had always managed to creatively and successfully augment their numbers and incorporate new blood and ideas. Outsiders, from Natives to Europeans, Africans, or others, were frequently welcomed into tribal communities through ceremonies and later through tribal governmental action. This openness was evidence of an inherent cultural confidence and generosity that were hallmarks of Native nations—qualities that for millennia were bolstered, not threatened, by inclusion.

Tribal lands, languages, spiritual beliefs and activities, and well-honed and long-standing kinship systems provided the sacred boundaries and frameworks necessary to enable each Native nation, and the individuals and clans constituting those nations, to generally rest assured in their collective and individual identities and to not have any questions about who they were.

As human communities, however, conflicts and deviance inevitably erupted within even these tightly knit societies. But Indigenous peoples had in place customs, values, and ceremonies that protected the integrity and personality of each member of the community. When problems arose or when offenses were committed, they were generally resolved through peacemaking, mediation, restitution, ostracism, or negotiation. Native peoples rarely engaged in the legal, political, or cultural termination of the rights of fellow tribal citizens because they were, after all, related to one another and much less draconian means were used to deal with the issue in an effort to restore community harmony.

It was well understood that the concept of nationhood, or sovereignty, meant that the tribal community members themselves were the sovereign, not the governing, bodies of those nations. Tribal leaders and other governing institutions have merely been delegated limited authority to fulfill the needs and to protect, not destroy, the rights of the people. These leaders and institutions did not have the power to sever an individual's relationship to their community by taking away the most important of statuses: the status of belonging to, of having citizenship or membership in, an Indigenous nation.

We saw in an earlier chapter that on rare occasions an individual might commit a grievous offense (e.g., premeditated murder) for which they might be killed or banished (*disenrollment* as a legal term did not appear until the allotment era) if all other attempts to resolve the conflict failed. But the available evidence and the oral traditions of tribes suggest that given the kinship structure of these nations, they were always focused on mediation, restitution, or compensation: permanent expulsion of relatives was rarely practiced.

Since the early 1990s, however, and coinciding with both the emergence of high-stakes gaming operations and increased criminal activity, we have witnessed a number of tribal governments throughout North America that have acted to dramatically redefine the boundaries and meaning of what it is to be a Native nation and a Native citizen. Many initiated formal banishment and legal disenrollment proceedings against increasing numbers of their own relatives or other citizens.

Why is legal, political, and cultural termination of Native individuals occurring at such a heightened level now? And what are some possible remedies to address these practices? As we established earlier, tribal nations have always enjoyed the sovereign right to decide who can be recognized as tribal citizens and have, in many cases, the treaty and constitutional right to evict nonmembers. But it was not until the Supreme Court definitively noted in the 1978 *Santa Clara Pueblo* v. Martinez opinion that tribal governments, as one of their retained powers, clearly had the right to decide membership questions that this issue began to draw attention. The federal government, Associate Justice Thurgood Marshall said, would generally not interfere with those internal decisions.

In the years after *Santa Clara*, the still sporadic cases of tribal disenrollments and banishment typically revolved around questions of family feuds, distribution of judgment funds, and political power struggles, sometimes masked by the alleged lack of sufficient blood quantum of those facing dismemberment.

By the early 1990s, however, as violent crime, drug activity, and gang strength had intensified, and with the Indian gaming revenue and judgment funds providing some tribal governments sudden and, in some cases, enormous increases in economic wealth, these factors—but especially the gaming revenue—provided some tribal officials with additional rationales on which to base dismemberment proceedings.

Of course, in some instances crime and economic benefits were simply grafted onto preexisting family conflicts, political and ideological power struggles, and racial criteria and blood quantum issues. Any one or combination of these factors could be and has been the basis on which to terminate tribal citizens.

In a few cases, especially those centered on criminal activity and in particular illegal drug distribution, Native nations have reluctantly determined that banishment (sometimes linked with disenrollment) is one mechanism they may employ in order to maintain community stability. They have carefully constructed clear guidelines and procedures to carry out this most difficult process, although banishment, as described in chapter 1, does little to address the deeper problems of deviant behavior and merely pushes the banished member into another jurisdiction that must now confront the person's criminal behavior.

But in a number of disenrollment (and some banishment) cases, some tribal officials are, without any concern for human rights, tribal traditions, or due process, arbitrarily and capriciously disenrolling tribal members as a means to solidify their own economic and political bases or to winnow out opposition individuals or entire families who disapprove of the actions or direction taken by the tribal leadership.

What was historically a rare event—the forced and sometimes permanent expulsion of a relative who had committed a terrible offense—has tragically become almost commonplace in Indian Country, leaving thousands of bona fide individuals without the benefits and protections of the nations they are biologically, culturally, and spiritually related to.

A detailed analysis of every nation currently involved in dismemberment actions would be a massive and extraordinarily difficult assignment to complete given privacy concerns and the tribal governments' and the BIA's insistence that enrollment data is confidential. Beyond that, each of the more than seventy Native governments and the thousands of individuals who have been or are now facing expulsion or disenfranchisement within those nations are unique cases that, in a perfect world, deserve book-length treatment. All we

Originally run March 4, 2007, on Indian Country Today Media Network. © 2016 Marty Two Bulls.

can do is identify and discuss what we believe are plausible factors, besides gaming revenue and crime, that have contributed to the rise of dismemberment proceedings and then lay out some potential remedies that might be employed to address these traumatic and nation-changing cases.

In the introduction we stated that the two dismemberment processes—banishment and disenrollment—can each be divided into two broad categories: nonpolitically motivated or politically motivated. Nonpolitically motivated disenrollments, at least theoretically, might be instituted because of fraudulent enrollment, mistake or error in enrollment, dual membership, and so on. And when disenrollments occur because of one of these reasons, and provided that due process safeguards have been rigorously followed for those facing expulsion, then the government's actions are arguably justified.

Politically motivated disenrollments, however, can be instigated because of economic greed, political power plays, personal vendettas, or the like. Of course, as noted in some of our analysis, some seemingly nonpolitically motivated disenrollments, be they dual membership or mistake, are actually deeply political actions, and what the tribal government says and does publicly is sometimes belied by the actual data presented by those facing disenrollment.

As regards banishment, an example of nonpolitically motivated expulsion would include the several Native nations (e.g., Cheyenne River Sioux, Standing Rock Sioux, and the Blood Tribe of Canada) that in 2015 banished drug dealers for their hawking of dangerously addictive drugs to tribal citizens. However, politically motivated banishments—like in the case of the five Seneca members discussed in the 1996 *Poodry* decision, or the several Snoqualmie of Washington State who were banished for a period of time (expelled for having allegedly committed treason)—are obviously more difficult to verify given their highly charged nature and the tribal governments unwillingness to appear retaliatory or to directly act in violation of the civil rights of those it is banishing.

Let us turn our attention to an additional set of factors we believe are linked with both political and nonpolitical disenrollments and sometimes political banishments: attorneys, enrollment audits, and per capita distribution plans.

ATTORNEYS

Petra Shattuck and Jill Norgren in their excellent study on federal Indian law, *Partial Justice*, pondered an important question: "Should the law be praised or cursed for what it has done to Native peoples?" On the negative side, our findings confirm some Native leaders have followed rather than directed their legal personnel with regard to enrollment and disenrollment matters. And there is evidence that some attorneys have prolonged or even fomented conflict to gain more resources for themselves and their law firms.

On the positive side, some Native and non-Native elements associated with the legal profession have been very supportive of the individuals facing dismemberment. First are those courageous tribal judges (some of whom are non-Indian) who have written well-reasoned opinions affirming the rights of those wrongfully denied membership or disenrolled. In their opinions they insist that the tribal government provide clear and unequivocal due process safeguards to those facing dismemberment. Second is the law firm of Galanda Broadman PLLC, one of the first Native law firms to represent those facing disenrollment, and which has done solid work for Nooksack, Grand Ronde, and other Native individuals. Finally, in 2015 the National Native American Bar Association adopted a resolution that, while respecting tribal governments' right to determine their own enrollment criteria, emphatically declared that those same governments and the attorneys who work for those nations must protect the due process rights of those facing disenrollment. They noted that "it is immoral and unethical for lawyers to advocate for or contribute to the divestment or restriction of the American indigenous right of tribal citizenship, without equal protection at law or due process of law or an effective remedy for the violation of such rights."[1]

ENROLLMENT AUDITS

In 1977 preeminent Native theorist Vine Deloria Jr. was asked to write a paper about the current state of Indian affairs in the United States. One of his recommendations was that tribal governments needed to clarify their membership rolls. This was important, Deloria intoned, because at the time "the present membership of most Indian tribes is a result of fortuitous circumstances, a dash of federal record-keeping, political favors among tribal members, and irrational administrative decisions made by federal employees."

A keen observer of Indian affairs, Deloria was aware that some tribal governments were already engaging in unscrupulous behavior toward their own citizens, saying that "the Indian exclusivity stance is very peculiar . . . Indians, their eyes on college scholarships, oil royalties, and special privileges, have taken the reverse attack, eliminating peoples unjustly from participation in the affairs of their communities." This could be remedied, he then suggested, if each Native community were to prepare an adequately documented roll with the help of qualified scholars. He urged that appropriate federal officials work closely with tribal peoples to help assure that the final rolls accurately "reflect the historical circumstances of each tribal situation" and emphasized that all the necessary federal, tribal, and private records be used to create a careful and accurate membership roll.[2]

While Deloria was a visionary, he was also a pragmatist, fully understanding that it would be challenging for all tribes to undertake this process. Unfortunately, numerous Native governments in the areas of constitutional reform and development, tribal membership, and enrollment policies and practices have entrusted some of these most intimate of governmental responsibilities to outside organizations like CSN (Creating Stronger Nations), the Harvard

Project For American Indian Economic Development/Native Nations Institute, Automated Election Services, the Falmouth Institute, J. Dalton Institute, and others. In the case of membership and enrollment, some of these organizations conduct what are arguably privacy invading audits.

These outside audits can be time consuming. For example, the Falmouth Institute, known for its training programs, recently conducted a nearly eight-year-long audit for the Eastern Band of Cherokee Indians at a cost of $900,000. The review of the nearly 14,000 individuals on the tribe's roll concluded that more than 10 percent of the members needed to correct their status and at least three hundred listed members appeared to have no direct connection to the 1924 Baker Roll, the tribe's official foundational enrollment document. Ironically, the Baker Roll was conceived as the tribe's final roll in preparation for their formal termination by the U.S. Congress, a process the Cherokees were fortunately able to fend off.

Worst of all, in these instances, the costs of this outside scrutiny are not limited to money and resources: there is also a debilitating toll exacted on the morale and cohesiveness of the community. The years of uncertain membership status eats away at the very fabric of trust and kinship that define a tribal nation. Native leaders who abdicate their responsibilities to outside enrollment auditors may even leave elected office and pass the problem on to the next governmental regime. Over time, there is a real danger that these auditors are the only ones with the long-term knowledge of a tribe's unique membership situation—a frightening proposition. No sovereign nation should ever be in such a vulnerable position.

What precisely is an enrollment audit? Why are so many Native nations turning to outside corporate and other organizations to investigate internal matters that should rightly be the province of tribal individuals and entities? Who are the consultants, lawyers, and accountants that provide advice and counsel to tribal governing officials? Are problems aggravated—either deliberately or through ignorance—by third parties who stand to make more money from a prolonged conflict? And most fundamentally, is reliance on so-called outside experts a hallmark of self-determined nations or an indication of ongoing tribal dependency?

These vital questions need deep investigation because Native governments are increasingly entrusting key elements of their fundamental powers of membership determination, and even constitutional reform, to outside organizations and businesses. No matter how well respected, these entities are making money from the strife and confusion Native peoples have inherited.

The very term *audit*, according to *Black's Law Dictionary,* means "inspection and verification by the Internal Revenue Service of a taxpayer's return or other transaction processing tax consequences." It also means "systematic inspection of accounting records involving analyses, tests, and confirmation." But citizenship or membership in a Native nation is, or should be, something much greater and more meaningful than an accounting transaction.

While tribal nations, like states and the federal government, have every right to outsource services like transportation, prisons, wastewater treatment, public benefits eligibility services, and even law enforcement, such privatizing entails real risks. It frequently raises costs. It does not always mean that the task is done better. It is sometimes a more wasteful approach and, in fact, there is frequently a decline in the quality of services under private contractors. It sometimes leads to corruption and unscrupulous behavior—as some tribal leaders learned when they linked up with Jack Abramoff and Michael Scanlon, two political lobbyists who exploited several tribes for economic and political reasons.

Deciding who belongs as a bona fide citizen or member is one of the most fundamental powers of a tribal nation. The difficult burden of creating an accurate tribal roll, as Deloria noted earlier, is an essential step in the maturation of Native nations.

There is more than sufficient knowledge within Indian Country to see that the important task of comprising an authentic and verifiable roll be done without having to resort to paying outside organizations or consultants, even those that identify as being Native or Native owned. These third-party entities will never have the same core values, historical understanding, or fundamental commitment that a group of competent, rightly empowered, and fully trained tribal members possess as long as they are armed with the necessary historical data and member-given authority to complete the task.

Tribal citizens must provide this authority by demanding that their leaders develop and employ sensible, transparent policies that offer a realistic pathway to gain or retain citizenship, as well as a fair process to question and appeal decisions. No nation should pit sovereignty against human and civil rights. In Deloria's words, "continued deprivation of the rights of individual Indians by tribal governments using the shield of tribal sovereignty is much more destructive of Indian communities in the long run than revision of the rolls."[3]

Native governments would do well to consider Deloria's good advice and seek to clarify and not deplete their nations' membership rolls. They should reconsider hiring outside firms for intimate and internal decisions, such as membership, since many of these businesses are, of necessity, generally more committed to revenue generation than Indigenous nation membership clarification. Native peoples should not consign the remembering of their nations to anyone other than themselves. Their private citizenship/membership rolls, with all their complexities, do not exist for profit.

PER CAPITA DISTRIBUTION PLANS

As described earlier, before the advent of Indian gaming revenue there were in a few instances some tribal nations who engaged in dismemberment activities when substantial judgment fund awards became available to the tribes via land claims or other settlements. But these were rare occurrences. There were also a few cases where blood quantum questions arose and some individuals—usually at the behest of the BIA—were disenrolled either by the BIA or with the BIA's concurrence.

It was not, however, until the explosion of Native gambling operations in the late 1980s that significant revenue acquisition began to have a direct bearing on tribal membership decisions. This period represented "a remarkable growth in Indian gaming activities and revenues, as the metric quickly shifted from the millions to billions of dollars."[4]

As of 2016, 286 Native peoples were operating well over four hundred gaming operations, generating some $28.5 billion in revenue. When Indian gaming was formally set in motion in 1988 following Congress's adoption of the Indian Gaming Regulatory Act (IGRA), three types of gaming were recognized. Class 1 entails traditional social games enjoyed by tribal peoples during social events or ceremonies. Class 2 consists of bingo, pull tabs, lotto, punch cards, and other games authorized by state law where players compete against each other as opposed to the house. Class 3 entails the more lucrative games, including casino-style gambling (e.g., blackjack, roulette, and craps), Keno, pari-mutuel racing, and jai alai where the players compete against the house. These games require a tribal ordinance, approved by the National Indian Gaming Commission, and a negotiated compact with the host state. Such compacts normally include provisions like division of regulatory authority between the two polities, establishment of terms of criminal jurisdiction and allocating of division of labor, payments to the state to cover enforcement or oversight costs, procedural remedies if there is a breach of the compact, and regulations for the operation of gaming, including licensing.

States may not insist that the compact contain a tax, charge, or other assessment. The compacting process is designed to balance the interests of the state (concerns over alleged crime, traffic congestion, and social ills generated by gaming) with the economic (pursuit of self-sufficiency) and political (respect of tribal sovereignty) interests of the tribe.

Indian gaming is solely the province of the sovereign tribal government, as revenues for gaming may only be used to fund tribal government operations, provide for the general welfare of the tribal government and its members, promote tribal economic development, or help the operation and funding of local governments. Tribal governments may also use some of the money to make charitable donations.

As a result of gaming revenue, some Native nations, for the first time since the late nineteenth century, have been able to attain a measure of economic self-determination, improve their relationships with local and state governments, and increase their political clout. Conversely, Indian gaming has also unleashed a powerful backlash from Nevada and New Jersey gaming operations, created tension between some tribes and state governments resulting in litigation, and, for our purposes, exacerbated tensions within and between tribes over concern about the cultural impact of gaming on tribal communities, particularly as this impacts a tribe's membership decisions.

Since two of the broad goals of the IGRA were to strengthen the tribal government through economic development and to support the general welfare of the tribe "and its members," Native nations must decide whether they are going to use the revenue generated to rebuild and enhance their nation's infrastructure (schools, cultural programs, health care facilities, etc.) or whether they are going to distribute the gaming revenue to tribal members on a per capita basis via a Tribal Revenue Allocation Plan (RAP)—or if they are going to have a hybrid arrangement that does both.[5]

Native governments that decide to distribute per capita payments must have a RAP plan. These plans must be approved by the Department of the Interior. To secure RAP approval "a tribe must demonstrate an ability to meet the needs of its members in the manner prescribed by the Indian Gaming Regulatory Act." Since 1993, 130 tribal governments have received federal approval to make per capita distributions of some portion of their gaming revenue.[6]

For instance, the Ho-Chunk Nation of Wisconsin had its RAP approved in 1996. For fiscal year 2005, of the revenues spent on general welfare, 71 percent was distributed by per caps, 15 percent went to education, health, labor, and general tribal assistance, and 14 percent was used for health insurance.[7]

There is still a lack of social science research on the social, economic, political, and cultural impact of per capita distribution payments among the 130 Native nations that have established such plans.[8] Some research suggests that per capita distribution produces tangible and positive economic growth, particularly for smaller gaming tribes that are "in a more advantageous position compared to larger nations."[9] One 2010 study involving the Eastern Band of Cherokee concluded that children in households that receive even a modest sum of $4,000 a year through per cap distribution plans have higher levels of education and a lower incidence of criminality for minor offenses.[10] Other research suggests that such payments have negative repercussions, including serving as a disincentive for those receiving substantial payments to continue their education.[11] Another possible problem, and one our data support for some Native nations, is that "reducing the size of the tribal population can potentially benefit existing tribal members if there are per capita distributions of gaming revenues."[12]

This is particularly evident in California where per capita plans sometimes promote membership decisions that culminate in disenrollments of otherwise qualified members because tribal officials want to limit the number of people who receive a portion of the money and thereby increase the size of each portion. When we scrutinize the number of tribal nations that have or are in the process of disenrolling or banishing—as seen in tables 5.1, 5.2, and 5.3—an interesting fact emerges: table 5.1 indicates that of the more than forty Native nations outside California that are dismembering their citizens, at least fifteen have instituted a RAP. Table 5.3, in contrast, shows that of the twenty-seven Native peoples in California practicing dismemberment, twenty-one have a RAP in place, a much more robust figure than in the rest of the country.

While the overall amount of revenue generated from Native gambling enterprises is significant—$28.5 billion in 2015—the amount earned by the over two hundred Native nations varies widely: from the enormous sums generated by tribes like the Mashantucket Pequot of Connecticut, the Shakopee Mdewakanton Sioux of Minnesota, and the San Manuel Band of Mission Indians in Southern California, to the many other gaming operations that produce much less revenue for the tribes.

Tribal governments are not required to publicly reveal their earnings, so it is difficult to ascertain precisely how much revenue is generated from nation to nation. What we do know is that, as in real estate, location matters a great deal. In other words, those Native nations with gaming operations located near large urban areas tend to be much better off economically than those situated in rural areas. California's population of nearly thirty-eight million, easily the largest of any state, means that in general more Native peoples in that state happen to be located near a sizable urban population, save for some of the communities in northern California.

In California, the 109 federally recognized tribes have memberships ranging from as little as five members to nearly five thousand, and depending on their geographic proximity to San Diego, Los Angeles, Fresno, San Francisco, or Sacramento, the nineteen communities with RAPs have per caps that range from several hundred dollars a year to $20,000 per month. A number of those who have been disenrolled in these communities assert that per caps were chief factors in their dismemberment.

The March 29, 2013, episode of the radio program *This American Life* featured a discussion about group membership and identity. One of the segments focused on the Chukchansi Tribe of California, which has disenrolled more of its citizens since 2003 than any other tribal nation. Several former citizens testified to how money and per capita payments directly affected their lives and their families. Here are excerpts from that segment:

DAVID FERRY *(broadcaster)*: The math is simple. If they [the tribal nation] have fewer people in the tribe, each person gets more of the sweet sound of cha-ching—more profit from the casino. Right now each Chukchansi only gets a few hundred dollars a month in casino profits. A tribal member named Nicki Livingston told me that when her friend Nancy was kicked out a few months ago, she could see it in her payment check.

NICKI LIVINGSTON: We got a raise on our per capita check after she got disenrolled.

DAVID FERRY: You got more money per month after your close friend was disenrolled from the tribe?

NICKI LIVINGSTON: Yeah. Me and my sister, my two older brothers and myself, we were together when we heard that news. And we saw it . . . in our bank statements and all three of us cried. It's done off the skin of someone's back.

DAVID FERRY: She says the checks were around $280 per month before Nancy and several dozen other people were kicked out. She says it jumped to about $380 a month after. There's another tribe just down the road from Chukchansi, and it has paid tens of thousands of dollars a month to each member. And that's because their tribe only has around seventy-five people. Chukchansi officials deny that disenrollment has anything to do with casino money. They say all they're doing is correcting the membership rolls. . . . But

Reggie Lewis, the tribal chairman who refused to step down when he was voted out of office, said to me, sure, money has something to do with disenrollments, but why shouldn't it?

REGGIE LEWIS *(former chair of Chukchansi)*: We don't have much to share. We've got tribal members who are living in gutted-out trailers with no sanitary facilities, without power. And then we have people who are trying to take advantage of being a tribal member when they're not entitled to be in.

Another Chukchansi disenrollee, Cathy Corey, pointed out in an interview that her nation did not have per caps prior to disenrolling six hundred citizens in 2006 and 2007.[13] Immediately following those disenrollments, when the tribe had been reduced by over one-third, it submitted a RAP to the Bureau of Indian Affairs (BIA) to institute per capita payments under the then chair Dustin Graham in late 2007; payments began shortly thereafter. Corey stated that she believed the tribe waited to start per caps until a significant number of members had been disenrolled, not only so that fewer would be required to receive them but also in order to prevent those being disenrolled from having enough funds to hire attorneys, travel to hearings, and so on, and to therefore be more easily disenrolled. And she reiterated and confirmed what had been revealed on the *This American Life* program: that the per cap payments to nondisenrolled Chukchansi did, indeed, increase when additional people were disenrolled in 2010 and 2012. Of course, the tribal council's presumed plan was dramatically derailed when federal officials ordered the Chukchansi casino closed in October 2014 after an armed showdown between vying tribal factions threatened public safety. The casino eventually reopened in January 2016.

Insufficient data and tribal privacy concerns prevents a detailed and accurate analysis of those tribal governments with RAPs that are engaging in dismemberment proceedings. Suffice it to say, this is a dimension that warrants close scrutiny. All the more because a 2015 report by the U.S. General Accounting Office shows that the National Indian Gaming Commission (NIGC), which is statutorily required to oversee RAP programs, has not taken any enforcement action for per capita violations since 2010.[14] Under the IGRA there are clear rules on who can share in per capita payments. Section 290.14 of title 25 states: "(b) If the tribal revenue allocation plan calls for distributing per capita payments to an identified group of members rather than to all members, you [the tribe] must justify limiting this payment to the identified group members. You must make sure that: (1) the distinction between members eligible to receive payments and members ineligible to receive payments is reasonable and not arbitrary; (2) the distinction does not discriminate or otherwise violate the Indian Civil Rights Act; and (3) the justification complies with applicable tribal law." Despite the clarity of this language, the NIGC has failed to fulfill its statutory obligations and violations in per cap distribution have led to gross membership terminations in several Native nations.[15]

IDEAS ON WHAT MIGHT BE DONE
TO ADDRESS DISMEMBERMENT

Since the explosion of disenrollments and banishments in the early 1990s, various proposals have been suggested, and a few already implemented by enterprising tribal governments, to address these attacks on the sovereign bodies of Native nations and the individual sovereign rights of those expelled or politically terminated. One way dismemberment has been addressed is through constitutional revisions wherein tribal peoples emphatically declare they will not disenfranchise members or will do so only with great reluctance. For example, the Passamaquoddy Tribe declared in its 1990 constitution that "notwithstanding any provision of this Constitution, the government of the Pleasant Point Reservation shall have no power of banishment over tribal members."

In 2013 the Federated Tribe of Graton Rancheria amended its constitution in advance of opening its casino and, while not completely disavowing disenrollment, did establish provisions that strictly limit that possibility. Citizenship can be terminated if an individual's enrollment resulted from fraud or error but, importantly, there is a three-year statute of limitations. Membership can also be terminated for dual enrollment or voluntary relinquishment. Another significant protection is that loss of citizenship is applicable only to the person in question; his or her descendants remain either citizens or eligible for citizenship. A final, crucial protection aimed at thwarting political power shifts is that the tribe's laws governing citizenship can only be amended by a two-thirds vote of the general council, which consists of all adult members of the eight-hundred-member nation.

Most recently, in 2015, the citizens of the Spokane Tribe of Washington State voted to amend their constitution by declaring that "except in instances where a citizen transfers enrollment to another Tribe, no Spokane Tribal law shall operate to strip citizenship from any person who has previously been recognized to possess citizenship." The vote was very close—369 to 268—but by constitutionally incorporating this protection of citizenship it at least prevents subsequent tribal councils or enrollment committees (unless another nationwide referendum is held) from arbitrarily acting to dismember citizens.

Another way Native nations have addressed dismemberment is by enacting statutory changes, via resolutions or ordinances that provide explicit to process safeguards. For example, the Grand Portage Band of Chippewa, who live in northern Minnesota, typify an Indigenous nation that has wrestled mightily with this issue and has arrived at a decision—largely because of rising crime and social disruptions by a small segment of the population—to formally add a new title on "exclusion" to their legal code. The nation's twelve-page law is one of the most detailed exclusion ordinances of any Native nation. It explains why the law became a necessity; describes who may be removed, the extent of the exclusion, and the reasons for expulsion; and outlines the procedural process for the banished individual and for enforcement.

The preamble to the law declares that "in order to properly secure the peace, health, safety, and welfare of the residents of and visitors to the band's territory, it is necessary to establish procedures and standards for the removal and exclusion from the lands subject to the territory authority of the band those persons whose conduct or associations become intolerable to the Community and threaten the peace, health, safety and welfare of the band."[16] The preamble states that the purpose of the law is to provide "standard criteria to review and identify persons who may pose such threats and to establish standards of removal and exclusion which are appropriate and proportionate to the threat posed by such persons."[17] The new law provides due process protections to any person facing expulsion.

Section 5202, titled "Grounds for Exclusion," specifies eighteen offenses that can be grounds for exclusion, including but not limited to the following: disruption of any religious ceremony or cultural events; "personal, impertinent, slanderous, or profane remarks" to tribal council members; gang activity; sale or distribution of illegal drugs; "mining, prospecting, or cutting timber" without tribal authorization; threatening or intimidating conduct or words to band members or others; child molestation; sexual abuse; homicide; rape; and designation as a level three sex offender.[18]

Importantly, explicit due process stipulations are spelled out, including written notice and a hearing that allow the individual to address the council, call witnesses, present evidence, and question and challenge the witnesses who are testifying against the person. Expelled individuals have the right to request that the council rescind or modify the expulsion order "once every year after it has been entered." The order may then be changed or terminated only if the excluded person can demonstrate "that the act or omission which constituted the grounds for the exclusion has been resolved, corrected, or is no longer an issue; or that the person no longer poses a threat to the citizens or residents of the band's territory."

According to Norman W. Deschampe, the tribal chairman, relative peace and quiet were restored once the government banished a mother, two mature sons, and a family friend who had been involved in a tribal fracas. This was the culminating event that had compelled the tribe to craft its exclusion law in the first place.[19]

We turn now to other ideas that commentators and dismembered individuals or their allies have proposed to address political and economic dismemberments that are deemed patently unfair, specious, arbitrary, capricious, and violative of due process rights.

One suggestion is the development of an independent, possibly intertribal, appellate body, an Indian Country Supreme Court, that would have the power to fairly and impartially review a tribal government's enrollment decisions. In theory, a tribal court would be the logical institution since presumably courts provide an unbiased assessment of a particular conflict. Unfortunately, not every tribe has a court system and not every tribal court system is sufficiently independent of the political branches it operates with, since sufficient separation of powers and checks and balances continues to be an issue for some Native governments.

On a related note, John Collier's original draft bill, that would have culminated in 1934 with enactment of the Indian Reorganization Act, contained a title calling for the creation of a dual system of tribal courts.[20] The first level would have consisted of local courts staffed by Native individuals. They would have been tasked with handling community-level issues as they arose. The second level would have been the creation of a national Court of Indian Affairs that would be staffed by seven presidentially appointed judges, subject to Senate ratification.

This would have been a permanent court that would have rotated to different circuits around Indian Country. This section of the bill was jettisoned early in the congressional hearing process, as it lacked the necessary support. Yet the idea and the need for a permanent court whose judges would acquire detailed knowledge about the intricacies of federal Indian law, treaties, land issues, and so on is one that Vine Deloria Jr. was keen on, as discussed in his book with Clifford Lytle, *The Nations Within*. "The fact remains," said Deloria and Lytle, "that this court would provide a focus to litigation dealing with Indian issues and attempt to bring a consistent source of expert knowledge to the solution of issues affecting Indians."[21]

In keeping with the intertribal theme, Wenona Singel proposed the negotiation of an intertribal treaty in 2012 that might prove a more effective mechanism to deal with human rights violations in Indian Country.[22] The idea for such a mechanism is not new, of course. Throughout history there have been several intertribal organs created or actively discussed. There have been regional structures like the confederated governing arrangement established by the Haudenosaunee (Six Nations) who created the Gayanashagowa, or the Great Law of Peace.[23]

In the Southwest, nineteen of the Pueblo peoples created the All Indian Pueblo Council in 1598 that enabled them to deal intergovernmentally with the Spanish, Mexican, and later the U.S. federal and state governments.[24] And in 1870, fifteen Native nations centered in what became known as Oklahoma organized an intertribal charter known as the Okmulgee Constitution.[25] Although it was never ratified by all the tribal nations, it established a diplomatic precedent that would later reemerge in 1906 with the writing of a constitution for numerous tribes in the same territory who set out to create an Indigenous state that would have joined the U.S. It was to be called Sequoyah.[26]

Historically, Native nations had long engaged in diplomatic affairs with one another, and they vigorously carried on the tradition when the European states began to arrive.[27] While many Native peoples agreed to surrender the right to negotiate treaties with other foreign powers as part of their negotiations with the United States, they never surrendered the right to negotiate treaties with other Native nations.[28] Deloria and DeMallie, for example, in their important treaty study remarked:

> Intertribal treaties and agreements represent a wide variety of situations. Sometimes the Indians resolved boundary disputes; at other times they agreed to share hunting and fishing areas. Still other occasions called for sharing annuities or guaranteeing that whites would not be molested in their lands. . . . Intertribal treaties and agreements still have considerable importance. No case law has ever suggested that any Indian nation surrendered the right power to make treaties with another Indian nation, even though the federal government itself insisted that treaties with Indians could no longer be made by the United States. In these days of consortiums and combinations of tribes for various purposes, tribal councils should

seriously consider the feasibility of conducting their own form of diplomacy
with other Indian nations.

One of the most frequently cited suggestions is that there needs to be an
amendment to the Indian Civil Rights Act (ICRA) and the largely hollow habeas corpus remedy it contains that would allow dismembered individuals to
sue the offending tribe in federal court. This could be achieved by waving
tribal sovereign immunity if the tribal government failed to fully comply with
the ICRA.[29] This idea was first championed by Senator Orrin Hatch in 1989.
But in 2005 it was renewed by members of a newly formed California-based
organization, the American Indian Rights and Resources Organization
(AIRRO), that was established to contest the increasing number of tribal
disenrollments.

In this vein, Laura Wass, a California Native activist who has long championed the disenfranchised in Indian Country, drafted a bill titled "The American Indian Legacy Act," which she sought to have introduced in Congress, that
would "reaffirm the inherent rights of American Indian individuals within
their historical groups/clans/tribes." This bill (see the appendix in this vol-
ume) calls for Congress to take a much more active role in Indian Country
when Native governments have unfairly violated the rights of bona fide tribal
members. The bill declares that if a Native government violates the civil rights
of tribal members by arbitrarily disenrolling them, that those governments
"will be subject to the suspension of their Federal Recognition status" unless
they correct their decision on disenrollment. Tribal officials will be given one
year to make the corrections. If they fail to reinstate all proven tribal members,
they will be terminated indefinitely.

While many Native governments would view such a law or amendment as
a deep intrusion to their inherent political authority over membership matters,
some believe that such measures are required because of the federal trust
relationship that extends not only to protect tribal governments but also to
protect the political and property rights of every tribal member as well.[30]

Native peoples have made significant strides in the last several decades in
an effort to apprise the international community and international bodies of
governance, like the United Nations, of their unique political, cultural, and
territorial status and to secure greater protections of their rights as self-determined peoples.[31] These efforts culminated in 2007 with enactment of the
United Nations Declaration on the Rights of Indigenous Peoples. While not an
internationally binding treaty, the declaration is an important document that

acknowledges the self-determined character of Indigenous peoples around the world and affirms their inherent rights to cultural autonomy, respect for their remaining territories, and support for treaty rights.

Interestingly, the United States, which hosts the United Nations, was the last signatory to this historic measure. When the Obama administration finally signed the declaration in 2010, some disenrollees hoped that the accord's language would be useful in their efforts to regain their Native citizenship. Thus far it has proven an ineffectual tool, but hope remains that it might one day yield benefits to dismembered individuals.

Another potential internal remedy that might help those who have been disenrolled or banished circles back to one of the important historical mechanisms used by tribal nations to augment their membership: adoption. If each Native nation that is not disenrolling or banishing would, at a minimum, adopt ten Indigenous refugees of the disenrollment epidemic, those nationless individuals who now feel their only avenues for help are within the federal or state legal system would have Native support and recognition of their humanity. Once Indian Country steps up to help their own, without casting blame against the nations who used their authority to purge their tribal rolls, the calls for federal or state intervention would likely be greatly diminished. Such unified action would protect the lives and liberties of those dismembered and the sovereign authority of all Native nations.

As leadership and political winds are ever changing, it is even possible that, with time, many disenrollees may find long-term remedies to their situations at home. There are a few examples where as soon as one set of tribal officials was voted out of office, disenrolled citizens were reinstated back into the community. In one case involving the Snoqualmie people of Washington, a former banished citizen, Carolyn Lubenau, was first readmitted and then elected as chairwoman of her nation.

If the idea of adopting ten persons seems overly ambitious, then tribal nations might at least take the step of adopting, at a minimum, one elder and one child. While this would not solve the problem of all those who have been outcast, it would at least give those most vulnerable some modicum of safety, stability, and dignity. Most importantly, they would retain their identities as Indigenous persons.

There are many examples of Natives who were born to one Indigenous community but who later joined a different one. In the 1840s, the Eastern Shoshone chief, Washakie, left Umatilla lands while an adolescent and was assimilated into the Eastern Shoshone, eventually becoming one of their most famous leaders. Richard Throssel, an early twentieth-century photographer of Crow life, was born in Washington and of Canadian Cree, Scottish, and English ancestry. He and his family moved into Crow country in 1902 and were adopted by tribal council action in 1906. As new Crow adoptees, the Throssel family also received land allotments, a generous gesture on the part of the Crow council, through a formal process that was approved by the commissioner of Indian affairs and the secretary of the interior in 1908.

At least 160 tribal constitutions contain clauses recognizing adoption as one of the chief processes available to expand tribal rolls; nearly two hundred others have the ability to incorporate such a clause into their organic charters. Those with more traditional types of governing structures and their governments may have adoption procedures as well. All sovereign nations certainly have the authority to authorize such a process. Ironically, the Nooksack Nation, one of the nations seeking to disenroll over three hundred of its citizens, is currently led by an adoptee, who, along with the council, recently oversaw an amendment to their tribe's constitution that suspends future adoptions. Not surprisingly, it does not go so far as to nullify existing adoptees' status.

Without delving into detail on constitutions, adoption provisions generally provide for the physical and economic incorporation of new members. We suggest that these be expanded to include a separate category of adoption of disenrollees or those formally exiled from other nations. Those willing to extend citizenship could initially do so in a limited way so that the dismembered were simply able to retain their basic social and health benefits that come to all federally recognized tribal citizens through the BIA or other federal agencies. There would be no immediate guarantee of land, per capita payments, housing, or other substantial economic benefits provided by the tribal government unless the tribes were so inclined. No one would be forced to leave their families or relocate from their home country to retain their identities.

Since a majority of tribal constitutions were drafted under the auspices of the 1934 Indian Reorganization Act (IRA), many of them contain language that declares that the tribal council has the authority to enact ordinances for the "adoption of new members," but that such procedures, like the Throssel family's adoption into the Crow nation, are "subject to approval by the Secretary of the Interior." While secretarial review is patently paternalistic, in this case it is an important provision as it reminds federal officials that they have a trust and, in many cases, a treaty obligation to provide a measure of protection to Indigenous citizens, who also happen to be U.S. citizens.

Organizations like the Native American Rights Fund and the National Congress of American Indians might provide guidance for those Native nations with existing adoption procedures or those who might wish to create adoption ordinances to help facilitate outreach to disenrolled tribal refugees who are suffering profound psychic, economic, and political losses due to their now tribeless status.

While Native peoples no longer live in a time where they find it easy, or even wise, to fully embrace outsiders into their communities, it is imperative that they protect those who have been or may become dismembered. Native nations can, at the very least, provide them with a sense of refuge and a basic set of rights that political refugees the world over receive when they seek asylum, like those fleeing Syria, Afghanistan, Iraq, and certain African states after having been forced out of their own territory.

Adoptions are one kind of medicine that might help heal, protect, and make Native communities whole again by harkening back to their ancestors' strategies to strengthen and augment their communities. By embracing those who have been disenrolled or banished, Native peoples would be protecting their own sovereign ability to make their own decisions, which might forestall the federal government from stepping in and imposing its will.

Two other options may be available to Native disenrollees who seek to restore, at the very least, their federally recognized status as Natives, if not their tribally derived citizenship. A provision in the IRA of 1934 provides the first potential route. Section 19 provides three definitions of the term *Indian*. First, it includes "all persons of Indian descent who are members of any recognized Indian tribe now under Federal jurisdiction." Second, it applies to all individuals who are descendants of those members who, as of June 1, 1934, reside within a given reservation's borders. And third, and of special importance for our purposes, the term includes "all other persons of one-half or more Indian blood."

While the IRA has been amended several times since 1934, the definition of *Indian* has not changed appreciably. In title 25 of the Code of Federal Regulations (2011), the term is defined in two ways: "all persons who are members of those tribes listed or eligible to be listed . . . as recognized by and receiving services from the BIA" . . . and "any person not a member of one of the listed tribes . . . who possess at least one-half degree of Indian blood."[32]

Current disenrollees who believe they meet the scientifically and politically problematic one-half blood quantum threshold might consider invoking this provision as a way of forcing the Department of the Interior and the BIA to meet their political and economic, if not their cultural, needs. Such a challenge might also allow an assault on the very notion of blood quantum itself—a phrase of dubious scientific and social credibility.

The second process that might prove useful also stems from the IRA period. The IRA did not initially apply to most Native nations in Oklahoma (or Alaska). But tribal complaints compelled Congress to enact a law two years later, the Oklahoma Indian Welfare Act (OIWA), which extended the principles of the act to the Native peoples in Oklahoma, if they voted for it. The act allowed recognized tribal nations or bands to organize and to adopt constitutions and bylaws if they so desired.

Article 4 of the OIWA laid out an organizational path that a group of Native disenrollees might be able to follow to meet their needs and provide for a restoration of federal services and benefits. It declares that ten or more Indians "who reside within the state of Oklahoma in convenient proximity to each other may receive from the Secretary of the Interior a charter as a local cooperative association for any one or more of the following purposes: credit administration, production, marketing, consumers' protection, or land management."

By organizing thus, the culturally and politically related group of disenrollees, living in "convenient proximity," of course, would be able to avoid the rigorous and highly politicized federal acknowledgment process since they would not be pursuing recognition as a tribe, but would instead be asserting their right to organize as an economic or political entity in order to receive needed benefits and rights.

Neither of these two paths is ideal, but until and unless Native governing officials return to the values that once precluded such egregious violations of their citizens' own identities, and until and unless Congress or the courts step in and provide a fair process that disenrollees can participate in to have their grievances heard, it behooves disenrollees, the Department of the Interior, and the federal government to consider alternative arrangements to support the inherent civil rights of these put-upon individuals.

The role of the secretary of the interior and, by extension, Congress, must be clarified in regards to tribal dismemberment decisions. As established in previous chapters, federal officials hold two seemingly irreconcilable positions on enrollment and/or disenrollment. On the one hand, federal courts—and tribal courts, obviously—have, as Felix Cohen pointed out, consistently recognized that "in the absence of express legislation by Congress to the contrary, an Indian tribe has complete authority to determine all questions of its membership."[33]

On the other hand, Congress and the secretary of the interior have long claimed and acted upon the premise that they possess plenary—that is, absolute—power over the broad field of tribal membership, especially when property rights are concerned, be they allotments or the distribution of tribal funds. In fact, Cohen, writing in 1942, noted in his important *Handbook of Federal Indian Law* that "property rights attached to membership are largely in the control of the Secretary of the Interior rather than the tribe itself."[34] And despite the litany of legislation and litigation since then, including the premier *Santa Clara* (1978) decision, that broad statement about property has not been challenged or minimized.

Presently, both Congress and the secretary of the interior frequently turn a deaf ear to the complaints and concerns of Native individuals facing dismemberment, claiming that they have no authority to intervene in such membership conflicts. The reasons given are fourfold: (1) there must be explicit tribal constitutional language authorizing such involvement, (2) they respect tribal sovereignty, (3) they cite the *Santa Clara* precedent, or (4) congressional policy supports the doctrine of tribal self-determination.

But every bona fide tribal citizen has an inherent property status in their personhood, while also holding and exercising a set of constitutional and civil rights as citizens of their tribal nation, the state they live in, and in the United States. Such rights, therefore, should be protected out of respect for the treaty relationship, the trust relationship, and the citizenship standing of the members facing termination.

The secretary of the interior should not be able to invoke the office's discretionary power to cherry pick which tribal dismemberment cases that office will decide to intervene in. The secretary, acting for the president, must carry out Congress's and the president's trust and treaty obligations in such conflicts if for no other reason that the sheer diversity of membership issues across Indian Country necessitates a consistent, unequivocal force that will ensure that complete due process protections are provided to every individual facing dismemberment. The only exception would be if it is clear that tribal enrollment was obtained fraudulently, with such alleged fraud having to be verified by an independent authority. As one federal court declared in a case involving Seminole Freedmen in 2002: "The Secretary of the Interior is charged not only with the duty to protect the rights of the tribe, but also the rights of individual member. And the duty to protect these rights is the same whether the infringement is by non-members or by members of the tribe."[35]

And Congress, which has a treaty and trust relationship with all Native nations, should respond when tribal governments engage in suicidal sovereignty by dismembering significant swaths of their populations. Under modern law, Native nations that pursued and attained federal recognition, and those, especially in California, that were terminated by federal decree in the 1950s and later restored to recognized status, were required to first identify members and then to create verifiable rolls of those incorporated into the nation. Thus, there was a clear incentive to incorporate and enroll as many members as possible in order to convince the Department of the Interior and Congress of their bona fides as an established community.

In a number of cases, however, particularly for rerecognized tribal nations, once significant revenue was later generated—say, via gambling operations or claims funds—tribes that had actively recruited members prior to recognition sometimes began to adopt dismemberment policies to reduce their enrollment numbers. This was done as a way to winnow out dissident voices and/or to enlarge the per capita distribution amount for remaining members. Rarely has Congress or the Department of the Interior stepped in to stop this carnage, quite possibly because it reduces both the amount of federal expenditures that are doled out to Native nations and the amount that tribal governments have to dole out to their own citizens. This incestuous process pits both the federal and tribal governments against the individual members facing dismemberment, a situation fundamentally at odds with the kinship and democratic traditions of most Native societies and the democratic values of the United States, as well as the treaty and trust relationship of the federal government to tribal nations.

Disenrollment and banishment of otherwise legitimate tribal citizens is a fundamental affront to the human rights of those being politically terminated or removed, and a violation of long-standing Indigenous and Western democratic traditions. As Joseph Hamilton, chairman of the Ramona Band of Cahuilla Indians, put it in 2015 when he emphatically came out against the practice, "disenrollment is common, in part because of big gaming revenues and internal power struggles. It is also a symptom of the breakdown of traditional tribal power structures. Simply put, some tribal leaders listen to lawyers instead of elders."[36]

Our analysis leads us to conclude that both nonpolitically motivated and politically motivated dismemberment actions primarily serve to expand the coffers of those lawyers, consultants, enrollment auditors, and other organizations that benefit from initiating and then perpetuating enrollment squabbles. They profoundly diminish the life circumstances and "rights bearing capacity of those who are targeted."[37] When Native nations engage in actions that are tantamount to suicidal sovereignty, their institutional and personal behavior represent not enrollment policy clarification but profound enrollment failure.

Beginning in the late nineteenth century, Australian officials aimed to deliberately eradicate the cultural identities and destroy the family networks of Aboriginal peoples by kidnapping children and sending them to be raised away from their families and traditions. This genocidal policy, which came to be known as the "Stolen Generations," lasted well into the 1960s, causing horrific multigenerational damage and suffering.

Those Native nations in North America that are now or have been engaged in the destruction of Native families through dismemberment policies are creating what we would term the "Exiled Generations."[38] One Indigenous national health organization, the Association of American Indian Physicians, representing over four hundred Native doctors, entered the fray in October 2015 and unanimously adopted a resolution imploring Native governments to reconsider their decisions on disenrolling members (and urging them to reenroll those already disenrolled) because of the devastating emotional, physical, cultural, and mental health problems associated with being cast out. One Native physician, Dr. Dale Walker, succinctly noted that "the critical issues concerning tribal disenrollment are the psychiatric implications and other medical issues that affect the morbidity and mortality of all members." Walker went on to say that "it is important to note that not just current families are affected but families of future generations as well."[39]

Native governments must be about strengthening and emboldening each and every member of their respective nations, especially the youngest of their citizens, not exiling them. We encourage Native officials to remember and act on our shared legacies of inclusion, respect, and humanity. Otherwise, as Gene Sloan (the disenrolled former chairman of the Cahto Tribe) put it in an interview in 2015: "What the federal government couldn't accomplish in the 1800s [the eradication of Native peoples], we're now doing to ourselves. We've got to stop this."[40]

APPENDIX

THE AMERICAN INDIAN LEGACY ACT OF 2016 (DRAFT)

An Act

To reaffirm the inherent birth rights of American Indian
individuals within their historical groups/bands/tribes

Be it enacted by the Senate and House of Representatives
of the United States of America in Congress assembled,

Section 1: Definitions of the Recognition Structure of Sovereign Indian Tribes

1) Findings—The Congress finds as follows:
   a. There exist 567 federally recognized Tribes in the United States;
   b. The act of federal recognition is granted by Congress after an Indian group/band/tribe has presented data showing a continuing historical relationship between Indian individuals through cultural patterns such as language, kinship, spiritual beliefs and practices, marriages, and political relationships with non-Indian political organizations and the federal government;
   c. The Congress created a system establishing Tribal federal recognition of the Tribes by which membership rolls were created and implemented within the Tribes through the directions of the Office of the Secretary of the Interior given to the Bureau of Indian Affairs;
   d. The act of federal recognition that is bestowed upon an Indian Tribe is granted by Congress in an effort to empower Tribes with the responsibility of self-determination for all persons of their race including the descendants of those persons;
   e. Tribes granted federal recognition have shown their willingness and desire for the responsibility of self-determination;
   f. Tribal governments of federally recognized Tribes have been given the ability to perform necessary governmental duties for the express

purpose of oversight of the economic, social and structural well-being of their race, which encompasses all persons of that race;

g. All federally recognized Tribal governments agreed to fulfill their governmental obligations to the members of their race;

2) Further—The Congress acknowledges the chronological relationship between the United States Government and the federally recognized Indians within the boundaries of the United States:

a. The Congress acknowledges historically allocating federal funds for the purpose of the extermination of the American Indian historically leading to the final extinction of many American Indian tribes and;

b. The Congress acknowledges devising a system implemented by the Secretary of the Interior, implemented through the Bureau of Indian Affairs, by which homeless and/or landless Indians were placed on parcels of government lands collectively after the extermination period without consideration of their individual tribal affiliations, thereby creating newly recognized Indian communities residing on reservations or Rancherias;

c. The Congress acknowledges in giving federal recognition to the Indians placed on government lands, and that Indian Tribes became "wards" of the United States Government which thereby assumed trust responsibility over said Tribes;

d. Furthermore, the United States Government assumed plenary power over the federally recognized Tribes therefore fracturing the Indian Tribes rights of Tribal Sovereignty;

3) Further—The Congress acknowledges the implementation of Congressional Acts following the federal Indian extermination period for the purpose of forcing Indian Tribes to abandon their tribal groups/bands, traditions, and heritage, therefore becoming assimilated for the purpose of ending the trust responsibility of the United States Government:

a. The Congress acknowledges implementing the Indian Removal Act of 1830 to disband individual Indian families from their Tribes;

b. The Congress acknowledges implementing the General Allotment Act of 1887 to disband individual Indian families from their Tribes;

c. The Congress acknowledges implementing the Termination Act of 1953 to disband individual Indian families from their Tribes;

d. The Congress acknowledges implementing the Indian Relocation Act of 1956 to disband individual Indian families from their Tribes;

4) Further—Under House Concurrent Resolution 108; the Termination Act:
  a. The Bureau of Indian Affairs, under the direction of the Secretary of the Interior, was instructed to notify all Indians of the newly created historic groups to seek approval through vote of Termination by the Indian individuals within the groups/bands/tribes, and failed to notify the entirety of said Indian groups;
  b. The tribal groups were Terminated by vote of a selected minority of Indians from said groups under the supervision and direction of the Secretary of the Interior and the Bureau of Indian Affairs;
  c. The Termination Act was later deemed an illegal Act passed by the Congress and the tribes are procedurally being restored to their original status as federally recognized Indian groups/bands/tribes;
  d. The Congress has expressly repudiated the policy of Termination whereby all federally recognized Indian groups/bands/tribes are to be restored into their original status, and all is to be returned to its originality prior to Termination, with only the exception of land exchanges during the Termination era;
  e. Under restoration of Indian groups/bands/tribes previously terminated by Congress, the Bureau of Indian Affairs interfered in the reorganization of tribal groups, ignoring the historical and traditional relationships between individuals of said Indian communities;

Section 2: Necessity and Justification for Congressional Relief

1) The Congress finds as follows:
  a. The Congress finds, through neglect or other actions of the Executive Branch, there are no oversight procedures in place to insure the welfare of individual Indians within the federally recognized Indian groups/bands/tribes;
  b. Federally recognized Indian groups/bands/tribes governments, through the suggestive instructions of the Bureau of Indian Affairs, have written their constitutions' membership criteria to exclude their Indian families who have direct Tribal connections prior to the Termination era if they did not reside on the land prior to termination;
  c. Federally recognized Indian groups/bands/tribes are being arbitrary

and capricious in their selections of new tribal members, enrolling selected individuals while leaving others who may or may not have stronger qualifications for membership without due process;

d. Individual Indians of federally recognized tribes are being denied their heritage, communal relationships, education, housing, medical benefits, and are being forever damaged mentally, emotionally and physically;

e. Federally recognized Indian groups/bands/tribes are disenrolling entire Indian families and their future generations who are fully connected to the tribes through customs, traditions, heritage and blood;

f. Federally recognized Indian groups/bands/tribes are placing illegal "moratoriums" on their enrollment procedures to ensure there is no increase in their tribal membership rolls;

g. Federally recognized Indian groups/bands/tribes have instilled fear and instability in members of their current rolls;

2) The Congress, upon passage of this act, formally declares that citizenship in the tribe is a right that is inherited at birth by American Indians; further;

a. The Congress, upon passage of this act, declares that all federally recognized Indian groups/bands/tribes must accept into membership those persons who are certified by the Bureau of Indian Affairs to be descendants of the same created historic group/band/tribe as members and meet the declared blood quantum criteria, and;

b. Further declares that no individual Indian of said federally recognized Indian group/band/tribe be stripped of their inherent birthright of tribal affiliation through tribal membership, and;

c. The Congress declares that those persons accepted into membership shall enjoy the same privileges, benefits, and services equal to all members of said groups/bands/tribes, and;

d. The Congress declares that each federally recognized Indian group/band/tribe will establish new enrollment criteria which does not allow proven Indian individuals to be denied their right to membership in said group/band/tribe, further;

e. The Congress declares that no federally recognized Indian group/band/tribe may increase their constitution's blood quantum in their membership criteria but may, upon vote of the majority of membership, decrease the blood quantum requirement, and;

    f. The Congress declares that any violation of a federally recognized Indian individual's civil rights as detailed under this act, and any violations of the civil rights of an American Indian as defined under the Indian Civil Rights Act, shall be given remedy jurisdiction of the federal court system, and;

    g. The Congress declares that every federally recognized Indian group/band/tribe shall, within a period of twenty-four months from the passage of this act, form an internal tribal court system through which any and all grievances may be heard and given redress prior to entering the federal court system;

Section 3: The Penalty for Noncompliance and Fraudulent Activities

1) Noncompliance by a federally recognized Indian group/band/tribe: Any federally recognized Indian group/band/tribe that is found to be in violation of this act shall be subject to loss of federal recognition;

    a. The notice: The Department of the Interior shall give notice to any federally recognized Indian group/band/tribe that is determined to be in noncompliance with this law, notifying them of their legal obligations, further;

    b. The group/band/tribe: The Department of the Interior shall give the group/band/tribe thirty days to present why they are not in compliance with the law, and;

    c. The hearing: The group/band/tribe shall have the right to a hearing within the federal court system, where the Secretary of the Interior or his representative must show cause as to why the group/band/tribe is in noncompliance with the law, and;

    d. The finding: If the group/band/tribe is found to be in violation of this law, they will be subject to the suspension of their federal recognition status should they refuse to comply after ninety days from the date of the federal court's finding. The suspension will be in effect for period of twelve months at the end of which time the Secretary of Interior will evaluate the group/band/tribe to determine if they have complied with this law. Should the group/band/tribe remain in noncompliance, they will lose their status of federal recognition everlastingly.

Laura L. Wass, American Indian Movement

INTERVIEWS

173

Allen, W. Ron. Jamestown S'Klallam Tribe. March 2015.

Anderson, Debi. Confederated Tribes of the Grand Ronde Community. May 2015.

Bernando, Erin. Confederated Tribes of the Grand Ronde Community. May 2015.

Brooks, Paul. Lumbee. September 2015.

Campbell, Jeannie. Nooksack. February 2015

Chavis, Francine. Lumbee. September 2015.

Cornsilk, David. Cherokee. May 2016.

Corey, Cathy. Picayune Rancheria of Chukchansi. August 2015.

Dreveskracht, Ryan. Galanda Broadman PLCC. May 2015.

Gladstone, Richard. Nooksack. February 2015.

Locklear, Reena Oxendine. Lumbee. July 2015.

Lubenau, Carolyn. Snoqualmie. May 2015.

Marquez, Deron. San Manuel Band of Serrano Indians. March 2015.

Maslin, Carla Foreman. Redding Rancheria. August 2015.

Maslin, Mark. August 2015.

Rabang, Angel. Nooksack. February 2015.

Rabang, Raenna. Nooksack. February 2015.

Roberts, Michelle. Nooksack. February 2015.

Sloan, Gene. Cahto Tribe of Laytonville Rancheria. August 2015.

Sloan-Langton, Alice. August 2015.

Spilde, Katherine. September 2015.

Vann, Marilyn. Cherokee Freedman. May 2016.

Wass, Laura. Mountain Maidu. August 2015.

Wilkinson, Russell. Confederated Tribes of the Grand Ronde Community. May 2015.

NOTES

NOTES TO INTRODUCTION

1   Vine Deloria Jr., *For This Land: Writings on Religion in America*, ed. James Treat (New York: Routledge Press, 1999), 43.

2   "Apparent" because historical and contemporary tribal case studies caution against simple rational choice utilitarian assumptions in the case of gaming's influence, as Henderson pointed out in 1998, and as our own research shows. Neither gambling revenue alone or civil or criminal violations alone are sufficient reasons to explain all cases of banishment or disenrollment. There tend to be a constellation of factors that push tribal officials to exile their citizens or terminate citizenship.

3   William Garth Snider, "Banishment: The History of Its Use and a Proposal for Its Abolition Under the First Amendment," *New England Journal on Criminal and Civil Confinement* 24 (1998): 460.

4   Thanks to Tom Biolsi for reminding us of this equally vital question.

5   85 F.3d 874 (1996).

6   Stephen L. Pevar, *The Rights of Indians and Tribes*, 4th ed. (New York: Oxford University Press, 2012), 92.

NOTES TO CHAPTER 1

1   "Cheyenne River Sioux Tribal Council Votes to Banish Drug Dealers for Life From Tribe," July 20, 2015, http://nativenewsonline.net/currents/cheyenne-river-sioux-tribal-council-votes-to-banish-drug-dealers-for-life-from-tribe/.

2   Statement of Chief Steve Pego, "Press Release: Banishment," February 26, 2015, www.sagchip.org/news.aspx?newsid=309#.Va63C-d_FOQ.

3   William Garth Snider, "Banishment: The History of Its Use and a Proposal for Its Abolition Under the First Amendment," *New England Journal on Criminal and Civil Confinement* 24 (1998): 476.

4   As quoted in Patrice H. Kunesh, "Banishment as Cultural Justice in Contemporary Tribal Legal Systems," *New Mexico Law Review* 37 (2007): 91.

5   Ibid.

6   Edward M. Peters, "Prison Before the Prison: The Ancient and Medieval Worlds," in *The Oxford History of the Prison: The Practice of Punishment in Western Society*, ed. Norval Morris and David T. Rothman (New York: Oxford University Press, 1995), 11.

7   David J. Reimer, "Exile, Diaspora, and Old Testament Theology," *Scottish Bulletin of Evangelical Theology* 28, no. 1 (Spring 2010): 3.

8   Snider, "Banishment: The History," 460.

9   http://avalon.law.yale.edu/subject_menus/hammenu.asp.

10   Christopher W. Close, "Review of Jason P. Coy's book, *Strangers and Misfits: Banishment,*

Social Control, and Authority in Early Modern Germany," *Law and History Review* 28, *no.
1 (2010):* 253–54.

11   Roger Scruton, *A Dictionary of Political Thought* (New York: Farrar, Straus and Giroux,
     1982), 161.

12   Ibid.

13   Reimer, "Exile," 15.

14   See, for example, Susan Lobo and Kurt Peters, eds. *American Indians and the Urban
     Experience* (Walnut Creek, Calif.: Alta Mira Press, 2001); Terry Straus, ed., *Native
     Chicago,* 2nd ed. (Chicago: Albatross Press, 2002); James B. LaGrand, *Indian Metropo-
     lis: Native America in Chicago, 1945–1975* (Urbana: University of Illinois Press, 2002);
     Reyna K. Ramirez, *Native Hubs: Culture, Community, and Belonging in Silicon Valley
     and Beyond* (Durham, N.C.: Duke University Press, 2007); and Rosalyn R. LaPier and
     David R. M. Beck, *City Indian: Native American Activism in Chicago, 1893–1934* (Lincoln:
     University of Nebraska Press, 2015).

15   Herman Diederik, "Urban and Rural Criminal Justice and Criminality in the Nether-
     lands since the Middle Ages: Some Observations," in *The Civilization of Crime: Violence
     in Town and Courts since the Middle Ages,*" ed. Eric A. Johnson and Eric H. Monkkonen
     (Urbana: University of Illinois Press, 1996), 158.

16   See Gwanda Morgan and Peter Rushton, *Banishment in the Early Atlantic World: Con-
     victs, Rebels, and Slaves* (London: Bloomsbury Publishing, 2013).

17   Nelson G. Karl, "Banishment from the Kingdom of Lake (County)," *Cleveland State Law
     Review* 21 (1972): 140.

18   Snider, "Banishment: The History," 461.

19   Morgan and Rushton, *Banishment in the Early Atlantic World,* 22.

20   Ibid. And see Titus Mooney Merriman, *The Pilgrims, Puritans and Roger Williams Vin-
     dicated: And His Sentence of Banishment Ought to Be Revoked* (Boston: Bradley and
     Woodruff, 1892), reprint ed.

21   Morgan and Rushton, *Banishment in the Early Atlantic World,* 109–12. Nan Goodman's
     Banished: Common Law and the Rhetoric of Social Exclusion in Early New England (Phila-
     delphia: University of Pennsylvania Press, 2012), chap. 4, is also a fascinating read.

22   Morgan and Rushton, *Banishment in the Early Atlantic World,* 112–13.

23   Michael F. Armstrong, "Banishment: Cruel and Unusual Punishment," *University of
     Pennsylvania Law Review* 111 (1963): 760n13.

24   Ibid., 759.

25   4 U.S. 14 (4 Dall. 14) (1800).

26   332 U.S. 388 (1947).

27   74 S. Ct. 737 (1954).

28   74 S. Ct. 822 (1954).

29   356 U.S. 86 (1958).

30   84 S. Ct. 580 (1964).

31   Matthew D. Borrelli, "Banishment: The Constitutional and Public Policy Arguments
     against This Revived Ancient Punishment," *Suffolk University Law Review* 36 (2003): 471.

32   See the constitutions of the following states: Alabama, Arkansas, Georgia, Kansas,
     Maryland, Massachusetts, Nebraska, New Hampshire, North Carolina, Ohio, Okla-
     homa, Tennessee, Texas, Vermont, and Virginia.

33   Snider, "Banishment: The History," 465.

34   See *State v. Collett,* 208 S.E. 2d 472 (Ga., 1974), *Cobb v. State,* 437 So. 2d 1218 (Miss. 1983),
     Flick v. State, 285 S.E. 2d 58 (Ga. Ct. App. 1981).

35 Borrelli, "Banishment: The Constitutional," 479.
36 Ibid., 469.
37 Snider, "Banishment: The History," 471.
38 Armstrong, "Banishment: Cruel and Unusual," 759.
39 Katherine Beckett and Steve Herbert, *Banished: The New Social Control in Urban America* (New York: Oxford University Press, 2009), 8.
40 Ibid., 9.
41 Ibid., 5.
42 Snider, "Banishment: The History," 476.
43 See the discussion of these amendments in Snider, "Banishment: The History," 493; Karl "Banishment from the Kingdom," and Armstrong, "Banishment: Cruel and Unusual," 773.
44 See, *People v. Baum*, 251 Mich. 187 (1930) and *Ex Parte Scarborough*, 173 P.2d 825 (Cal. Ct. App. 1946).
45 Armstrong, "Banishment: Cruel and Unusual," 784.
46 Snider, "Banishment: The History," 495.
47 Armstrong, "Banishment: Cruel and Unusual," 786.
48 Beckett and Herbert, *Banished: New Social Control*, 22.
49 Ibid., 16.
50 Snider, "Banished: The History," 458.
51 231 N.W. 95, 96.
52 Snider, "Banishment: The History," 496.
53 356 U.S. 86, 101 (1958).
54 Lutisone Salevao, *Rule of Law, Legitimate Governance and Development in the Pacific* (Canberra, Australia: Asia Pacific Press, 2005), 132–33.
55 Ibid.
56 www.indianz.com/news/2009/016220.asp; also see Colin Miller, "Banishment from Within and Without: Analyzing Indigenous Sentencing Under International Human Rights Standards," vol. 80 *North Dakota Law Review* (2004): 253–88.
57 Special thanks to John Borrows, a law professor at the University of Victoria, for helping clarify the complicated situation of Indigenous status under Canadian law.
58 See Mary Swift, "Banishing Habeas Jurisdiction: Why Federal Courts Lack Jurisdiction to Hear Tribal Banishment Actions," *Washington Law Review* 86 (2011): 943; and Miller, "Banishment From Within and Without," 255.
59 See Vine Deloria Jr. and Clifford M. Lytle, *American Indians, American Justice* (Austin: University of Texas Press, 1983), 112, and Kunesh, "Banishment as Cultural Justice," 92.
60 See www.law.ou.edu/hist/iroquois.html for one version of the Iroquois Constitution.
61 Ibid.
62 Karl L. Llewellyn and E. A. Hoebel, *The Cheyenne Way: Conflict and Case Law in Primitive Jurisprudence* (Norman: University of Oklahoma Press, 1941), 132.
63 Ibid.
64 Ibid., 133.
65 Ibid., 137–44.
66 Ibid.
67 Ibid., 158.
68 Rennard Strickland, *Fire and the Spirits: Cherokee Law from Clan to Court* (Norman: University of Oklahoma Press, 1975), 25–39.
69 Strickland describes "outlawry" as the placing of "individuals guilty of specified crimes

beyond the protection of the tribe" (*Fire and the Spirits*, 170–71). This was a long-standing procedure utilized by Cherokees before white contact. When an individual was declared an outlaw, that person could be killed by any person within the Cherokee nation. The killer of an outlaw would not be subject to any penalties under tribal law. In the 1830s, Chief John Ross relied on the sanction and applied it to those Cherokees accused of "political crimes" like selling tribal lands or negotiating treaties without the consent of the entire nation.

70   Ibid., 36.

71   Ella Cara Deloria, *Waterlily* (Lincoln: University of Nebraska Press, 1988), 214.

72   Ibid., 216.

73   Correspondence with Christina Black, an Aboriginal scholar who is a senior research fellow at Charles Darwin University in Australia, August 2, 2015.

NOTES TO CHAPTER 2

1   Ten western states, home to nearly 80 percent of the Indigenous population in the United States, have explicit clauses that prohibit those governments from taxing or otherwise interfering in the internal affairs of Native nations without Native and federal consent.

2   We say "constitutionally problematic" because when a branch or agency of the federal government wields virtually absolute—plenary—power over tribal governments or tribal citizens, this, by definition, violates the essence of democratic government, which is based on the concept of limited power. Absolute power is fundamentally irreconcilable with both democratic theory and the doctrine of tribal sovereignty, and yet these concepts coexist in law, policy, and the intergovernmental relationship. Associate Justice Clarence Thomas in his concurring opinion in *U.S. v. Lara* (2004) correctly noted that nothing in the Constitution's treaty or commerce clauses supported the majority's view that the federal government's claim to plenary power over Indian nations is moored in those clauses. Lacking a constitutional basis, and since treaty language also does not empower the federal government to exercise boundless authority over tribal nations, the United States purported claims to superior power over Native nations rests on nothing more than mere verbal assertions, and not on constitutional, treaty, or statutory authority.

3   See the Winnebago Treaty with the United States, signed in 1859. And see Paul Spruhan's article, "A Legal History of Blood Quantum in Federal Indian Law to 1935," *South Dakota Law Review* 51, no. 1 (2006): 1–50, to gain a solid background on this contentious and confusing concept.

4   45 U.S. 567.

5   Ibid., 572–73.

6   Ibid., 573.

7   Ibid.

8   7 Stat., 478.

9   Ibid.

10   4 Stat., 729.

11   162 U.S. 499 (1896).

12   Ibid., 501.

13   164 U.S. 657 (1897).

14   Ibid., 661.

15   168 U.S. 218 (1897).

16   Ibid., 222.

17   Ibid., 223.

18   Eric Reitman, "An Argument for the Practical Abrogation of Federally Recognized Indian Tribes' Sovereign Power over Membership," *Virginia Law Review* 92 (2006): 852.

19   168 U.S. 218, 222 (1897).

20   70 S.W. 8 (Indian Terr., 1902).

21   See Reitman, "An Argument for the Partial Abrogation," 852–53, for a good summary of this case.

22   203 U.S. 76 (1906).

23   *New York Times*, November 6, 1906, 12.

24   203 U.S. 76, 79 (1906).

25   Ibid., 76, 86.

26   U.S. Commissioner of Indian Affairs, *Annual Report* (1907), 104.

27   Ibid.

28   U.S. *Congressional Record*, Senate, vol. 41, 2688.

29   34 Stat. 1220.

30   U.S. Commissioner of Indian Affairs, *Annual Report* (1873), 372.

31   D. S. Otis, *History of the Allotment Policy*, ed. Francis P. Prucha (Norman: University of Oklahoma Press, 1973), 3.

32   24 Stat. 388.

33   Annual Messages of the President (1901), 2047.

34   Felix S. Cohen, *Handbook of Federal Indian Law* (1942; repr., Albuquerque: University of New Mexico Press, 1972), 98.

35   24 Stat. 388–91.

36   48 Stat. 985.

37   Cohen, *Handbook of Federal Indian Law*, 216.

38   Messages of the President (1891), 1698.

39   27 Stat. 612, 645.

40   Angie Debo, *And Still the Waters Run: The Betrayal of the Five Civilized Tribes* (Princeton, N.J.: Princeton University Press, 1940; repr. 1973).

41   U.S. Senate. Report of the Dawes Commission. S. Report No. 377, 53rd Cong., 2nd Sess. (Washington, D.C.: Government Printing Office, 1894), 12.

42   29 Stat. 321, 339.

43   30 Stat. 62, 83.

44   Sen. Doc. No. 190, 1896: 1; See also Choctaw Petition, Sen. Doc. No. 274, 1898.

45   30 Stat. 495.

46   House Report, No. 593 (1898), 1.

47   174 U.S. 445 (1899). This was a consolidated case that also involved the Creek, Choctaw, and Chickasaw.

48   Ibid., 478.

49   Ibid.

50   Ibid., 483–84.

51   Ibid., 483.

52   Ibid., 488.

53   204 U.S. 415 (1907).

54   205 U.S. 80 (1907).

55   235 U.S. 441 (1914).

56 34 Stat. 1015, 1018.

57 34 Stat. 1221.

58 204 U.S. 415, 425.

59 Ibid.

60 Ibid., 424.

61 Cohen, *Handbook of Federal Indian Law*, 100.

62 Ibid.

63 101 U.S. 753 (1879).

64 Ibid., 769.

65 205 U.S. 80, 85.

66 Ibid., 84.

67 Ibid., 85.

68 Cohen, *Handbook of Federal Indian Law*, 135–36.

69 The Osage, because of their enormous oil reserves, have long employed the concept of "headrights," which are defined as "any right of any person to share in any royalties, rents, sales, or bonuses arising from the Osage mineral estate" (98 Stat. 3163).

70 Gabriel S. Galanda and Ryan D. Dreveskracht, "Curing the Tribal Disenrollment Epidemic: In Search of a Remedy," *Arizona Law Review* 57, no. 2 (Summer 2015): 417. The issue of fraudulent enrollment arose again in 2015 when the Osage Nation Membership Department mailed out twenty-seven letters of disenrollment to individuals deemed, by the Attorney General's Office, not Osage and who had allegedly enrolled through fraudulent means. This prompted a conflict between Principal Chief Geoffrey Standing Bear and members of the Osage Congress. Standing Bear said those facing disenrollment were milking the nation of valuable resources that rightfully belonged only to bona fide Osage who could trace their descent back to the 1906 roll. Several Osage legislators, in contrast, were concerned that the process was not being carried out fairly. But by the end of December 2015, the two parties agreed to a compromise law that provides clearer guidelines on membership criteria and the grounds upon which membership can be terminated if fraud is involved. See www.osagenews.org/en/article/2015/12/08/chief-and-osage-congress-odds-over-disenrollment-members/ and www.osagenation-nsn.gov/news-events/news/chief-signs-negotiated-membership-bill.

71 See Dennis McAuliff, *Bloodland: A Family Story of Oil, Greed and Murder on the Osage Reservation* (San Francisco: Council Oak Books, 1999), 226, as quoted in Galanda and Dreveskracht, "Curing the Tribal Disenrollment Epidemic," 417.

72 Kirsty Gover, *Tribal Constitutionalism* (New York: Oxford University Press, 2010), 96n145.

73 211 U.S. 249.

74 U.S. Commissioner of Indian Affairs, *Annual Report* (1907), 108.

75 211 U.S. 249.

76 Ibid., 262.

77 235 U.S. 441 (1914).

78 Ibid., 445–56.

79 Ibid., 448.

80 Ibid., 447.

81 Ibid., 449–50.

82 283 U.S. 753 (1931).

83 Ibid., 763.

84 244 F. Supp. 808 (1965).

85 60 Stat. 968.

86 244 F. Supp. 808, 813.

87 Ibid.

88 Ibid., 814.

NOTES TO CHAPTER 3

1   Cited in Angie Debo, *A History of the Indians of the United States* (Norman: University of Oklahoma Press, 1973), 261.

2   See *Standing Bear v. Crook*, 25 F. Cas. 695 (C.C.D. Neb. 1879), which describes the Ponca's efforts to secure the right to return to lands they had previously been forced to relocate from.

3   See David E. Wilkins, ed., *Documents of Native American Political Development: 1500s to 1933* (New York: Oxford University Press, 2009), which contains a variety of documents showing how tribal nations were modifying their governing structures in the face of colonial intrusions.

4   48 Stat. 984.

5   See Dalia Tsuk Mitchel, *Architect of Justice: Felix S. Cohen and the Founding of American Pluralism* (Ithaca, N.Y.: Cornell University Press, 2007), 199.

6   48 Stat. 984, Sec. 16.

7   Stephen Haycox, "Felix Cohen and the Legacy of the Indian New Deal," *Yale University Library Gazette* 64 (April 1994): 140.

8   Elmer Rusco, *A Fateful Time: The Background and Legislative History of the Indian Reorganization Act* (Reno: University of Nevada Press, 2000), 307n7.

9   See David E. Wilkins, ed., *On the Drafting of Tribal Constitutions* (Norman: University of Oklahoma Press, 2006) for a detailed discussion of Cohen's work in this important field and for a copy of his basic memorandum on constitutional development.

10 Other questions that merit further discussion: what do the structure and content of Native constitutions tell us about how the competing federal and Indigenous impulses toward self-determination or assimilation played out in tribal governance? And are the tribal nations that chose to draft formal written constitutions under federal auspices more or less sovereign than those nations who rejected the IRA or who never adopted constitutions?

11 Solicitor's Opinion, "Powers of Indian Tribes," 55 I.D. 14, October 25, 1934. *Decisions of the Department of the Interior*, ed. George A. Warren, 14–67 (Washington, D.C.: Government Printing Office, 1938).

12 Ibid.

13 Solicitor's Opinion, M. 27810, Dec. 13, 1934. See *Opinions of the Solicitor of the Department of the Interior Relating to Indian Affairs, 1917–1974,* (Washington, D.C.: Government Printing Office, 1974), 1:484–94.

14 Howard Meredith, *Modern American Indian Tribal Government & Politics* (Tsaile, Ariz.: Navajo Community College Press, 1993).

15 While every IRA constitution has language specifying membership requirements, language on how membership can be terminated is sometimes spelled out in separate legislative ordinances dealing with enrollment.

16 See "Laws of the Pamunkey Indian Town, 1886–1887," in Wilkins, ed., *Documents*, 228–31.

17 This constitution was adopted in 1936.

18 Derek Heater, *A Brief History of Citizenship* (New York: New York University Press, 2004), 3.

19 Kirsty Gover, *Tribal Constitutionalism* (New York: Oxford University Press, 2010), 83.

20 Ibid., 85.

21 Ibid., 94.

NOTES TO CHAPTER 4

1 See "Indian Claims," in *The Legal Conscience: Selected Papers of Felix S. Cohen*, ed. Lucy Kramer Cohen (New Haven: Yale University Press, 1960), 265.

2 Russel L. Barsh, "Indian Land Claims Policy in the U.S.," *North Dakota Law Review* 58 (1982): 14.

3 David E. Wilkins, *Hollow Justice* (New Haven, Conn.: Yale University Press, 2014).

4 Joseph G. Jorgensen, *The Sun Dance Religion: Power for the Powerless* (Chicago: University of Chicago Press, 1972), 150.

5 Eric Henderson, "Ancestry and Casino Dollars in the Formation of Tribal Identity," *Race and Ethnic Ancestry Law Journal* 4 (1998): 22.

6 Jorgensen, *Sun Dance*, 151.

7 68 Stat. 868.

8 Eric Henderson, "Ancestry and Casino Dollars," 22.

9 68 Stat. 868, 869.

10 Ibid., 877.

11 Henderson, "Ancestry and Casino Dollars," 22.

12 82 Stat. 73, 77–81.

13 436 U.S. 49.

14 Reitman, "An Argument for the Practical Abrogation of Federally Recognized Indian Tribes' Sovereign Power over Membership," *Virginia Law Review* 92 (2006): 802; quoting from *Quair v. Sisco*, 359 F. Supp. 2nd 948, 977 (2004).

15 Vine Deloria Jr. and David E. Wilkins, *Tribes, Treaties and Constitutional Tribulations* (Austin: University of Texas Press, 1999), 158.

16 Stephen Pevar, *The Rights of Indians and Tribes*, 4th ed. (New York: Oxford University Press, 2012), 247.

17 Gabriel S. Galanda and Ryan D. Dreveskracht, "Curing the Tribal Disenrollment Epidemic: In Search of a Remedy," *University of Arizona Law Review* 57, no. 2 (Summer 2015): 446.

18 Pevar, *The Rights of Indians*, 247.

NOTES TO CHAPTER 5

1 Normally, each table would list sources for each case. But as will be seen in the next two chapters, due to the complexity of many of these cases, tribal governments, the entity responsible for these dismemberments, were not always willing to release data. Neither is the Bureau of Indian Affairs, which claims that researchers must approach tribal officials for the information. As a result, most of the data is drawn from tribal and federal court cases—many of which are analyzed in chapter 6—some tribal legislative data that has been made available for the public, newspaper accounts, social science and law review article, books, and interviews with disenrollees. Virtually all of those sources are identified in the endnotes and the bibliography.

2 Suzianne D. Painter-Thorne, "If You Build It, They Will Come: Preserving Tribal Sovereignty in the Face of Indian Casinos and the New Premium on Tribal Membership," *Lewis & Clark Law Review* 14 (2010): 321.

3 Ibid., 320.

4 Stephanie J. Kim, "Sentencing and Cultural Differences: Banishment of the American Indian Robbers," *John Marshall Law Review* 29 (1995): 239–67.

5 *Time Magazine*, August 1, 1994, 74.

6 William C. Bradford, "Reclaiming Indigenous Legal Autonomy on the Path to Peaceful Coexistence: The Theory, Practice, and Limitations of Tribal Peacemaking in Indian Dispute Resolutions," *North Dakota Law Review* 76 (2000): 593.

7 *The Economist*, August 13, 1994, A29.

8 *State v. Roberts*, 894 P.2d 1340 (Wash. App. Div. I 1995).

9 Bradford, "Reclaiming Indigenous Legal Autonomy," 596.

10 Kim, "Sentencing and Cultural Differences," 262n128.

11 85 F.3d 874 (2nd Cir. 1996).

12 Ibid., 879.

13 Ibid.

14 Ibid., 877–78.

15 Ibid., 879.

16 Ibid., 878.

17 Ibid., 889.

18 Ibid., 895.

19 117 S.Ct. 610 (1996).

20 85 F. 3d. 874, 897.

21 Ibid., 900.

22 Ibid.

23 Ibid.

24 82 Stat. 92.

25 Everett Saucedo, "Curse of the New Buffalo: A Critique of Tribal Sovereignty in the Post-IGRA World," *The Scholar: St. Mary's Law Review on Minority Issues* 3 (2000): 79–80.

26 Ross E. Milloy, "Texas Casino Shutdown as Hope for Reprieve Dies," *New York Times*, February 13, 2002.

27 Saucedo, "Curse of the New Buffalo," 81.

28 Pamela Colloff, "The Blood of the Tigua," *Texas Monthly* (August 1999): 131.

29 Saucedo, "Curse of the New Buffalo," 81.

30 Ibid., 84.

31 Ibid.

32 Ibid., 84–85.

33 Montoya-Lewis and the other plaintiffs in *Shattuck v. Lucero* (No. CIV 04–1287 JB/RHS., D. N.M. August 26, 2005) began to receive notice from the Isleta Pueblo in 2003 that they were "no longer eligible for membership in the Pueblo" because they did not meet the tribe's one-half blood quantum standard. They filed a federal lawsuit seeking a "declaration that [the defendants—tribal officials] have taken cruel, arbitrary, and invidiously discriminatory actions [by] denying Plaintiffs' fundamental rights by disenrolling them, or reducing their official blood quantum." Their lawsuit was unsuccessful and they were disenrolled.

34 Nina Shapiro, "Nooksack River Casino Shuttered Abruptly," *Seattle Times*, December 3, 2015.

35 See the works of Robert F. Heizer, particularly *The Destruction of California's Indians: A Collection of Documents from the Period 1847 to 1865 in Which Are Described Some of the Things That Happened to Some of the Indians of California* (Lincoln: University of Nebraska Press, 1993).

36 Joanne Barker, *Native Acts: Law, Recognition, and Cultural Authenticity* (Durham, N.C.: Duke University Press, 2011): 149–51.

37 No. C. 79–1710 SW.

38 Chris Collins, *Fresno Bee*, March 1, 2009.

39 Marc Benjamin, *Fresno Bee*, April 17, 1998.

40 Lisa Aleman-Padilla and George Hostetter, "Chukchansi Casino Opens under Shadow of Disenrollment," *Fresno Bee*, July 15, 2003.

41 Chris Collins, *Fresno Bee*, March 1, 2009.

42 Ibid.

43 Marc Benjamin, "Chukchansi Tribe Disenrolls 57 Members," *Fresno Bee*, November 25, 2011.

44 Ibid.

45 Marc Benjamin, "Near Riot at Chukchansi," *Fresno Bee*, February 29, 2012.

46 Marc Benjamin and Carmen George, "Feds Give Chukchansi New Tribal Council," *Fresno Bee,* February 13, 2014.

47 Marc Benjamin, "Leadership Questioned by Judge," *Fresno Bee*, April 19, 2014.

48 Marc Benjamin, "Chukchansi Audit Reveals $49.6m Deficit," *Fresno Bee*, October 30, 2014.

NOTES TO CHAPTER 6

1   We emphasize court opinions because the judicial branch is uniquely positioned to protect citizens' rights from real and potential abuses by the legislative or executive arms of government.

2   www.tribal-institute.org/lists/justice.htm.

3   See Carole Goldberg-Ambrose, *Planting Tail Feathers: Tribal Survival and Public Law 280* (Los Angeles: UCLA American Indian Studies Center, 1997).

4   Matthew Fletcher, email correspondence, May 5, 2016. A recent report, the "Tribal Crime Data Collection Activities, 2014: Technical Report," by Steven W. Perry (July 2014, NCT 246917, Bureau of Justice Statistics, U.S. Department of Justice), says that altogether there are some 426 tribal court units in the United States.

5   Stephen Pevar, *The Rights of Indians and Tribes* (New York: Oxford University Press, 2012, 18.

6   1999 WL 34986342. All of the quoted material is from this case unless otherwise indicated.

7   2004 WL 5748376.

8   2005 WL 6458622 (Yurok Tribal Court of Appeals).

9   2006 WL 6369535.

10 No. SAU-CIV-10/05–106 (Court of Appeals).

11 *Equitable estoppel* is a defensive doctrine preventing one party from taking unfair advantage of another when, through false language or conduct, the person to be estopped has induced another person to act in a certain way, which resulted in the other person being injured in some way. This doctrine is founded on principles of fraud.

12 No. 2013-CI-CL-001 (Tribal Court).

13 No. 2013-CI-CL-003 (Court of Appeals).

14 No. C-13–09–002; No. C-14–021; No. C-14–022.

15 Eric Peters and Alan Prendergast, "Interview: Vine Deloria Jr.," *Leviathan* 3, no. 4 (1977): 6.

16 Vine Deloria Jr. and Clifford Lytle, *The Nations Within: The Past and Future of American Indian Sovereignty* (Austin: University of Texas Press, 1984), 242.

17 *Crocker v. Tribal Council for the Confederated Tribes of the Grand Ronde Community,* C-13-09-002 (2015).

18 No. C-14–021.

19 *Shakopee Mdewakanton Sioux Community v. Acting Minneapolis Area Director, BIA,* 27 IBIA 163 (1995).

20 Case No: C-14-22.

21 http://turtletalk.wordpress.com/2015/09/02/66-grand-ronde-treaty-desecendants -judicially-disenrolled/.

22 Ibid., "Respondent's Motion for Order Prohibiting Release of Briefs," 3.

23 Ibid.

24 No. C-14–022 through C-14–088.

25 2000 WL 357 49822.

26 6 NICS App. 132.

27 www.themorningsun.com/article/MS/20150923/NEWS/150929852.

28 No. 04-CA-1017.

29 Of course, some tribes, like the Lumbee of North Carolina, do employ such language but place it in an ordinance, rather than their organic document. The Lumbee adopted such a measure and titled it "An Act to Provide Tribal Enrollment Ordinance" on January 21, 2010, amended on August 18, 2011 (CLLO-2010–0120–01). Section 10 declares that "a tribal member who is found to have been erroneously or fraudulently enrolled . . . shall be subject to disenrollment."

30 2006 WL 6358356.

31 JAT-04–09.

32 For a thorough overview of this complicated history, see Lolita Buckner Inniss's article, "Cherokee Freedmen and the Color of Belonging," *Columbia Journal of Race and Law* 5, no. 2 (2015): 100–118.

33 Rennard Strickland, *Fire & the Spirits: Cherokee Law From Clan to Court* (Norman: University of Oklahoma Press, 1975).

34 Greg Rubio, "Reclaiming Indian Civil Rights: The Application of International Human Rights Law to Tribal Disenrollment Actions," *Oregon Review of International Law* 11 (2009): 7.

35 No. CV-07–40.

36 2007 WL 6900788.

37 No. 09-CA-1040.

38 *Littlegeorge v. Hall,* 9 Am. Tribal Law 161 (2010).

39 NHBP Tribal Court.

40 No. CA13–001 (Oct. 30, 2013).

41 Ibid.

42 *Las Vegas Tribe of Paiute v. Phebus,* No. 2: 13-CV-02000-RCJ-CWH (March 24, 2014), 14–15.

43 Largely because of treaties, the U.S. Constitution's commerce clause, the trust doctrine, and the doctrine of tribal sovereignty, the most important political relationship for

Native nations is with the federal government. States, of course, play an ever-increasing role as more tribal nations look to improve their relationship with those governments via child welfare compacts, sovereignty accords, tax agreements, and gaming compacts. One of the most important laws that deepened state involvement into tribal affairs was Public Law 280, adopted by Congress in 1953. That law authorized several designated states to wield full criminal and some civil jurisdiction over most Indian reservations in their borders and allowed the assumption of such jurisdiction by any other state that chose to do so. In a few cases, such as *LaMere v. Superior Court* (131 Cal. App. 4th 1059) and *Salinas v. Barron* (2008 Cal. App. Unpb. LEXIS 2251), state courts, when confronted with disenrollment, have generally deferred to federal law and tribal sovereignty by declaring that "Public Law 280 does not give California's courts' jurisdiction over tribal membership disputes" (*Salinas*, 4). As recently as November 10, 2015, a California court of appeals decision of the fourth appellate district, *San Diego County Health and Human Services Agency v. Michelle T.*, held that two children, K. P. and Kristopher, who had been disenrolled by the Pala Band in February 2012 for insufficient blood quantum—although their mother, Michelle T., had not been disenrolled and their father had never been an enrolled member—were not "Indian children" for purposes of the Indian Child Welfare Act. Michelle T. had contended that the state juvenile court had violated the Indian Child Welfare Act by terminating her parental rights to her children. But the state's juvenile court had deferred to the tribe and ruled that the children were not Indian, adhering to the general rule that state courts may not substitute their own determination for that of the tribe regarding a child's membership or eligibility for membership in the tribe. And the appellate court in affirming the juvenile court ruling followed suit and concluded that the Pala Band of Mission Indians' determination of membership was conclusive in state court custody proceedings.

44   See, e.g., Colin Miller, "Banishment From Within and Without: Analyzing Indigenous Sentencing under International Human Rights Standards," *North Dakota Law Review* 80 (2004): 253–88; Eric Reitman, "An Argument for the Partial Abrogation of Federally Recognized Indian Tribes' Sovereign Power over Membership" *Virginia Law Review* 92 (2006): 793–866; Rubio, "Reclaiming Indian Civil Rights," Suzanne D. Painter-Thorne, "If You Build It, They Will Come: Preserving Tribal Sovereignty in the Face of Indian Casinos and the New Premium on Tribal Membership," *Lewis & Clark Law Review* 14 (2010): 311–53; Gabriel S. Galanda and Ryan D. Dreveskracht, "Curing the Tribal Disenrollment Epidemic: In Search of a Remedy." *University of Arizona Law Review* 57, no. 2 (Summer 2015): 383–474.

45   See, e.g., *Sac & Fox Tribe of Indians of Oklahoma v. Andrus*, 645 F.2d 858 (10th Cir. 1981); *Smith v. Babbitt*, 875 F. Supp. 1353 (1995); *Olquin v. Lucero*, 87 F.3d 401 (10th Cir. 1996); *Ordinance 59 Assoc. v. Babbitt*, 970 F. Supp. 914 (D. Wyo. 1997); *Torres v. Acting Muscogee Area Director, BIA*, 34 IBIA 173 (1999); *Alire v. Jackson*, 65 F. Supp. 2d 1124 (D. Or. 1999); *Moore v. Nelson*, 270 F.3d 789 (9th Cir. 2001); *Davis v. U.S.*, 199 F. Supp. 2d 1164 (2002); *Shenandoah v. Halbritter*, 275 F. Supp. 2d 279 (N.D.N.Y. 2003); *Payer v. Turtle Mountain Tribal Council*, No. A4–03–105, 2003 WL 22339181 (D.N.D. Oct. 1, 2003); *Quair v. Sisco*, 359 F. Supp. 2d 948 (E.E. Cal. 2004); *Custalow v. Commonwealth of Virginia*, 2004 WL 1091771 (Va. App. 2004); *Lewis v. Norton*, 424 F. 3d 959 (9th Cir. 2005), *Arviso v. Norton*, 129 Fed. App. 391 (9th Cir. 2005); *Alvarado v. Table Mountain Rancheria*, 509 F.3d 1008 (9th Cir. 2007); *Sweet v. Hinzman*, 634 F. Supp. 2d 1196 (W.D. Wash. 2008); *Hendrix v. Coffey*, No. CIV-08–605-M, 2008 WL 2740 901 (W.D. Okla. 2008); *Sweet v. Hinzman*, No. C08–844, 2009 WL 1175647 (W.D. Wash. Apr. 30, 2009); *Jeffredo v. Macarro*, 590 F.3d 751

(9th Cir. 2009); *Timbisha Shoshone Tribe v. Kennedy*, 687 F. Supp. 2d 171 (E.D. Cal. 2009); *Quitiquit v. Robinson Rancheria Citizens Business Council*, No. C11–0983PTH, 2011 WL 2607172 (N.D. Cal. 2011); *Cahto Tribe of the Laytonville Rancheria v. Dutschke*, No. 2:10CV01306, 2011 U.S. Dist. LEXIS 54398 (E.D. Cal. May 20, 2011); *Cahto Tribe of Laytonville Rancheria v. Dutschke*, No. 2:10CV01306, 2011 U.S. Dist. LEXIS 108393 (E.D. Cal. Sept. 21, 2011); *Aguayo v. Salazar*, No. 12 CV0055-WQH-KSC, 2012 WL 1069018 (S.D. Cal. 2012); *Allen v. U.S.*, 871 F. Supp. 2d 982 (N.D. Cal. 2012); *Alto v. Salazar*, No. 11 CV2276-IEG (BLM), 2012 WL 2152054 (S.D. Cal. 2012); *Cahto Tribe v. Dutschke*, 715 F.3d 1225 (9th Cir. 2013); *Cahto Tribe v. Dutschke*, 524 Fed. Appx. 362 (9th Cir. 2013); *St. Germain v. U.S. Dept. of Interior*, No. C13–945RAJ, 2013 WL 3148332 (W.D. Wash. 2013); *Allen v. Smith*, No. 12 CV1668-WQH-KSC, 2013 WL 950735 (S.D. Cal. 2013); *Alto v. Black*, 738 F.3d 1111 (9th Cir. 2013); *Las Vegas Tribe of Paiute Indians v. Phebus*, No. 2: 13-CV-02000-RCJ-CWH, 2014 WL 1199593 (D. Nev. 2014); *St. Germain v. U.S. Dept. of Interior*, No. C13–945 RAJ, 2014 WL 2765219 (W.D. Wash. 2014; *Tavares v. Whitehouse*, No. 2: 13-CV-02101-TLN-CKD, 2014 WL 1155798 (E.D. Cal. 2014); *Allen v. Smith*, No. 13–55552, D.C. No. 3: 12-CV-01668-WQH-KSC (March 6, 2015); and *Germain v. U.S. Dept. of Interior*, No. C13–945RAJ (May 20, 2015).

46 Wenona T. Singel, "Indian Tribes and Human Rights Accountability," *San Diego Law Review* 49 (2012): 567.

47 2003 WL 22339181, 6.

48 424 F.3d 960.

49 Mary Swift, "Banishing Habeas Jurisdiction: Why Federal Courts Lack Jurisdiction to Hear Tribal Banishment Actions," *Washington Law Review* 86 (2011): 943.

50 *Shenandoah v. U.S. Dept. of the Interior*, 159 F.3d 708 (2nd Cir. 1998).

51 Ibid., 714.

52 335 U.S. 601 (1949).

53 Cited by Judge Wilken, dissenting, in *Jeffredo v. McCarro*, 590 F. 3d 751, 764.

54 590 F. 3d 751, 761.

55 Ibid., 769.

56 359 F. Supp. 2d 948 (E.D. Cal. 2004).

57 2007 WL 1490571 (E.E. Cal. May 21, 2007).

58 359 F. Supp. 2d 948, 971.

59 Ibid., 964.

60 Kunesh, "Ibid: A Postscript on *Quair v. Sisco*," *New Mexico Law Review* 37 (Spring, 2007): 480.

61 Ibid., 485–86.

62 Ibid., 484.

63 359 F. Supp. 2d 948, 977.

NOTES TO CONCLUSION

1 Resolution No. 2015-06.

2 Vine Deloria Jr., *A Better Day for Indians* (New York: Field Foundation, 1977), 24–25.

3 Ibid., 25.

4 Thaddieus W. Conner and William A. Taggart, "Assessing the Impact of Indian Gaming on American Indian Nations: Is the House Winning?" *Social Science Quarterly* 94, no. 4 (December 2013): 1027.

5 See Title 25–Indians–*Code of Federal Regulations*, Pt. 290-Tribal Resource Allocation Plan.

6   Thanks to Thaddieus Conner and William Taggart who shared their data with us on this important figure.

7   www.ho-chunknation.com/government/the-office-of-the-president/budget-and-finance/trap.aspx.

8   Conner and Taggart, "Indian Gaming and Tribal Revenue Allocation Plans: A Case of Play to Pay," *Gaming Law Review and Economics* 15, no. 6 (2011): 355–63.

9   Conner and Taggart, "Assessing the Impact," 163.

10 Randall K. Q. Akee et al., "Parents' Incomes and Children's Outcomes: A Quasi-Experiment Using Transfer Payments from Casino Profits," *American Economic Journal-Applied Economics* 12, no. 1 (2010): 86–115. Also see Randall K. Q. Akee, Katherine A. Spilde, and Jonathan B. Taylor, "The Indian Gaming Regulatory Act and Its Effects on American Indian Economic Development," *Journal of Economic Perspectives* 29, no. 3 (Summer 2015): 185–208.

11 See Kathryn R. L. Rand and Stephen A. Light, "Virtue or Vice? How the Indian Gaming Regulatory Act Shapes the Politics of Native American Gaming, Sovereignty, and Identity," *Virginia Journal of Social Policy and the Law* 4, no. 2 (1997): 381–437.

12 Akee, Spilde, and Taylor, "The Indian Gaming Regulatory Act," 199.

13 Interview via email on September 17, 2015.

14 U.S. General Accounting Office, "Indian Gaming: Regulation and Oversight by the Federal Government, States, and Tribes," GAO-15-355 (2015), as cited in Gabriel S. Galanda, "Tribal Lawyer Ethics: Gaming Per Capita Disputes" (paper presented at the 13th Annual Northwest Gaming Law Summit, Seattle, Washington, December 10, 2015), 1.

15 Ibid., 4.

16 "Exclusion" (copy of this ordinance in authors' possession).

17 Ibid.

18 Ibid.

19 Sarah Kershaw and Monica Davey, "Plagued by Drugs, Tribes Revive Ancient Penalty," *New York Times*, Jan. 18, 2004, 23.

20 Vine Deloria Jr. and Clifford M. Lytle, *The Nations Within: The Past and Future of American Indian Sovereignty* (Austin: University of Texas Press, 1984), 76.

21 Ibid., 266.

22 Wenona Singel, "Indian Tribes and Human Rights Accountability," *San Diego Law Review* 49 (2012): 568–625.

23 For one version of this historic document see David E. Wilkins, ed., *Documents of Native American Political Development: 1500s to 1933* (New York: Oxford University Press, 2009), 14–37.

24 Ibid., 37.

25 For a copy of this constitution, see Wilkins, *Documents of Native American Political Development*, 133–41.

26 Ibid., 299–359.

27 See Vine Deloria Jr. and Raymond DeMallie, comps., *Documents of American Indian Diplomacy: Treaties, Agreements, and Conventions, 1775–1979* (Norman: University of Oklahoma Press, 1999).

28 Ibid., 680–81.

29 Suzanne D. Painter-Thorne, "If You Build It, They Will Come: Preserving Tribal Sovereignty in the Face of Indian Casinos and the New Premium on Tribal Membership," *Lewis & Clark Law Review* 14 (2010): 337.

30 Gabriel S. Galanda and Ryan D. Dreveskracht, "Curing the Tribal Disenrollment Epi-

demic: In Search of a Remedy," *University of Arizona Law Review* 57, no. 2 (Summer 2015): 383–474, citing *St. Paul Intertribal Housing Board v. Reynolds*, 564 F. Supp. 1408, 1413 (D. Minn., 1983).

31 See, e.g., Franke Wilmer, *The Indigenous Voice in World Politics* (Newberry Park, Cal.: Sage Press, 1993); Chris Tennant, "Indigenous Peoples, International Institutions, and the International Legal Literature from 1945 to 1993," *Human Rights Quarterly* 16, no. 1 (February 1994): 1–57; Alexandra Xanthaki, *Indigenous Rights and United Nations Standards: Self-Determination, Culture and Land* (Cambridge, UK: Cambridge University Press, 2007); S. James Anaya, *International Human Rights and Indigenous Peoples* (New York: Aspen Publishers, 2009); and Charmaine White Face, *Indigenous Nations' Rights in the Balance: An Analysis of the Declaration on the Rights of Indigenous Peoples* (St. Paul, Minn.: Living Justice Press, 2013).

32 25 CFR 81.1 (1).

33 Felix S. Cohen, *Handbook of Federal Indian Law* (1942; repr., Albuquerque: University of New Mexico Press, 1972), 133.

34 Ibid., 133n78.

35 *Seminole Nation v. Norton*, 223 F. Supp. 2d 122, 137 (2002).

36 http://indiancountrytodaymedianetwork.com/2015/10/05/tribal-leaders-must-talk -about-disenrollment.

37 Katherine Beckett and Steve Herbert, *Banished: The New Social Control in Urban America* (New York: Oxford University Press, 2009), 20.

38 Special thanks to our friend Maralise Hood Quan for coining this haunting and perfectly descriptive term.

39 See the resolution on the organization's website: www.aaip.org (October 20, 2015).

40 Personal interview, August 2015.

SELECTED BIBLIOGRAPHY

Akee, Randall K. Q., William E. Copeland, Gordon Keeler, Adrian Angold, and E. Jane Costello. "Parents' Incomes and Children's Outcomes: A Quasi-Experiment Using Transfer Payments from Casino Profits." *American Economic Journal: Applied Economics* 12, no. 1 (2010): 86–115.

Akee, Randall K. Q., Katherine A. Spilde, and Jonathan B. Taylor. "The Indian Gaming Regulatory Act and Its Effects on American Indian Economic Development." *Journal of Economic Perspectives* 29, no. 3 (Summer 2015): 185–208.

Anaya, S. James. *International Human Rights and Indigenous Peoples*. New York: Aspen Publishers, 2009.

Armstrong, Michael. "Banishment: Cruel and Unusual Punishment." *University of Pennsylvania Law Review* 111 (1963): 758–86.

Barker, Joanne. *Native Acts: Law, Recognition, and Cultural Authenticity*. Durham, N.C.: Duke University Press, 2011.

Barsh, Russel L. "Indian Land Claims Policy in the U.S." *North Dakota Law Review* 58 (1982): 7–82.

Beckett, Katherine, and Steve Herbert. *Banished: The New Social Control in Urban America*. New York: Oxford University Press, 2009.

Borrelli, Matthew D. "Banishment: The Constitutional and Public Policy Arguments against This Revived Ancient Punishment." *Suffolk University Law Review* 36 (2003): 469–86.

Bradford, William C. "Reclaiming Indigenous Legal Autonomy on the Path to Peaceful Coexistence: The Theory, Practice, and Limitations of Tribal Peacemaking in Indian Dispute Resolutions." *North Dakota Law Review* 76 (2000): 551–604.

Close, Christopher W. "Review of Jason P. Coy's *Strangers and Misfits: Banishment, Social Control, and Authority in Early Modern Germany*." *Law and History Review* 28, no. 1 (2010): 253–54.

Cohen, Felix S. *Handbook of Federal Indian Law*. Washington, D.C.: Government Printing Office, 1942. Reprint, Albuquerque: University of New Mexico Press, 1972.

Colloff, Pamela. "The Blood of the Tigua." *Texas Monthly* (August 1999): www.texasmonthly.com/politics/the-blood-of-the-tigua/.

Connor, Thaddieus W., and William A. Taggart. "Assessing the Impact of Indian Gaming on American Indian Nations: Is the House Winning?" *Social Science Quarterly* 94, no. 4 (December 2013): 1016–44.

———. "Indian Gaming and Tribal Revenue Allocation Plans: A Case of Play to Pay." *Gaming Law Review and Economics* 15, no. 6 (2011): 355–63.

———. "Indian Gaming and Tribal Revenue Allocation Plans: Socio-Economic Determinants of Policy Adoption." *Social Science Journal* 50 (2013): 162–67.

Debo, Angie. *A History of the Indians of the United States*. Norman: University of Oklahoma Press, 1973.

———. *And Still the Waters Run: The Betrayal of the Five Civilized Tribes*. Princeton, N.J.: Princeton University Press, 1940.

Deloria, Ella Cara. *Waterlilly*. Lincoln: University of Nebraska Press, 1988.

Deloria, Vine, Jr. *For This Land: Writings on Religion in America*. Edited by James Treat. New York: Routledge Press, 1999.

Deloria, Vine, Jr., and Raymond DeMallie, comps. *Documents of American Indian Diplomacy: Treaties, Agreements, and Conventions, 1775–1979.* 2 vols. Norman: University of Oklahoma Press, 1999.

Deloria, Vine, Jr., and Clifford M. Lytle. *The Nations Within: The Past and Future of American Indian Sovereignty* (Austin: University of Texas Press, 1984).

Deloria, Vine, Jr., and David E. Wilkins. *Tribes, Treaties and Constitutional Tribulations.* Austin: University of Texas Press, 1999.

Edwards, Lydia. "Protecting Black Tribal Members: Is the 13th Amendment the Linchpin to Securing Equal Rights within Indian Country?" *Berkeley Journal of African-American Law and Policy* 8, no. 1 (2006): 122–54.

Galanda, Gabriel S. "Tribal Lawyer Ethics: Gaming Per Capita Disputes." Paper presented at the 13th Annual Northwest Gaming Law Summit, Seattle, Washington, December 10, 2015.

Galanda, Gabriel S., and Ryan D. Dreveskracht. "Curing the Tribal Disenrollment Epidemic: In Search of a Remedy." *University of Arizona Law Review* 57, no. 2 (Summer 2015): 383–474.

Goldberg, Carole. "Members Only? Designing Citizenship Requirements for Indian Nations." *University of Kansas Law Review* 50 (2002): 437–70.

Goldberg-Ambrose, Carole. *Planting Tail Feathers: Tribal Survival and Public Law 280.* Los Angeles: UCLA American Indian Studies Center, 1997.

Gover, Kirsty. *Tribal Constitutionalism.* New York: Oxford University Press, 2010.

Haycox, Stephen. "Felix Cohen and the Legacy of the Indian New Deal." *Yale University Library Gazette* 64 (April 1994): 135–56.

Heater, Derek. *A Brief History of Citizenship.* New York: New York University Press, 2004.

Henderson, Eric. "Ancestry and Casino Dollars in the Formation of Tribal Identity." *Race and Ethnic Ancestry Law Journal* 4 (1998): 7–24.

Inniss, Lolita Buckner. "Cherokee Freedmen and the Color of Belonging." *Columbia Journal of Race and Law* 5, no. 2 (2015): 100–118.

Jorgenson, Joseph G. *The Sun Dance Religion: Power for the Powerless.* Chicago: University of Chicago Press, 1972.

Karl, Nelson G. "Banishment from the Kingdom of Lake (County)." *Cleveland State Law Review* 21 (1972): 139–46.

Kim, Stephanie J. "Sentencing and Cultural Differences: Banishment of the American Indian Robbers." *John Marshall Law Review* 29 (1995): 239–67.

Kunesh, Patrice H. "Banishment as Cultural Justice in Contemporary Tribal Legal Systems." *New Mexico Law Review* 37 (2007): 85–145.

———. "Ibid: A Postscript on *Quair v. Sisco.*" *New Mexico Law Review* 37 (2007): 479–86.

LaGrand, James B. *Indian Metropolis: Native America in Chicago, 1945–1975.* Urbana: University of Illinois Press, 2002.

LaPier, Rosalyn R., and David R. M. Beck. *City Indian: Native American Activism in Chicago, 1893–1934.* Lincoln: University of Nebraska Press, 2015.

Llewellyn, Karl L., and E. A. Hoebel. *The Cheyenne Way: Conflict and Case Law in Primitive Jurisprudence.* Norman: University of Oklahoma Press, 1941.

Lobo, Susan, and Kurt Peters. *American Indians and the Urban Experience.* Walnut Creek, Cal.: AltaMira Press, 2001.

Meredith, Howard. *Modern American Indian Tribal Government & Politics.* Tsaile, Ariz.: Navajo Community College Press, 1993.

Merriman, Titus Mooney. *The Pilgrims, Puritans and Roger Williams Vindicated: And His Sentence of Banishment Ought to Be Revoked.* Boston: Bradley and Woodruff, 1892.

Miller, Colin. "Banishment from Within and Without: Analyzing Indigenous Sentencing under International Human Rights Standards." *North Dakota Law Review* 80 (2004): 253–88.

Mitchell, Dalia Tsuk. *Architect of Justice: Felix S. Cohen and the Founding of American Pluralism*. Ithaca, N.Y.: Cornell University Press, 2007.

Morgan, Gwenda, and Peter Rushton. *Banishment in the Early Atlantic World: Convicts, Rebels and Slaves*. London: Bloomsbury Publishing, 2013.

Otis, D. S. *History of the Allotment Policy*, edited by Francis P. Prucha. Norman: University of Oklahoma Press, 1973.

Painter-Thorne, Suzianne D. "If You Build It, They Will Come: Preserving Tribal Sovereignty in the Face of Indian Casinos and the New Premium on Tribal Membership." *Lewis & Clark Law Review* 14 (2010): 311–53.

Pevar, Stephen. *The Rights of Indians and Tribes*. 4th ed. New York: Oxford University Press, 2012.

Ramirez, Reyna K. *Native Hubs: Culture, Community, and Belonging in Silicon Valley and Beyond*. Durham, N.C.: Duke University Press, 2007.

Rand, Kathryn R. L., and Stephen Andrew Light. "Virtue or Vice? How the Indian Gaming Regulatory Act Shapes the Politics of Native American Gaming, Sovereignty, and Identity." *Virginia Journal of Social Policy and the Law* 4, no. 2 (1997): 381–437.

Reimer, David J. "Exile, Diaspora, and Old Testament Theology." *Scottish Bulletin of Evangelical Theology* 28, no. 1 (2010): 3–17.

Reitman, Eric. "An Argument for the Partial Abrogation of Federally Recognized Indian Tribes' Sovereign Power over Membership." *Virginia Law Review* 92 (2006): 793–866.

Rubio, Greg. "Reclaiming Indian Civil Rights: The Application of International Human Rights Law to Tribal Disenrollment Actions." *Oregon Review of International Law* 11 (2009): 1–41.

Rusco, Elmer. *A Fateful Time: The Background and Legislative History of the Indian Reorganization Act*. Reno: University of Nevada Press, 2000.

Salevao, Lutisone. *Rule of Law, Legitimate Governance & Economic Development in the Pacific*. Canberra, Australia: Asia Pacific Press, 2005.

Saucedo, Everett. "Curse of the New Buffalo: A Critique of Tribal Sovereignty in the Post-IGRA World." *St. Mary's Law Review on Minority Issues* 3 (2000): 72–113.

Scruton, Roger. *A Dictionary of Political Thought*. New York: Farrar, Straus and Giroux, 1982.

Singel, Wenona T. "Indian Tribes and Human Rights Accountability." *San Diego Law Review* 49 (2012): 568–625.

Snider, William Garth. "Banishment: The History of Its Use and a Proposal for Its Abolition under the First Amendment." *New England Journal on Criminal & Civil Confinement* 24 (1998): 455–509.

Spruhan, Paul. "A Legal History of Blood Quantum in Federal Indian Law to 1935." *South Dakota Law Review* 51, no. 1 (2006): 1–50.

Strauss, Terry. *Native Chicago*. 2nd ed. Chicago: Albatross Press. 2002.

Strickland, Rennard. *Fire and the Spirits: Cherokee Law from Clan to Court*. Norman: University of Oklahoma Press, 1975.

Swift, Mary. "Banishing Habeas Jurisdiction: Why Federal Courts Lack Jurisdiction to Hear Tribal Banishment Actions." *Washington Law Review* 86 (2011): 941–79.

Tennant, Chris. "Indigenous Peoples, International Institutions, and the International Legal Literature from 1945 to 1993." *Human Rights Quarterly* 16, no. 1 (February 1994): 1–57.

White Face, Charmaine. *Indigenous Nations' Rights in the Balance: An Analysis of the Declaration on the Rights of Indigenous Peoples*. St. Paul, Minn.: Living Justice Press, 2013.

Wilkins, David E., ed. *Documents of Native American Political Development: 1500s to 1933*. New York: Oxford University Press, 2009.

———. "Exiling One's Kin: Banishment and Disenrollment in Indian Country." *Western Legal History* 17, no. 2 (Summer/Fall 2004): 235–62.

———. *Hollow Justice*. New Haven, Conn.: Yale University Press, 2014.

———, ed. "A Most Grievous Display of Behavior: Self-Decimation in Indian Country." *Michigan State Law Review* 2013, no. 2 (2013): 325–38.

———, ed. *On the Drafting of Tribal Constitutions*. Norman: University of Oklahoma Press, 2006.

Wilmer, Franke. *The Indigenous Voice in World Politics*. Newberry Park, Cal.: Sage Press, 1993.

Xanthaki, Alexandra. *Indigenous Rights and United Nations Standards: Self-Determination, Culture and Land*. Cambridge, UK: Cambridge University Press, 2007.

INDEX

Please note that page numbers with *n* indicate notes; page numbers with *t* indicate tables; page numbers with *f* indicate figures.

Charlotte Cotè and Coll Thrush,
Series Editors

Indigenous Confluences publishes innovative works that use decolonizing perspectives and transnational approaches to explore the experiences of Indigenous peoples across North America, with a special emphasis on the Pacific Coast.

A Chemehuevi Song: The Resilience of a Southern Paiute Tribe
by Clifford E. Trafzer

Education at the Edge of Empire: Negotiating Pueblo Identity in New Mexico's Indian Boarding Schools
by John R. Gram

Indian Blood: HIV and Colonial Trauma in San Francisco's Two-Spirit Community
by Andrew J. Jolivette

Native Students at Work: American Indian Labor and Sherman Institute's Outing Program, 1900–1945
by Kevin Whalen

California through Native Eyes: Reclaiming History
by William J. Bauer Jr.

Unlikely Alliances: Native and White Communities Join to Defend Rural Lands
by Zoltán Grossman

Dismembered: Native Disenrollment and the Battle for Human Rights
by David E. Wilkins and Shelly Hulse Wilkins